W9-DFJ-396

LISTEN
TO THE
BLUES

ALSO BY BRUCE COOK

The Beat Generation

LISTEN TO THE BLUES

BY BRUCE COOK

New Introduction by the author

DA CAPO PRESS • NEW YORK

Library of Congress Cataloging in Publication Data

Cook, Bruce, 1932–
Listen to the blues / by Bruce Cook; new introduction by the author.—1st Da Capo Press ed.
p. cm.
Reprint. Originally published: C. Scribner's Sons, 1973.
Includes index.
Discography: p.
ISBN 0-306-80648-7 (alk. paper)
1. Blues (Music)—History and criticism. I. Title.
ML3521.C56 1995
781.643'09—dc20 95-21600
CIP

First Da Capo Press edition 1995

This Da Capo Press paperback edition of *Listen to the Blues* is an unabridged republication of the edition originally published in New York in 1973, with the addition of a new introduction and discography by the author and new photos. It is reprinted by arrangement with the author.

Published by Da Capo Press, Inc.
A Subsidiary of Plenum Publishing Corporation
233 Spring Street, New York, N.Y. 10013

Manufactured in the United States of America

CONTENTS

INTRODUCTION

ORIGINALLY, the title I had in mind for this book was "The Blues Trip." As with many titles, there was a bit of a pun intended there, for this was the time of LSD and those day-long voyages of discovery undertaken by the spiritually bold and the merely curious. If you had a reassuring experience, saw the face of God, or whatever, then you'd had a good trip; if you had been plagued by demons of paranoia or black-dog depression along the way, and perhaps seen the face of the Devil, then you had had a decidedly bad trip. But soon, "trip" came to be used by extension and analogy to mean any passionate involvement with practically anything at all. Well, ever since I was a kid and had discovered those old records at the bottom of the drawer (more about that in the first chapter), I'd had a passionate involvement with the blues. In that sense then I'd been on a blues trip for a long, long time.

But in another sense, this book is, at least in part, the product of a literal trip which I took in January 1972 to meet the bluesmen, as many as I could, on their home ground. I'd interviewed others all over the country—and Memphis Slim in Paris—when they were on the road (before gigs, after gigs, and once, in the case of Son House, at intermission). But this trip was important because it put me in touch not just with the music, which I had known ever since I was a kid, but also with the remarkable region where it had come to be created. I'd been down South before on reporting trips for the newspaper I worked on, but I didn't know the country well, and except for one visit to Memphis and another to New Orleans, I didn't know the Mississippi Delta at all.

I flew to Memphis, rented a car, and searched out Bukka White and Furry Lewis there in town. Then I drove south and a little east on two-lane country blacktop to Brownsville, Tennessee to talk to Sleepy John Estes and his partner Hammie Nixon; then down into Mississippi along the famous, or infamous, Highway 61. I had just one stop to make in the state, so I was in no hurry. I moseyed along, stopping frequently to talk to people along the way and maybe just to stretch my legs and take a look. I still remember one early-morning view of a bend in the great river with mist rising from it that obscured the tops of the near-naked winter trees. My appointment there was in Batesville with Mississippi Fred McDowell, a great bottle-neck guitarist and songster—then a detour east to Tuscaloosa, Alabama to meet Johnny Shines, who as a young man had traveled with the legendary Robert Johnson. Back along the river, I entered Louisiana and found my way along back roads to Robert Pete Williams's place outside Baton Rouge. Then I made the run from Baton Rouge to New Orleans in the rain, past swamps where stunted tree trunks rose from the brown water. And while I talked to only one there who had much to say—Babe Stovall, the street entertainer—I did attend Sunday services at the Morning Star Baptist Church and found things to say later about that.

Now, you may have noticed something about that list of those I looked in on during my blues trip through the Delta. With the possible exception of Hammie Nixon, they are all now dead and gone. Fred McDowell, whom I interviewed in the hospital, passed on just months after we talked.

That does a lot to explain just why I wanted to write this book in the first place. A whole generation of bluesmen was growing old in the 1970s. Many, like Son House and Mance Lipscomb, were well into their eighth decade; others not so old were nevertheless showing signs of wear and tear from the tough conditions of the lives they'd led. I would have called most of them the second-generation bluesmen. A few had dropped out of sight only to emerge when they had been rediscovered. Others had kept right on playing and singing through it all, even managing a precarious living in dingy urban clubs and country roadhouses. But the renewed interest in the blues in the sixties, the new enthusiasm for the authentic source of rock 'n' roll by that generation, brought sudden celebrity to these blues survivors, opportunities to record on major labels, and for a few the chance to make a little real money for the first time in their lives.

That was long overdue. Yet the audience for the blues was mostly white and young, and black soul performers and their black fans were indifferent to the blues at best (and at worst ashamed of it). I was fearful that this second generation of bluesmen, which included Howlin'

Wolf, Memphis Slim, and Little Brother Montgomery, might die off, and with them would be lost direct contact with that first generation—the Charley Pattons, the Big Bill Broonzys, and the Blind Lemon Jeffersons. I determined to interview as many of that second generation as I could while they were still around. And along with them I talked to a few of the younger men involved in the music—B.B. King, Junior Wells, and Buddy Guy. I was trying to decide if the blues would continue as a viable, separate genre of American music. Frankly, I was doubtful that it could.

I'm happy to say that I was wrong. Far from dying, blues has picked up strength in the two decades since *Listen to the Blues* was first published. The audience, still predominantly white, has grown. There are more blues festivals, more college dates, more blues clubs today than ever before—and therefore, probably more bluesmen actually making a living from the music than at any time. More important, younger bluesmen have emerged, a few of them white. To mention just three: Blues guitarist Stevie Ray Vaughan came out of Texas and blazed bright across the sky before he died in 1990 at the age of 35. Albert "Icepick" Collins, who had been around for years, emerged as a major figure when recorded by Alligator Records, but died suddenly in 1993. However, the hero and reigning champion of the blues revival is, of course, Robert Cray. He seems to have it all—good voice, good looks, better than average skills on the guitar, and a certain genius for coaxing original content from blues lyrics. His recordings on a major label—Mercury—have won him listeners beyond the blues audience; he's alive and well and spreading the gospel among the unwashed, unbaptized fans of hip-hop and punk rock.

But it's true that even with the resurgence the music has enjoyed during the last decade, the blues remains a somewhat specialized taste, its audience small, passionate, and well-informed. That's why I'm more than happy to have this book out again: It was written with readers like that in mind.

Even when it was first issued in 1973, most of the writing about the blues was done with a tape recorder. Interviews are important—get it from the source!—but there was also information to impart. The blues does have a history and a pre-history. It is a form with content, both musical and poetic. It is, I maintain in what follows, the fundamental music that gave foundation to all forms of original American popular music in the twentieth century—jazz, country, rock, and all their sub-genres. There was no way all this could be communicated in a book of interviews, so I insinuated myself into the text as an eye, an ear, a voice, a memory. It helped a lot that I grew up in Chicago and had known the music since my childhood. So in a way, this became a very personal book for me.

Although I have altered nothing in the text from its first edition, I should back off a bit from the high moral tone of some of my pronouncements. For instance, I was critical of John Lomax and his son Alan for what seemed to me a certain high-handedness and a patronizing attitude in their handling of the black bluesmen whom they recorded in the field for the Library of Congress. I am happy to concede that whatever their attitude (and I wasn't present, so how could I be certain?), they did invaluable work in preserving the blues and American folk music of all kinds. After all, John Lomax personally interceded on behalf of Leadbelly and helped instrumentally to win a commutation of his life sentence for murder from the governor of Louisiana. In this alone he far exceeded the mark.

I stand firmly behind some of my more controversial critical judgments—for instance, regarding Lightnin' Hopkins and John Lee Hooker. Even though they were first-rate singers and truly inventive bluesmen in that nearly all the material they recorded was reasonably original, they were at best guitarists of only primitive skill. Johnny Lee seems to know it and has never tried anything fancy; the irascible Lightnin' Hopkins was more ambitious and frequently got into trouble when he tried to improvise.

When *Listen to the Blues* was first published, a reviewer or two complained about the lack of a discography. I have attempted to remedy this in a modest way with a short basic list of blues recordings at the end of the text.

Finally, I want to make explicit what should be fairly plain from the frequent mention of a name in the pages that follow. This book could not have been written without the help of Dick Waterman. He provided names, addresses, phone numbers, and a personal reference whenever necessary. He did not, however, review the manuscript; the mistakes, whatever they may be, are my own. I acknowledge his help and thank him again.

BRUCE COOK
March 1995

PART
ONE

CHAPTER ONE

MY FATHER was a jazz musician who could never make a living at it. He tried a couple of times. The first was when he came to Chicago from Iowa in the late twenties and began to jam around the speakeasies and roadhouses that were going full blast just then. But he got married after a while, bowed to his responsibilities, and settled down to his job as a railroad telegrapher, sneaking out only occasionally to play a gig when somebody got sick on bad gin and they needed a cornet man in a hurry.

He lost the railroad job in 1932, a couple of months before I was born, and from that time until he got it back in 1934, about the only work that came his way during those Depression years was as a musician. But you couldn't really say he made a living at it even then. People ask me who he played with, as if in this way to establish just how good he was. Well, I don't know how good he was exactly. But I do remember him mentioning Chet Roble, who became fairly well known as a piano player and bandleader in Chicago during the thirties and forties, Boyce Brown, an alto saxophonist who played with various Eddie Condon units before going into a monastery (that's right, he became a monk), and the best known of them all, a guitar player named Lester Polfus. Is that a frown? Well, when my father was playing around in a little band with him in taverns on the north side of Chicago, Lester was also singing hillbilly as Rhubarb Red on station WJJD. But if Rhubarb Red doesn't help either, the year he left Chicago Lester Polfus shortened his name to Les Paul and did well as a jazzman and finally as a kind of combination pop guitarist-electronic wizard.

For years, whether he was playing regular dates or not, my father kept at his music. I think it gave him a sense of identity and purpose that the job he did for money never could. He thought of himself as a "jazzman." It was a word he used a lot. To be ready to play every date every now and then he would practice for at least an hour every day "just to keep the lip up." Practice consisted of scales, a bit of reading, and lots of jamming—that is, improvising along with records by the jazzmen he respected most: Bix Beiderbecke, Louis Armstrong, and Red Nichols.

Yes, those records—they are just the point, for I grew up hearing them over and over again. I got to know them so well that to this day I can hear solos and even whole records through in my mind's ear. And I am sure that on the day I die, whether it be tomorrow or forty years from tomorrow, I shall be able to hum, whistle, or pick out on a piano that marvelous trumpet fanfare that begins Louis Armstrong's "West End Blues."

Those were the records my father played, and while he was scrupulously careful of them himself it was always understood that if I were careful of them, too, I could play them when I wanted. And when I grew old enough to be curious about them —say, at the age of ten or eleven—I began to do just that, digging through the drawer in which they were kept, looking over those blue-label Vocalions and the red-label OKehs, playing one or two as I continued on down to those odd items at the bottom of the drawer. These were the records he didn't play, and when I asked him about them he shrugged and said, sure, he listened to them once in a while. They were just sort of . . . different from the Louies and the Bixes. Of course I could play them if I wanted to. He said he'd like to know what I thought of them, indicating by the tone of his voice and the expression on his face that he didn't think I'd like them much.

Well, I was of such an age and turn of mind that that was all I needed to like them a lot. With him away one afternoon I began playing those records at the bottom of the drawer. My mother passed through the room several times, making awful faces of disapproval, all but holding her nose. Yet I pretended not to notice and just sat there listening to them one after another. There was a scratchy old thing on the Paramount label, a piano solo that was unmistakable boogie, called "Cow Cow Blues," by one Cow Cow Davenport. There was a crazy Tampa Red record on Bluebird, "Stop Truckin' and Suzy-Q," and others on the same label by Memphis Slim and Jazz Gillum. And then there was some fascinating moaning and groaning by ladies whose very names stirred my imagination—Victoria Spivey, Hociel Thomas, Mamie Smith, and Bessie Smith. Well, let me qualify that last—Bessie's name, powerful voice and unmistakable style were known to me from her record of the "St. Louis Blues," which was one my father played often, chiefly because Louis Armstrong played back-up trumpet on it. But here were others by her: "One and Two Blues," "Down-Hearted Blues," and a couple of others.

It was quite an afternoon. I sat, if not quite amazed then deeply impressed by this new sound I heard coming through the speaker. For it was a new sound to me. The voices changed from disc to disc, but there was a unity of style and feeling in all of them that told me that this was a separate musical idiom. It was very *like* the jazz I had grown up listening to, but at the same time it was different—somehow more basic and more direct. There were strong echoes of this music through all those Louis Armstrong Hot Five recordings that I knew so well, but it was there not so much perhaps in Satchmo's flashing horn work as in his groaning, scatting vocals, and particularly in the doleful smears of Kid Ory's Creole trombone. But I heard some of it in Bix and Red Nichols, too. I had the feeling that even though some of these records at the bottom of the drawer were fairly recent, I had found on them a music that was older than the jazz on which I had been brought up.

And in a way, I *had* found something older, for I had discovered the blues. It was funny. It seemed I was hearing it for the first time then, yet at the same time I was vaguely aware that there were hints, bits, and pieces of it in nearly all the music

I heard all around me—certainly in the big-band stuff that was so popular in the forties, but even dimly in some of the most banal of the popular music that spewed forth endlessly from the radio.

Yes, the radio. It suddenly became interesting again when, not long after my first afternoon with the blues, I found out that if you fooled around with the dial far to the right of the network stations you could catch an approximation of that same blues sound in the twanging guitars and the down-home moans of the one or two black stations then broadcasting in Chicago. I became a special fan of a disc jockey named Al Benson—or that's not quite right, for the old swing-master, as Benson called himself, actually put me off a bit with his Jamaican accent and his corny line of jive. What I liked was the music he played. Some of it, though not enough, was straight blues, but most shaded into what they soon began calling rhythm-and-blues. There was something nice called "Drifting Blues," by Johnny Moore's Three Blazers, a kind of funkier version of the King Cole Trio; there were various pieces by Ivory Joe Hunter; something lusty by Helen Humes called "Ee-Bobba-Lee-Bob"; and a delicate, confidential bluesy thing by one Cecil Gent called "I Wonder," which I can hear in my head to this day.

Hearing blues on the radio this way was particularly good for me, for it saved me from the error of supposing that all the blues that was worth listening to was on those few discs at the bottom of the record drawer. I don't mean that quite as facetiously as it may sound, for there are blues scholars today that will tell you that the only true blues was played in the Mississippi Delta during the second and third decades of this century, or that no authentic blues has been recorded since Robert Johnson died in 1938, or that once the blues moved north of Memphis it stopped being blues. Tuning it in on the radio every night and listening in as I did saved me from such dogmatic certainties—and a good thing, too. I knew that blues were still being written and sung. I knew that the form was being bent and squeezed to fit personal styles and particular audiences. I realized—though I would have been hard put to articulate it at the age of twelve—that the blues was a living tradition and not some dead and ancient form fit only for the attention of folklorists and musical antiquarians.

Any vague doubts I may have had about all this were quickly dispelled the moment I set eyes and ears on my first bluesman. His name was Lonnie Johnson, and he was the real thing. I came upon him almost by accident at a jazz concert—my first —to which my father had taken me probably sometime in 1944. It was a session sponsored by a group that called itself, I think, the Hot Club of Chicago, and it was a program of traditional jazz in the old New Orleans style. The front-line men were all excellent New Orleans musicians—Lee Collins, trumpet; Preston Jackson, trombone; Tony Parenti, clarinet—all of whom would have been better known if they had recorded more. Also from there was the drummer Warren "Baby" Dodds, who did record a lot and was very well known; he was the drummer on all those Louis Armstrong Hot Five records I knew so well.

But Lonnie Johnson—what about him? When he was introduced, it turned out that, whether by the intention of the program planners or merely by coincidence, he was from New Orleans, too, one of the few blues *singers* to come out of the Crescent City. Lonnie Johnson was born there in 1894, and although he became best known when he left home, he is well remembered by the early Storyville musicians as one of the most talented members of a large musical family. In his autobiography, New Orleans bassist Pops Foster speaks of Johnson playing guitar on street corners along with his father, an excellent violinist, for whatever change came their way. In 1917 he went overseas with a troupe to entertain American soldiers in France. While he was there, the deadly influenza epidemic of that year hit New Orleans and killed nine members of his family, leaving only one older brother.

There was nothing to hold him there after that, and so he left New Orleans for good and started to ramble with his guitar, playing and singing the blues wherever he could gather a crowd to listen—through Texas, up and down the Mississippi on riverboats, gradually working his way farther north. In St. Louis, in 1925, he won a blues-singing talent contest at a theater that brought him a seven-year recording contract with OKeh Records. He became one of the most prolific of all the recording bluesmen, playing and singing his own fine songs, playing backup guitars for others, and even doing a series of excellent guitar duets in which he took great pride with the white jazz guitarist Eddie Lang. By the time I saw and heard him, he had been active in Chicago for a number of years, playing at the old 3 Deuces and other clubs and recording for Decca and Bluebird. He was to fall on hard times in a few years, but the afternoon I listened to him Lonnie Johnson, at the age of fifty, must have been close to his prime.

He had to be! I remember my own impression in listening to him was that it would be hard to imagine anybody playing better. There is a quality that the real virtuoso communicates, an added dimension to his playing, that makes it immediately and recognizably distinct from that of one who is merely proficient. Lonnie Johnson had it that day, and he may always have had it, for Pops Foster, though then hardly more than a boy, remembered him as "the only guy we had around New Orleans who could play jazz guitar. He was great on guitar. Django Reinhardt was a great jazz player like Johnson." And here he was, at fifty, playing deep rolls and treble runs that he extended with amazing subtlety, torturing out the last nuance of melody from those simple blues chords.

But the blues is essentially a vocal art, and Lonnie Johnson was pre-eminently a blues singer. I remember his voice as hushed and rather insinuating in tone; he was a singer with a style that managed to say more than words alone might allow. He was a dapper man, light-complexioned, with a pencil mustache, and dressed in a careful and precise way that reminded me a little of my father. (I remember he kept his hat on as he played and sang, and that struck me as odd.) He was the very picture of the urban bluesman, and that was the image he projected as he sang—knowing, world-wise, a man who had no illusions left but who still had pride in himself, a kind of played-out masculinity that you might associate with Bogart. All that was Lonnie Johnson. I won't pretend to remember what he sang. Diligent digging and listening have turned up any number, from "Backwater Blues" and "Falling Rain Blues" to "Careless Love" and "When You Fall for Someone That's Not Your Own," that he *might* have sung. But what seems important as I look back now is that he presented me with a figure, a living, breathing person to go with the brooding music I had started to listen to. I could see it as well as hear it: I knew it was real.

My father's attitude about all this was interesting. I remember asking him on the way home what he thought of Lonnie Johnson. He said he was a good guitar player, one of the best he had heard—and that's all he would say. I tried to draw him out on the blues we had heard, the odd, hushed style in which they'd been sung: I asked him what he thought of the blues and how come he didn't play them more himself. He just smiled, and shrugged, and changed the subject. It was only gradually, over a period of years, that I got the kind of answers I was looking for, and even then I apprehended rather than heard them from him. I came to understand that he, like most of the white jazzmen of his generation—and many of the black, too—was a little ashamed of the music's primitive beginnings. The juke joints and whorehouses from which jazz had sprung represented a world he had not known and one he would just as soon not know. The blues were much closer to this world, closer to the beginnings, and I think he (quite rightly) perceived them as the dark underside of jazz, the music he played and loved. Still, there were those records at the bottom of the drawer: they were his; he had chosen them and yes, he did listen to them from time to time. What about them? Well, I can only say that his attitudes in this were complicated and for the most part undefined, even to himself. There was a contradiction there, and he knew it, but he managed to live with it.

And that was how I grew up—or at least one of the ways I grew up—listening to jazz and blues, hearing the former more and more on records and the latter on the radio. I would go to jazz concerts when I could and I started collecting records on my own, buying a few of the modern things that my father didn't go for at all, by Dizzy Gillespie and Charley Parker. But as for blues, I found those records couldn't be bought at the North Side record shops I patronized. I remember being annoyed by that but not especially troubled: I was quite willing to listen to what Al Benson played every night on the radio.

Back in the late forties and early fifties in Chicago you were never really very far from the blues anyway. Get off the El at any stop between Cermak and Sixty-third, walk down the stairs, and you'd hear the music rise up to meet you. For a white kid from the North Side there was always a thrill in going into the South Side, as if traveling to another country—and in the cultural sense, that is what it was. Not an unfriendly country, just a place where people walked and talked a little differently and where you might keep an eye and an ear open for the unusual. I remember taking a State Street streetcar clear across town once when a blind street singer got aboard with his dog around Thirty-first Street. He sat down near the front of the car, unslung his guitar, and began serenading us all with blues and gospel songs. Everybody liked it just fine, and he collected a fair share of change before he got off someplace in the Fifties.

Time passes. Think of me as in college now, and still right in the city. I was acting hip, going to jazz spots mostly—the Bee Hive, the Streamliner, the Rag Doll—until I started working at a Michigan Avenue bookstore, Werner's. The porter at the bookstore was named Ernest Crawford, and portering was just something he did for money; in real life he was "a old ham-fat bass player" (in his own phrase). I used to sell the paperbacks downstairs, which left me more or less alone with Ernest, whose domain was the shipping room next door. When no customers were around, and I was supposed to be dusting the shelves, I was usually hanging out in the shipping room, talking to Ernest, asking him questions about his music. He liked to talk about the time he went on tour with Nellie Lutcher, that lusty, shouting two-handed piano lady from Kansas City. That was his taste of the big time, I guess, and he never forgot it.

I asked who he was playing with right then, and he just shrugged and said, "Muddy and Slim mostly." That turned out to be Muddy Waters, his steady gig, and Memphis Slim, for whom he played occasionally at Sylvio's. I extracted a kind of halfhearted invitation from him to come up and listen to him play sometime, and I think I astonished him when I actually did show up one Friday night around midnight. He was with Muddy then at a place on Forty-third Street that must have been Pepper's Lounge. I was with a friend, and I remember I was slightly intimidated by the place at first. The crash and holler of the music was something I wasn't quite prepared for. The Chicago blues sound, electrified and fully amplified, would shake an auditorium; inside a place as small as that one it seemed almost to explode around you, bouncing off the walls and punishing your ears. Or that's how it seemed at first. As my friend and I settled in to listen, we found that we were able to take it pretty well by the end of a set, we felt a little easier about having come to listen.

I went back to Pepper's a couple of times after that. Ernest decided he didn't mind at all having me come by. He even had me out one weeknight when he sat in with Memphis Slim at Sylvio's, on Lake Street. But I never went back. The place had a kind of forbidding atmosphere that made me uncomfortable. The West Side made me uneasy, and the South Side never did. I hit the blues spots pretty regularly out there the year that I was a senior in college. That was when Willie Mabon's "I Don't Know" was such a big hit, and I remember catching him at a big loud bar on Forty-seventh Street. I went to the Crown Propeller Lounge often to hear the brand of jazz and slick-blues they dished out there. And farther up Sixty-third Street, at the corner of Cottage Grove, there were spots on each corner that were worth hitting any weekend. I remember hearing Big Joe Williams at one of them. Across the street from it was a place I kept going back to again and again. Eddie Vinson was there —"Mr. Cleanhead," the Houston alto sax player and blues singer whom I had heard years before at the Oriental Theater when he was with the Cootie Williams big band. Yes, I remember sitting there when it was close to 4:00 a.m. on a Saturday morning, listening to Eddie Vinson sing "Juice-Head Baby" for the third time that night, looking in the long bar mirror and realizing mine was the lightest face in the place: there hadn't been any of those white guys in since one o'clock or so.

IF I SEEM to dwell a bit on these memories of all those years of listening in Chicago, it is because I am trying to establish my credentials for what will follow. It is not a question of knowledge. There is plenty of that around, for the blues has become a whole field of scholarship all its own. Serious young fellows with tape recorders have been combing the Mississippi Delta for the last dozen years or more looking for blues singers who might still be active in the territory, or maybe just for people who still remember the ones who were. The oral history thus amassed is impressive enough—and I'll admit I've made plenty of use of it myself in gathering facts, information, and opinions in my own research—but it all seems to have more to do with anthropology than with music. This "folklore" approach to the blues tends, ultimately, to diminish it, for it isolates the form, defining it all too narrowly and delimiting it to a style and an era that are for the most part long gone, and to a locale from which it has since gone forth, spreading its influence wide and deep throughout the world into all sorts and styles of music.

The blues is a living tradition. It has changed a time or two in the recent past and will probably change again. It has had a shaping influence on *all* native American music of this century—from jazz to country and western, and to rock-and-roll. You could even call it the *fundamental* American music. It is the tough, hard, durable stuff that all our styles and genres have in common. If a particular kind of music should lose contact with its origins in the blues it will go into an at least temporary decline. This is what happened to jazz in the forties and fifties, when musicians who had gained greatly in musical sophistication began emphasizing non-native elements more and more so that what was promised as jazz by some—the Dave Brubecks, the John Lewises, and the Lennie Tristanos—was delivered as a kind of hybrid, half-European form that may have intrigued some but excited none. The more arid and intellectual the music became, the smaller was its audience. It looked for a while as though jazz would lose its popular audience altogether, until some black jazzmen began injecting certain down-home blues and gospel elements into the music, and a little later on blues-based rock became an important element in jazz. And now, little by little, the audience is being won back.

If in that last paragraph you seem to detect the suggestion of a kind of musical chauvinism from me, then you are only partly wrong. I did, of course, contrast European music with American music. The difference between the two, I think, is self-evident. The point is that they can and should be compared —and they have been by the music critic Henry Pleasants. In three books—*The Agony of Modern Music, Death of a Music?,* and *Serious Music—and All that Jazz*—he has developed a thesis that has put the music world on its ear, infuriating some (Mark Schubart, dean of the Juilliard School of Music called his first book "scurrilous, unfair, destructive, and specious"), but gradually winning over others with the force of his argument (Erich Leinsdorf called it "frighteningly sound and logical").

Put briefly, Henry Pleasants' thesis is this: To remain vital and to continue to grow, a music must be sustained by popular taste and living popular music traditions. But toward the end of the nineteenth century, following the great explosion of harmonic innovation that began with Beethoven and ended roughly with Wagner, gradually music began to lose the support of popular taste, was no longer fed by the streams of popular music that had nourished it in the past. The reason for this is that European music became technically exhausted: there were fewer and fewer new tricks to pull. But because composers felt themselves in a sort of competition with the innovators of the past, they felt obliged to keep right on trying. The result of their efforts—atonality, serial and twelve-tone composition—only served to alienate what popular support they had left. It is significant that all this came to a crisis at just about the time that American music had established a separate identity of its own. As Henry Pleasants writes in *The Agony of Modern Music:*

> This time factor is essential to the critical comprehension of what has happened to serious music. Technical exhaustion coincided with sociological obsolescence and esthetic decay. All coincided with the ultimate agony of the nineteenth century on the battlefields of Europe in the First World War. Until then Western music had been a European affair in a European culture. Thereafter cultural leadership passed to America. Western civilization is now well into its American phase, and its music is the popular music of America.

So that today European music—and this, of course, includes all music by American composers in the European idiom, all "serious" music—is at a dead end. It has no popular appeal and it has no relation to any spontaneous popular tradition. Today the new music—the music that has supplanted the European idiom—is American music.

Now, what does Henry Pleasants mean by "the popular music of America"? In the beginning—say, at the time he wrote *The Agony of Modern Music*—he would have answered forthwith "jazz," yet (as he himself later indicated) he would not have been entirely sure what he meant by it—that is, how broadly or narrowly he would have defined the term. The reason for that is that he is himself a product of that European tradition whose agonized end he has described so well. He studied voice and piano at the Curtis Institute and went on to become the regular classical music critic of the Philadelphia *Eve-*

ning Bulletin from 1930 to 1942 and was subsequently a musical correspondent and critic for the *New York Times.* The point in delving into his *curriculum vitae* is to demonstrate how firmly he was at one time attached to the musical tradition he has now to some extent rejected.

His theory on the death of European music and the new dominance of American music was developed inductively, step by step—that is, he seemed to know that European music was in trouble and what the trouble was before he was really very intimate with American music. As his familiarity with this music grew, he sensed it offered the way out—and today he is the only music critic around who can speak with real authority on both; he had actually broadened his notion of the American musical idiom, which he contrasts with the European. In *Serious Music—and All That Jazz* he included rhythm-and-blues, country and western, rock, and pop along with jazz, remarking on the diversity of Afro-American music as a clear sign of its vitality. He would say that all these are elements in the new idiom that is American music. And I would add, of course, that blues is the element common and basic to them all.

My reason for presenting Pleasants' view at such length is twofold. First, I think he is right and that his theory deserves to be widely known and accepted. Second, I think it is terribly important that he is right, for it is a rare thing when such an epoch is begun in the history of music; the last such, which has been called the harmonic era by Pleasants, began about 1600 with the development and use of the musical key. But this is also notable as an important phenomenon of American culture —probably the *most* important because the most far-reaching in its implications. In a way, what is remarkable about American music is that it came to be at all. To call it Afro-American music, as is done so often today, is merely to acknowledge its dual nature. It is not to say that it is African music that is made in America—although for reasons that don't have much to do with music some seem to believe it is just that. No, American music is distinctive and separate. If it is different from European music, it is perhaps even more different from African music. It is a new music, an idiom, a whole new language that represents a synthesis of the two. Having written that, my immediate impulse is to go back and alter that last sentence to remove the word "synthesis"; it sounds programmatic, tendentious. But a synthesis is what it is, and the analogy to language in that same sentence is exactly to the point. For it is a synthesis in the same way that English is also one: that is, a whole new language that cannot be reduced to its original constituents of Anglo-Saxon and Norman French. That is how the American musical idiom has developed: as a language will—organically, naturally, and popularly with no special respect for what is "high" or "low," what is acceptable usage or unacceptable, or which of the original elements came from which group. It would be easy enough to dispose of the problem if one could say that American music combined European harmony with African rhythm—as it does more or less—but this would be to generalize our way too quickly through a vast complex of musical borrowing, trades, and thefts that went back and forth between white and black over a couple of centuries.

But if it is a music apart and a true synthesis of separate idioms, it is so not because anybody planned it that way but because in one of the more abominable episodes of history the black man was brought to America by the white man and kept here for centuries—in captivity but not in isolation. For the process of musical exchange and assimilation that ultimately brought forth American music as a separate idiom began very early. A change of sorts could be perceived in our folk and popular music during the first half of the nineteenth century. What this means is that even in slavery days a kind of cultural exchange was under way. American culture—the musical part of it, anyhow, which may well be the part that matters most—was even then being shaped by the black man.

There wouldn't be an American music if African culture had not had that prolonged encounter with the European down there in the American South. That was how the process began. The black man provided its essential element, the fuel for this engine of change. This is not quite the same thing as saying he is responsible for creating the music. So what is it exactly that I'm trying to sidestep here? Fundamentally, these are rhetorical evasions of the old nature-versus-nurture question, which is, of course, the root of the problem: Was it the peculiar genius of the black man that was responsible? Or the environment—slavery, Christianity, European music, and all—into which he was thrust? Flip Wilson caps his routine, "The Blues Singer," with an exchange that catches the essentials of this dilemma: The earnest young white blues singer tells the black lady who owns the club at which he has been playing, "You should be very proud because everybody knows the Negro gave the blues to America." She replies: "Just a minute, honey. The Negro didn't give the blues to America. America gave the blues to the Negro."

And perhaps took it away from him again when it began to look as though he had made a pretty good thing of it. Because when we talk about a synthesis we are using a nice neutral term that clouds an untold number of plagiarisms, a good deal of outright cheating on copyright material, and a general pattern according to which the black man makes the music and the white man makes the money.

And one of the ways that the white man makes the money is by writing *about* the music the black man makes—as, of course, I am doing now. Yes, I know full well that I myself am caught up in the ironies of this situation. And that, fundamentally, is why I took the time and space to go into my own early relations with the blues. I wanted to show that I have a personal, emotional investment in what I'm writing about here. For in criticism generally, and particularly in the critcism of something as wide open as popular music, it seems to me that this sort of personal investment is really the authority that matters most. This is my stake in all that follows.

But back to Chicago, that city so fabulous to southern black people in general and to bluesmen in particular. Only a place with a potent myth could have attracted such gifted people from Louisiana, Mississippi, Texas, and Tennessee. All along the Illinois Central right-of-way, clear down to New Orleans, people must have responded with a kind of longing to Robert Johnson's erroneous exhortation:

Oh, baby, don't you want to go
Back to the land of California, *
To my sweet home, Chicago?

*Don't laugh too hard: Remember, Keats attributed the discovery of the Pacific to Cortez in a sonnet.

And so it was more or less in that spirit, objectively—as a kind of pilgrimage to the single Northern city that had sustained and extended the blues tradition—that I returned not long ago to my sweet home, Chicago, and looked for some blues to listen to.

I had been primed for the visit when a little while before I met Bruce Iglauer, a young man from Louisville who came to Chicago because he is a passionate blues fan and stayed to edit a magazine, *Living Blues,* and founded a blues record label, Alligator. I had come to know about him through the first release on that label, a good album by a bluesman named Hound Dog Taylor. Talking to Iglauer once at a concert at Notre Dame, I had heard from him where I might catch Hound Dog. "If you go on a Monday," he had told me, "you'll be able to hear anybody who's in town. They all come out and jam. Blue Monday, they call it—at Pepper's and Theresa's."

When it came time to start, though, I found out that Pepper's had moved from Forty-third Street to what was considered a "safer" location on Michigan Avenue just south of Roosevelt Road. The idea, it turned out, was to be in a location that was still south yet close enough to the Loop that it would be easily accessible to the white college-age kids who have taken up Chicago blues as a kind of crusade.

I met one of these young aficionados only minutes after I had stepped inside the place. His name was Wesley Race, and he was, coincidentally, co-producer with Bruce Iglauer of that Hound Dog Taylor LP that had started me out on my Blue Monday quest. Hound Dog was there, too—just setting up with the drummer, apparently waiting around for a musician or two more before starting the jam.

Wesley Race told me he was from Wichita, Kansas, "where all they play is country music." How did he get into blues, then? "Well, when I was thirteen," he said, "my mother bought me a Bessie Smith album and said, 'Here, get off that rock-and-roll stuff.' She did me a favor, all right. I was hooked from then on."

That, he said, was how he happened to come to Chicago: "It was either here or Houston, and Chicago had more of what I wanted. You think it's so unusual for somebody to come here to live just to hear the blues? There are people here from England who came here just to listen to the music. I know twenty or thirty people who moved here just for that reason."

The place was beginning to bustle and fill up a bit. It was still early, they said, only ten o'clock, and Junior Wells would be in any minute. A few of the tables were a little loud, shouting to compete with the all-soul jukebox. This one didn't look a thing like the old Pepper's. It is dark and sort of Moorish, with a whole wall of mirrors to make it look twice its modest size.

Suddenly, a tall young black man strode up to the stand, a guitar under his arm, and from a table or two away Wesley Race signaled me they would soon be starting. He was right. After a bare moment given to the preliminaries of plugging in and tuning up, the trios—two guitars and drums—began in earnest. They swung beautifully through a couple of Hound Dog's own slow blues, which the man himself shouted with authority, looking black and haughty, as he told Baby just what she could do when she cried his name. And they played breakdowns—boogies to you—on which, in the absence of a bassman, Hound Dog played the bass line on his guitar with a funny kind of bloop-bloop-bloop inflection due to the higher pitch of his instrument.

The surprise was the late arrival; he played a good strong lead throughout, more than holding up his own, and soloed fluently in a somewhat more modern style than Hound Dog's. At the end of the set he sat down with Wesley Race. I was called over then and introduced to young Lefty Diz, a twenty-four-year-old guitar man out of Kankakee, Illinois, who had started out playing jazz and rock-and-roll. "But I'm into this Delta blues thing all the way now. Maybe I had to learn it, but it's me. This is what I feel."

Lefty Diz clearly has a lot of respect for Hound Dog Taylor, but he would rather talk about Junior Wells, the brilliant young harp player who, with guitarist Buddy Guy, leads the boss Chicago blues band. There are elder statesmen around, like Muddy Waters and Howlin' Wolf, but Buddy and Junior are the movers today on the Chicago blues scene. Lefty Diz told me a little about the tour he had made with their band in Africa and ended his encomium by urging me to stick around until Junior came. "We'll do a few of his things then because I know his music," he assured me.

I did wait through a couple of sets but then ducked out and

headed for Theresa's, telling myself I could look in at Pepper's on the way back. It's out south on Indiana Avenue, an inconspicuous little walk-down right on the corner of Forty-eighth Street. At this point Indiana is a dark, mean street, and just a little scary. I parked directly across the street from Theresa's, locked up tight, and went inside. The band at the far end of the club was grinding out "Hoochie-Koochie Man," laying it down with that electric panache and verve that when heard is quite unmistakably Chicago blues. There was a somber-looking individual at the door, holding a cord and looking over the customers as they entered. And beyond him, greeting those deemed worthy of admission, was Junior Wells.

Although he owns no part of the club, you get the sense that he is presiding there, almost holding court—if not quite a king, then a reigning prince of the realm. Junior Wells is a quick, shrewd, intelligent young man, one who has learned a good deal from his travels and social contacts. It was one of these contacts, a mutual friend, whose name I tossed to him as we shook hands. "Sure, man! You know him? We're like *that!*"

Junior has the natural host's ability to concentrate fully on whomever he is talking to. He called the bartender over and told him to set me up and listened attentively to my questions about his beginnings in the blues. He told me he is originally from Arkansas and learned to play harp there, listening to Sonny Boy Williamson on the old King Biscuit show, so he knew a little when he came. I asked him if he started playing clubs right away. "At my age then? Oh, man, I was twelve!" No, what he used to do was to play riding the streetcars and set up on the street corners. "Me and Earl Hooker, we'd do that. We'd catch those streetcars at one end and ride them clean on through to the other, just playing and singing all the way.

"My first band? You mean in a club? They're right over here —well, two of them are anyway. Come on, let me introduce you." And in another moment he had guided me artfully down the bar and passed me on to a couple of friendly and slightly older men, Louis Myers and Freddy Bellow—and then Junior was gone, back to his post near the door. The perfect host.

I had heard about both Myers and Bellow, a guitarist and drummer of some standing. They had a nice way of listening and talking in a completely relaxed way so that they were able to divide their attention between what was being said and the music that was being played, dropping a remark in response after a pause as they listened to a chorus or two of a solo. Or to a vocal. I remember we were listening to a young man in a visored cap delivering an impassioned "Every Day I've Got the Blues." I asked who he was.

"Him? That's B. B. King," said Louis Myers.

"B. B. *King?"* I repeated skeptically. It seemed unlikely that B.B. would jam in such an informal way anywhere.

"B. B. King, *Junior,"* Fred Bellow clarified.

"His son?"

"Well, he looks a lot like him, doesn't he?"

Well, it was true enough: he did look like the Blues Boy. When he came down off the stand and mixed with the crowd, I noted the resemblance—though as it turned out, the two are not actually related. I was just shaking hands with him there at my place at the bar when a party of four young white kids entered rather hastily and were ushered to an empty table that had suddenly come vacant directly in front of the stage. I asked if many white kids came to Theresa's.

"Some do," said B.B., Jr. "Usually just Mondays and the weekends."

I said in a kind of neutral way to the group at large that I was about that age when I started going out to listen to the blues bands around town. There was some interest in that, and so I added that I had started because somebody I knew used to play bass with Muddy Waters.

"Yeah?" Louis Myers leaned forward with interest. "Who was that?"

"Ernest Crawford," I said. "I used to work with him at a bookstore."

"Sure, Big Crawford! I remember that bookstore job of his. So you used to work with him there?" I could tell I had gained a bit of stature in his eyes.

"Yeah. You remember him?"

"Remember him?" said Myers. "Man, I used to *play* with him. Yeah, him and me used to gig at the 108 Club on Forty-seventh. That's closed now. I closed that place up with Otis Rush in 1958."

"That must have been just before he died," I prompted.

"Yeah, must have been. Doesn't seem that long ago I was gigging with Big Crawford, though," he mused. "He was some bass player, he was, on that upright bass of his. He was the onliest cat I ever heard play who could get a real big sound on an upright bass."

In the world of the blues, where competition is tough and memories are short, Louis Myers' tribute to Big Crawford qualifies as high praise indeed. Ernest would have been pleased to hear himself talked about that way. And listening to it made me glad I had come out that night to make the old scene. It made up for the uneasy feeling I had that things had changed on the South Side, perhaps permanently, that the four white kids who now sat up front near the stage digging the sounds were a bit braver and more aware of what they were doing than I had ever been.

Junior Wells came back over to me and said he had just been wondering where I had parked. I told him I had parked directly across the street.

"Uh-oh. Wrong side of the street. I think B.B. should walk you to the car whenever you think you want to go." I protested, told him I was quite capable of taking care of myself, but he dismissed all this with a shake of his head. "No," he said, "listen, when you go to a place you always want to park right by the club and not on a side street and not across the street or down the street, either. And don't go for any walks."

I felt intimidated. It was hard to listen to the music after that. Had I been invited to leave? I didn't think so. Was Junior Wells trying to scare me? No, he seemed genuinely concerned for my . . . what? Safety, I guess.

I finished my drink after a while and decided to leave. With goodbyes and shakes all around, I made for the door and found B. B. King, Jr., already there ahead of me, leading the way. Outside it seemed a little colder than when I had come in. Just as we were about to start across Indiana a cab pulled right up to the door and another couple of white kids jumped out and scurried for the shelter of Theresa's.

"We call cabs for them when they go," said B.B., Jr., without my asking.

We walked across the street then, and I stood for a moment with the car door open as we tried to make small talk and act casual. And then I left the scene.

Things sure have changed there.

CHAPTER TWO

IN SEARCH OF A DEFINITION

OFTEN PEOPLE seem not quite sure what you mean when you talk about the blues. They may have the general idea without getting the particulars down quite right—sometimes without being sufficiently aware that there are particulars of any sort to settle.

"The blues? That's black music, isn't it?"

Yes, that's right, but not all American black music is blues. And it may be, too, that not all blues are black, a proposition that we shall examine briefly a few chapters from now.

"The blues is soul, right? James Brown, Chuck Berry, Bo Diddley, and all the rest?"

That's a big hasty, too. When we talk about soul music, we're talking about a wide spectrum of styles that would include singers and shouters as different as James Brown, Otis Redding, Aretha Franklin, Wilson Pickett, the old Supremes, and on high up into that rarefied atmosphere where only songbirds such as Diana Ross and Dionne Warwick seem to survive. Soul has blues in it—as nearly every variety of American popular music does today—but its line of descent is circuitous and rather complicated. On the other hand, the line from blues to what was called rhythm-and-blues—Chuck Berry, Bo Diddley, Little Richard, and all the rest—is straight and direct. In point of time, the difference between the two is a matter of a generation (Bo Diddley, for instance, played guitar for Muddy Waters early in his career). In style, it is a matter of tempo and attack. But perhaps the real significance of rhythm-and-blues is as a station on the way from blues to white rock-and-roll. Which is just the sort of complication this book is all about.

"All right then, what about this? Blues is that old-time music that the jazz bands used to play, like the 'St. Louis Blues' and 'The Birth of the Blues' and so on."

The relationship of the blues to jazz was, it is true, simple and straightforward back in the beginning. They were more or less different styles of the same music: jazz chiefly instrumental (heavy on the brass), and blues chiefly vocal (usually with string accompaniment). As jazz developed, however, and became the virtuoso music it was even by the 1920s, its relationship to the blues became tenuous, but more complex and even symbiotic. Jazz needed the blues. That's where the roots were, and that's where they are to this day.

"St. Louis Blues," a jazz standard if there ever was one, is an example of the sort of blues that gave jazz its foundation. It is a true blues. Although it is credited to W. C. Handy, it may only have been adapted by him from one or more folk blues that he heard in his travels from Memphis; certainly lines in the lyrics are interchangeable with those in many others that came from as far away as Texas. I suspect that W. C. Handy's chief contribution was the interpolation of the bridge between the basic blues figures, which in this case came, oddly enough, in the form of a tango. (Just listen to Louis Armstrong's early recording of it, where this is unmistakable.) It may have made it a little less a blues in the bargain, but it introduced the "Spanish tinge" that Jelly Roll Morton used to claim was absolutely essential to jazz.

You may have heard "The Birth of the Blues" played *ad nauseam* down in New Orleans, but that doesn't make it a blues; it is still just a popular song *about* the blues. In this case, when we talk about a popular song, we are not implying one of those tired value judgments that exalts true folk art over what is merely manufactured for public consumption. No, we mean something much more specific. It is in the thirty-two-bar form in which nearly all American popular songs have been written up to and even into the rock-and-roll era. It consists of an eight-bar figure that is repeated once before a new eight-bar figure is introduced as a "bridge" to the original eight-bar figure, which is then repeated to conclude the chorus. That is the form of "The Birth of the Blues," just as it is the form of "Stardust," "Up, Up and Away," and countless other songs.

But it is not the form of the blues. Although simpler, the blues chorus is just as precise in formulation. Examples of short eight-bar chorus blues can be cited, and there are extended sixteen-bar blues choruses, as well. But the most common—no, call it the classic—blues chorus consists of twelve bars that are divided in an interesting way that is just right for the easy improvisation of lyrics. In it, a four-bar line is stated:

When a woman gets the blues she wrings her hands and cries.

Then it is repeated with the addition of a pickup word or phrase:

I said, when a woman gets the blues she wrings her hands and cries.

And then the final "answering" line comes, concluding the chorus and completing the rhyme:

But when a man gets the blues he grabs a train and rides.

Each of the three lines consists of four bars, giving us the standard twelve-bar blues chorus. Yet it is no more than a couplet stretched to three lines, simply by repeating the first line before following through with the second. This gives the singer, if he happens to be making up his words as he goes along, a little extra time to come up with the last line. In almost any folk blues the figure that carries each line fills its allotted four bars rather slackly, so that, again, there is room for both musical and verbal improvisation. All this emphasizes the blues as vocal art.

Harmonically, blues was—at least in the beginning—a very simple form, but one that had a trick or two in store for the performer who thought he could pick it up just by reading the right notes. Most of the early bluesmen began by learning three common chords on the guitar; they could sing a lot of songs just knowing these chords alone. (Many, of course, have gained overwhelming skill on this difficult instrument—Lonnie Johnson, Scrapper Blackwell, and Shirley Griffiths, for example—but a few talented shouters—John Lee Hooker, for one—have never gotten much beyond that basic primitive skill.) The trick in blues harmony is in the so-called "blue notes." The third, fifth, and seventh notes of the major scale are flatted, diminished to produce chords that can only truly come together in quarter tones. The human voice can sing a quarter tone; horns and stringed instruments can "bend" into them; but a piano can only suggest it with a dissonant chord, for the true quarter tone lies, as they say, "between the keys." These "blue notes" are now heard in American music of all kinds, not just in the blues. They and certain distinctive elements of rhythm have given American music its distinctive sound. And the blue notes were there even before the blues—well back in the nineteenth century, when all this was taking shape. Some say these quarter tones were brought from Africa; they are the black contribution to Western harmony.

And so if, in the blues scale, we drop certain tones from major to minor, the effect is basically a *sad* sound. And that, of course, is what the blues is all about: sadness, despondency. Just look in the *Oxford English Dictionary,* and you can see such a definition taking shape as far back as the sixteenth century. Blue was the color of the Devil; candles were said to burn blue when he was near (probably because blue flame was associated with brimstone). From this came the expression "blue devils"—a man who was plagued by them was despondent, felt a depression of spirits. And as early as 1807, Washington Irving could dispense with the devils entirely and remark that he was "in a fit of the blues," and have it perfectly well understood that he felt depressed.

It may well be that I am making too much of something simple, for elementary color psychology designates blue as the color of melancholy. And whenever it has been used in a figurative or poetic sense in the past it has carried this meaning, though sometimes with connotations that shaded into fear and anxiety (all of which goes well enough with the music). And when this melancholy music began to be heard as something in itself, it may only have seemed the natural thing to call it "blue" music, or, simply, the blues.

When was this? When did blues first come to be perceived as a distinctive style or form? If we were to go by copyrights, dates of publication, and so on, we would mark the beginning at 1912, for that's when something called "Baby Seals Blues" was published in St. Louis, "Dallas Blues" was published in Oklahoma City, and "Memphis Blues" was published in Memphis. But actually, of course, the form was well set years before. In New Orleans, that black-hearted cornet man who is said to have led the first real jazz band used to play his "Buddy Bolden Blues" as a kind of musical signature as early as 1897. And Big Bill Broonzy recorded something he called "Blues in 1890," actually a version of the old "Joe Turner Blues," which he said his uncle used to play and sing back then; this, to Big Bill, was the "first" blues.

It was something different, a sad and personal kind of music. Once you heard it you knew it was different and you remembered it. And right from the start, the people who played it knew there was something special about it, too.

> . . . I think that the blues is more or less a feeling that you get from something that you think is wrong, or something that somebody did wrong to you, or something that somebody did wrong to some of your own people or something like that . . . and the onliest way you have to tell it would be through a song, and that would be the blues . . . but the blues is really aimed at an object of some kind or an indirect person. It's not aimed at the whole public; the blues cannot be aimed at the whole public.

That's Li'l Son Jackson, quoted in *The Blues Line,* an anthology of blues lyrics. It is a huge collection, 270 songs that fill well over 400 pages. There is not a note of music. The lyrics are laid out on the pages like so many pieces of verse. Read through them this way, and you will be struck again and again, I think, by the points cited by Li'l Son Jackson in that modest little commentary quoted above. He's saying it's trouble-music, sad music, but there is nothing abstract about it; no, its miseries are specific and personal, and the way they come out best is in a song.

And it's true enough, for just look how specific the songs are in *The Blues Line.* Place names and personal references abound. In many, experiences are described with the kind of precise detail that has to come straight from life. Take Li'l Son Jackson's own "Charlie·Cherry":

If the shack get raided
ain't no body run
If the shack get raided
ain't no body run
You stay right here till
Charlie Cherry come
Well he cut you if you stand
shoot you if you run
Well he cut you if you stand
shoot you if you run
You better stay right here
till Charlie Cherry come
Now he arrested my brother
tied him to a tree
Well now he arrested my brother
tied him to a tree
You could hear him crying,
Please don't murder me
Well now Charlie Cherry
meanest man I know
Well it's Charlie Cherry
meanest man I know
Well now you meet him in the morning
you don't know which-a-way
to go
Well now where was you baby
when the wind blowed cold
Well now where was you
when the wind blowed cold
Well now you was in the bottom
by the red hot stove

There are no notes here to inform us who Charlie Cherry was, but it seems fairly obvious that he was a sheriff against whom Li'l Son Jackson brushed a time or two, and it is just as evident that Charlie Cherry was a mean son of a bitch ("You could hear him crying, Please don't murder me"—that says it pretty well). It kind of calls to mind that picture of Sheriff Jim Rainey (who was tried and acquitted for the murder of civil-rights workers James Chaney, Michael Schwerner, and Andrew Goodman in

Philadelphia, Mississippi), chewing on that gob of tobacco and smirking in the courtroom.

Turn the pages of this or any other blues collection, read through the lyrics, and you will be impressed by the evocative and very specific quality of the language. You will note a limited but sometimes very compelling use of metaphor, as here in Blind Lemon Jefferson's stanza:

Blue jumped a rabbit, run him one solid mile
Blue jumped a rabbit, run him one solid mile
This rabbit sat down, crying like a natural child.

Or the sort of resonant images that say more than words can tell:

Well the sun's gonna shine in
my back door some
day
Well the sun's gon' shine
in my back door some
day
Ahhhh it's one more drink
gonna drive these
blues away

What I am saying, in effect, is that the more we read of blues lyrics the more we are struck by their poetic qualities. It is not just seeing the songs set down in printed lines that persuades us. You can look at rock lyrics presented in the same way in any number of collections, then read through them quickly, and be impressed merely by how pitifully they are diminished, languishing there on the page without music to support or charisma to sustain them. The poetic qualities of the blues are right there in the lines.

Does this mean that the blues is poetry? There has been a tacit assumption that it is since the time—late in the 1920s—when white intellectuals first began to listen seriously to the music that blacks were singing. And, indeed, the blues have been emulated in imagery and diction by some black and white poets ever since then. But does this make it poetry? Samuel Charters takes up the matter in a book that seems to beg the question in its very title, *The Poetry of the Blues.*

And yet though Charters notes the poetic qualities of the

blues early in his little book, just as I have done here, he seems to withhold final sanction on what for him seems to be no less than a point of doctrine. The question is one of authorship. He says even in a note on sources preceding his text, "Most of the verses of the blues are used by every singer, and they have become the root language for the more personal singers like John Estes and Robert Johnson. I have not mentioned a particular source for these verses, since this would tend to imply that there is someone who could be thought of as having written them." Does Charters really mean this? It seems to me that it comes awfully close to saying that the blues were not written but, instead, they just happened. This may make a case for the blues as folk art of a kind, but it doesn't really convince us that it is poetry, for poetry implies single authorship, a direct expression of individual human experience.

And this seems to be exactly what Samuel Charters is saying, because a little later in the text, where he ought to be talking about the bluesman writing a song, he speaks of him "creating a verse pattern." And then he goes on to say: "Because so much of the blues is concerned with the disappointments of love there are hundreds of verses using this idea, and a singer can simply put four or five of these second-hand verses together and have a blues that will have little individuality but will give him something to sing without much effort involved." As an alternative to this, he goes on to extoll not authorship, but the arrangement of verses by "an emotional association." He stops just short of insisting that there are no original lines in the blues, but he strongly suggests that the best one can hope for from any bluesman is good editorial work of the scissors-and-paste sort.

Why? Why is Samuel Charters so determined to reduce the poetry of the blues to mere folklore? What does he hope to prove by generalizing authorship in this way? Not to belabor this, but it seems self-evident that blues are and have been written. Pushed back to their sources, stanzas and whole songs had to have come from specific composers, even if we are unsure of their identity (and in most cases we know precisely who wrote them). No, the beginnings of the blues are not shrouded in quite the obscurity that Charters pretends. But it suits his purposes to present the blues as folklore, for—and here we come to that point of doctrine that he tacitly defends—group authorship of the kind he seems to insist upon implies that the music could only have come out of a very specific set of conditions and circumstances. For Samuel Charters, as for a number of others who have written on the subject, the blues is purely a product of the black man in the rural South—more specifically, a product of the black in the Mississippi Delta region. Its origin, he insists in *The Poetry of the Blues* and elsewhere, is social, growing directly out of racial segregation: "From this separatedness of white and Negro there have come not only differences in social attitude, but also in social expression. The lives of the two groups are so insistently kept apart that there has grown up within the Negro society its own artistic self-expression."

And while there is no disputing that the blues is essentially Negro music, we can certainly question the implication that it was cut from whole cloth (or at least that the cloth was quite so black in color). And we are hardly giving the music its due if we allow to go unchallenged the tacit assumption that the only true blues is that which came from a limited territory and time; the corollary to this is that whatever may follow in time, or derives from it in style or is adapted from it, is unauthentic and probably debased. Such a purist's position reduces ultimately to the stubborn insistence that the blues is what *I* say it is.

But because blues is what it is—a *living* tradition—there are still blues being made today in just about the same way they always were. Muddy Waters, Willie Dixon, and Sunnyland Slim still *write* them, of course. They are blues composers; they write them (often in far more interesting and subtle patterns than that of the old three-line couplet of the classic blues form), and record them, and play and sing them ever after in just about that way. Fine. Theirs is an important, respectable, and certainly vital part of the blues tradition today. But travel down to the blues country, take a look around, and, above all, take a listen, and you will find that there are bluesmen who survive even now in the backwaters of the South, not just playing the blues but *making* them, too. Blues-makers, if you will, innovators, improvisors of the word, poets: most of them are conscious artists who can and do draw from their own experience and intense personal feelings the very stuff of their music.

Let me tell you about one of them.

IN 1958, a folklorist named Harry Oster, who was then a member of the English Department at Louisiana State University, visited the state prison farm at Angola, Louisiana, and with the permission of the warden began holding auditions among the prisoners. He was collecting songs and looking for singers for a series of field recordings that he would be undertaking under university auspices. But once made, these recordings were eventually released commercially (they are, in fact, still available). Dr. Oster got more than he bargained for. Two of the men he found there at Angola—Mathew "Hogman" Maxey and Robert "Guitar" Welch—were more or less conventional bluesmen who had learned most of their material from recordings and from itinerant singers like themselves. But the third was an exceptional man named Robert Pete Williams, then thirty-five and serving a life sentence for murder.

Robert Pete could and did play some familiar material—"Levee Camp Blues" and "Motherless Children"—but he showed himself as something special when Richard Allen, who was assisting Oster in recording the material, asked if he knew a blues about doing time in prison. Robert Pete said that he did not, but he could make up one for him. And with that, he began picking away and singing the blues that appears on the recording, *Angola Prisoner's Blues,* as "Some Got Six Months." This is how it goes:

Some got six months, some got a solid year.
But me and my buddy we got life time here.
Some got six months, some got one solid year,
But me and my buddy we got life time here.

Six months, oh baby, let me go to bed,
I've drunk white lightnin', gone to my head . . . it
gone to my head.

I've got so much time, darlin',
It worryin' me, oh babe,
You know this time killin' me,
But I just can't help it, darlin', I just got to roll.

You know that old judge must been mad.
Yeah, hey, that old judge must have been mad,
darlin',
When he gave me my sentence,
He throwed the book at me.

First time in trouble, I done get no fair trial at all,
Oh Lord, seem like to me, baby, they locked the poor
boy in jail.

It's kind of ragged. The inequality of lines in the stanzas are not quite as noticeable on the recording as they are here on the page, for the lines are chanted, almost spoken, against a steady guitar rhythm. The effect is something slightly closer to a spoken poem than to a sung blues. And that is why, too, the imperfections in the rhymes seem less obvious as we listen to Robert Pete Williams' improvised rendition. What is sung may be expected to rhyme; what is spoken may not.

And yet what cannot be denied and what need not be excused is the simple, direct power of these lines. If it is not poetry, than it is something very close to it, for this sort of eloquence born of experience raises the simple blues as far above the level of the ordinary popular song as Grünewald's *Crucifixion* stands above a Hallmark Easter card. It is a kind of talent for truth-saying that Robert Pete Williams has. He possessed it, has developed it, and uses it just as any other artist might—with the difference that his poems are sung and spoken against the rhythm of a guitar and within the loose conventions of the blues form.

This ability of his to extemporize poetry is shown even more impressively in another number recorded by Oster and Allen at Angola, listed in the album as "Prisoner's Talking Blues." Although too long to quote here, it is worth searching out and listening to. For that matter, it is only that way—actually hearing it spoken and sung—that you can perceive the real power of it. His blues, like that of any original bluesman, is essentially oral poetry; it must be heard to be truly appreciated. Shadings of tone and enunciation, the interplay of the musical background with spoken and sung phrases—these are what make "Prisoner's Talking Blues" the moving experience it is.

Dr. Harry Oster knew that he had found someone special in Robert Pete Williams. He not only came back to Angola to record him again—one full album, *Those Prison Blues,* was recorded while Robert Pete was still there at the prison farm—but he set about to see what he could do to secure his release. Oster sent letters and copies of the albums on which Robert

Pete had appeared to Governor Russell Long and members of the Louisiana pardon board; and in December, 1959, parole was granted.

Even then it was not easy for Robert Pete Williams, for he had been released to a farmer in Denham Springs, Louisiana, for whom he worked about eighty hours a week during the seven years of his parole period. He could not travel outside the state, so he was unable to make appearances as a blues singer in the North, where he had been invited on the strength of his prison albums. He continued to be recorded by Oster, however, and just as his Angola recordings mirror his prison experiences, so his first album afterward (*Free Again*) is filled with material—"Hay-Cutting Song," "Hobo Worried Blues," and "A Thousand Miles from Nowhere"—drawn from his life as a farmhand.

Eventually, he was permitted to travel, and the first trip that he made was up to the Newport Folk Festival, where he was well received—although what he offered was not quite what the crowd there was used to. He is not essentially a performer. Before going to jail, he had only played for family and friends in a small hometown circle. Even when he recorded in prison and afterward, there were only himself, the tape recorder, and one or two others present to run it. In the beginning he had trouble coping with a crowd as immense as the one that looked up at him the afternoon he made his debut as a professional bluesman, and it is only gradually that he has learned a few of the tricks that most real performers seem born with. He is still uncertain of himself on stage, and the best possible place to hear him—as I discovered—is in his own living room in Rosedale, Louisiana, where he now makes his home.

Robert Pete Williams was born not far away, in Zachary, and before going to prison he farmed in Scotlandville. All the towns in which he has resided during his lifetime are within a few miles of one another and lie on the outskirts of Baton Rouge. In fact, on the day I set out to find him, driving through intermittent rain along Route 190, I passed through Denham Springs, where he had served his parole, and it seemed almost suburban compared to the raw, rural communities I had just driven through.

There had very recently been trouble in Baton Rouge. You

may remember it: A rally led by newcomers to the city who claimed to be Black Muslims (Elijah Muhammed subsequently denied knowledge of them) erupted into a shoot-out with the local police. They were burying the dead that day; I was just as glad to be skirting the city rather than driving through it. And apparently I was not the only one made uneasy by the situation. I remember pulling up behind an International pickup truck, noting the two very red necks displayed in the rear window of the cab—and just behind the seat, trigger up, was a Browning semiautomatic shotgun. Memories flashed through my head of the last few minutes of *Easy Rider*. I cut out around the pickup at the earliest opportunity, and quickly put some distance between me and it.

Rosedale lies northwest of Baton Rouge at the end of a back-country road. Robert Pete had given me explicit directions to the town, but because I had never driven there before it seemed to take a little longer than it should. The rain was gone and the sky was clear by the time I got to Rosedale—a good omen, I thought—and I turned in at the crossroads post office and got further directions from a helpful white postal clerk. And finally, I checked at the black general store off on a sideroad, and I was told precisely where I might find the house. They said to keep an eye open for the red truck—that I couldn't miss Robert Pete's house if I just kept an eye open for that truck with "Williams" on the side.

It is with this truck that he plies the scrap-iron trade. He makes rounds of the farms and businesses in the area, collecting what he can and then taking it in to Baton Rouge to sell. He also does a bit of light farming out the back door of his house—chickens, a few hogs, and a vegetable garden. This, combined with the money he makes from the few personal appearances he makes each year at colleges and coffeehouses around the country, gives him and his family a pretty good living. He works hard and is conscientious about his responsibilities.

He met me at the door of the single-story house that he and his wife built together when they moved to Rosedale from Denham Springs. It is not only well kept but well constructed: he pointed out to me that it is put together in "the old way," with joists at the corners, and has stood up through hurricanes without so much as a wobble. As Hattie, his wife, was preparing what turned out to be quite a feast, Robert Pete and I broke out a bottle and sat down in the living room. Although he is not a hard drinker, he likes a taste now and then, and as he drinks the only real change to be noted is that he becomes more relaxed and outgoing.

Assuming I'd like to hear him play something, he went into the bedroom and brought out a guitar. It was a narrow-necked, slightly undersized affair that he said was given to him by a fellow once in Bertrand (Berkeley) "just because he liked me." It is one of two guitars he owns. This one he keeps for bottle-neck work. He produced a piece of conduit that was just about finger-sized, and I asked him when he had started to use that.

"That would be about 1964, I guess, or after that," he said, "when I met Fred McDowell at Newport. He was the first man I saw with one of these on his fingers." Robert Pete held up the piece of conduit, which he had now attached to the little finger of his free hand. "Around here they always use a pocketknife for a slide. But I sure like the sound he got with this, so I been practicing."

He demonstrated what he had picked up on his own of the bottle-neck technique—the Delta style of guitar, in which notes are bent or flattened by touching the strings with metal or glass (bottle necks were first used) as they are struck for a whining, nasal sound that is oddly appealing. I had never heard him play bottle-neck on records and was surprised at the facility he had developed with it. He is a good, if unorthodox, guitarist—one with quick, caressing fingers, who is far more daring harmonically than others who are more polished musicians.

He sang nothing, merely played for a few minutes and talked sporadically in phrases that were loosely timed to the music. He talked about his travels. Something like: "Yessir, I been to Bertrand. . . . Been to Europe, too, in Germany. . . . Yessir, played in England and Czechoslovakia. . . . Played at Newport and got five hundred at Ann Arbor. . . . Cut a tape, and I got five more hundred. . . ."

I asked him about his first guitar. When had he gotten it? When had he started playing and singing the blues?

"I made my first guitar," he said. "I made it out of a cigar box and a good stout long board, and it had five strings of baling wire. Hurt my fingers on it. That was when I was just a farm boy." Robert Pete stopped playing, set down the guitar, and started remembering: "That was right here in Louisiana. We made cotton, corn, potatoes, and raised hogs and chickens. We worked on the halves back then. The boss man got half of everything, all but the peanuts. I was just a kid of fifteen then and I took care of my mother. Back then, see, my mother had parted from my father, and she made me work for the milk dairy to take care of the family. I'd get up, oh, at two a.m. and had to milk seventy-five head of cattle.

"I have all those old-country talents. I can cook and milk cows, and all. And I'm going to tell you something, I learned all that by *doing* it. Why, I picked moss to fill a mattress, and learned how to skin cows and mules so I could sell bones for fertilizer. And I did all that to take care of my mother and sisters and brothers. They were all dead on my father's side, so there was no one but me to take care of them."

He glanced up and smiled then, remembering my question. "Now, you asked me when did I start. That must have been in 1943, when I was about twenty years old. That was when I first started looking at men playing the blues. I remember back then was Walter Green, Eddie Ticette, and Bill Chaney. I'd listen to them and beat on the bucket—that was my style. Good rhythm! But then I built this old cigar-box guitar I'm telling you about, and this fellow Walter Green he showed me a few things. He started me out with something sound like this—" Robert Pete picked up his guitar again and played a simple bass pattern, kind of a walking boogie. "Then he showed me how to add this." He added a treble line to it, and he called it "this little bumble-bee thing."

But, he reminded me, this was just a homemade guitar, and he wasn't able to do much with it. "But finally one day a colored lady working for a white lady, she told me to go over there because they had a guitar, a Simon, that might be for sale. So I went over like she said and I knocked on the door—knock-knock-knock—and the white lady comes, and I say to her, 'Yes, ma'am, I heard you had a guitar here.' And she looks at me, and she says, 'Yes, we do, and it's a mighty good one, a real eighty-five-dollar box.' Then she looks at me again, and she says, 'Do *you* have any money?' And I say, 'Yes, ma'am, but I only have four dollars.' And she says, 'I bought this for my son to learn, and he just wasn't interested, so I believe I'll teach him a lesson and sell you that guitar for four dollars.' And that was it. She got it, and I gave her the four dollars, and I got an eighty-five-dollar guitar.

"And that was my first real guitar. Pretty soon I was playing those country suppers for the colored people. And white folks would hear me playing, and they'd get me to come to their parties and play for them. I'd get a kazoo and blow on that, and they'd say, 'Come on, Pete! Come on, Pete!' Everywhere I play there's white folks there."

He looked up at me and smiled. There is this that is disturbing to me, a city-bred white from the North with the usual liberal responses: As Robert Pete Williams talks with me, I notice that whenever there is eye contact between us, he smiles automatically. It is a reflex that must have been developed long before he was an adult and must have helped him immeasurably in getting along with white people. Yet, as at least one story he told convinced me, he is not to be dismissed as anybody's "good nigger." His relations with white people have been very complicated, and still are. He is interested in getting along, but not in getting along at any price.

He was chuckling now. "Before I had trouble with my throat, I used to whoop and holler when I sang the blues, and I'd get quite a crowd around me among the colored, too. They got a man over there, his name was Willie Hudson. He was a great guitar player, too. But when I got started, he was trying to learn from me. I was a kid, and he knew I play, and he was looking at what I play and making notes on it, then he'd go out do the same thing his own self."

Robert Pete shook his head and laughed, remembering. Then he picked up the guitar and began playing softly. "I didn't have no picks," he remarked. "I had to have tough fingers." He found his way into a steady rhythm, a figure repeated. "Hear that?" he asked. "That's something like Lemon used to play, you know?" And then he began to sing against that rhythm, crooning softly as he looked out the door:

Why you treat me so mean?
Way you treat me, yeah, baby, ooh yeah.
I'm a long way from home.
I'm a stranger here, baby.
Please don't treat me wrong.

It didn't rhyme, as many of his lines do not, but that didn't matter, for again it was almost spoken against the guitar accompaniment. The steady rhythmic figure was almost a setting for the lines that came from him. And then he added, as an afterthought:

I'm gonna leave.
I'm gonna leave, baby, oh yeah.

Then he played a little swinging ride on the guitar, an improvisation on that same rhythmic pattern he had set down before, and stopped suddenly and looked up with a smile. "With the blues you make your own beat," he said.

I asked him where he got his songs, how his blues came to him. "It's just air music," he answered. "It just comes to me, is all. When I ride in a car or I'm in a field working I might begin to hear sort of an echo, as an echo of singing, like. And then maybe I start to sing with the echo, or maybe I just keep it on my brain until I get home and then pick up my guitar and start to play those blues. Yessir, it's just air music, but I remember it."

What about a blues he might want to write to say something in particular? "Oh, I write them, too. I sit here and look at you from the head on down, and I could make a song of you. Or say you misuse and scold me, I could make a record of that." He began playing idly at the guitar once more, picking with his fret hand as well as the other in a little virtuoso touch.

He continued to pick as I asked him if that is what the blues is—a song about being misused and scolded. "Well, sure," he said with an easy nod of his head. "Like me and my wife. If she's mad at me and get to fussin', then I just get my guitar and sit down like I am now, and I just pick it off. Just pick those blues away. It'll be all right then."

There was an uneasy laugh from farther in the house, and Robert Pete turned and smiled and must have realized that what he had just said embarrassed his wife, Hattie. She was setting the table now, working quietly and efficiently, eyes downcast.

"She never gives me trouble I don't deserve, though," he added after a moment. "This child I got here for a wife, she's my third wife. See, I'm the father of eight head of boys and two girls, and if I live to see this March come I'll be fifty-eight years old. But Hattie, I'll tell you, I been in love with her since the first day I met her. And I'll tell you something else, if you knock me down in a ditch, she'll pull me out—that's how she sticks by me. When we got married I was on parole and making fifteen dollars a week, had to live on grits and cheap rice and all, but she stuck by me, even though she knowed I was a convict. This was on that farm I worked when I was on parole that I met her.

"I had some trouble on that farm, too, and she stuck by me in that. Somebody there, one of the white folks, put it out to the parole officer that I was throwing wine and whiskey bottles around, and this same somebody he start giving orders to my son, who was with me then. So I tell him, 'You want my boy to do something you ask me. I'm the father.' And he gets upset then and real nasty, and he comes down on me and says, 'Why don't you thus-and-so,' and with Hattie standing right there he sort of run out of words and say, 'Aw, shit!' And I shake my finger at him then, and I say, 'Now, watch your mouth. Hattie is a black woman, and your wife, she's white, but I think I respect Hattie just like I respect your wife, and I think you should, too.' " He paused with a sober nod to let that sink in.

What happened then? I asked him.

"Well, then I was call up to the parole man and had to defend myself. And I found then that that white man had changed his story. He said no, Robert Pete didn't throw bottles, but he was waving a gun around at a party. Well, now, that wasn't true. I didn't have no gun then, and they knew that, but it was hard to get the parole man on my side. Oh, I'll tell you, parole is hard to be!"

With that, Hattie called us to the table to sit down to lunch. It was good, and there was a lot of it—pork chops, peas, and mashed potatoes, with a real country taste to the peas that said ham fat to me. Hattie seemed to do more serving than eating. We got to talking about the blues again over coffee. I think it began with a question of mine about his unusual style—the sort of setting in which he can talk the blues or chant them freely. Had he known any bluesmen earlier who played the way he does?

"Well, I'll tell you," pausing to light the filter cigarette he had pulled out of the pack on the table. "I'm just a straight-out bluesman. I'm a finger man, a picker. Fred [McDowell], he'll use that slide, and he's not too much with his fingers. A lot of people like slide and a lot don't. It's best to learn both ways. You never know. You may get in a place where you want to use it. That's why I been practicing slide.

"Let me tell you some more about the blues."

He started talking then in the rhythmic way he had earlier —but this time without his guitar. The phrases came with slight pauses between them; imagine them that way.

"The blues is something gonna tame your mind. You got a girl friend. She's in New York. Say you left her, and she wants to see you. She may start moanin' and whistlin'. She got you on her mind. *You* is the blues. I is the blues. Hattie is the blues. Say Hattie is gone. I take a few drinks and start to sing. Got Hattie on my mind. Don't help me to talk to other people. I just start to pick the blues. You got your wife on your mind. No woman you can pick up can satisfy your mind. Ain't gonna be satisfied until you get back to her."

It was a kind of recitation. He concluded it with a nod and took a puff of the cigarette, satisfied that he had had his say.

"You know," he began in a more conversational manner, "I was raised up with a white boy. He didn't have no experience of life. He was rich and married rich where what you should do is marry somebody that love you." Robert Pete told the story, a sordid one, that had involved him indirectly as an observer. The young husband bullied his wife and beat her when he suspected her of infidelity, and finally she left him. When she returned with her mother the next day for her things, he was waiting for her; he shot his wife and then himself.

"Love *means* something," said Robert Pete, commenting on his story and returning to that measured, rhythmic style of speech. "It makes you do anything. Love means a whole lot. Love makes the blues." He nodded for emphasis, and then repeated: "Love makes the blues. That's where it comes from. There wouldn't be no love and there wouldn't be no blues if there was just men. Men shootin' bull. Men shootin' dice, wrestlin'. Men don't mean nothin' together. The blues is not there. They don't have time to make the blues. The most blues you can make is when you go out with another man's wife. When a man want to see a woman he want to *see* her. Man thinks the sweetest woman is another man's wife. He want to *see* that woman —he can't help himself. . . ."

He might have continued on this subject for a while, but suddenly he started coughing. And what began as a mild smoker's hack developed into a fit. Hattie brought a glass of water, and finally it passed. "Can't get to talk like I want to," he said unhappily with a shake of his head.

It was clear he attributed to love and to the blues a kind of occult power. This got him talking specifically about occult powers—spells and the like, of the power of a black hen's egg. "If I get your name, Mr. Cook, and write it seven times across a black hen's egg, then you leave here and go to Washington, I can draw you right back to this house in three days' time. That's why it never pays to give people your full name."

He suddenly broke off and stood up, assuming a dramatic posture. "How did you think I kept those people from executing me?" he asked. Then he went on to explain: "When I knew the names of the jury, I took their names and wrote them down on a piece of paper just like that, see, and then I covered them over with my name and folded it real tight, and then I breathed my breath of life on it. So then what happened? I got up in court and I told them, 'You can send me to your prison, but I won't be there long.' This confounded the jury. I said, 'You can't kill me because I got help from somebody.' And then they want to know from where, and I tell them, 'I got help from God.' "

They took him to Angola on April 6, 1956, he said, and then he stopped, realizing perhaps just where he had come in his story and what really needed telling now.

"All my life," he began, "I been just like you see me around here. I been a humble man and a good man all days. You ask colored and white, and they tell you, 'That's a good man.' But I got in this trouble, not for being biggety and not for being bad. That was back in Scotlandville. I used to carry a gun then. I had a big family and I used to take them to the picture show and go to the store and drink a beer and then bring them home when the show was out. That was how it was that one night. I was just there drinking my beer, and there was these two men standing up against the bar, one of them I knew. The other was a stranger, just a huge man, he was.

"I say to the one I know, 'Hello, Lee.'

"He say, 'Hey, Pete.'

"And the other man, the big man, he say to me, 'Where you from?'

"I say, 'I'm from Zachary.'

" 'You're a lyin' son of a bitch.'

"And I just look at him, see, and I say, 'I wouldn't call you that.'

"Then this big man act real mean to me, and he says, 'Why don't you go back there to Zachary and pick cotton?'

"And all I said to him was 'I don't need to do that.'

"And what does he do? He hauls out this knife, and he says, 'See that, motherfucker?'

"I start moving out, and I say, 'I'm goin', you all.' He had this big hook-'n'-bill knife, and he's coming at me, and then I find my way behind is barred by that other man, the one I knew. But I had a gun in my pocket, so what could I do? I pulled it out, and still he kept on coming at me, and so I told myself, 'Shoot at the navel, and he'll live,' and so I did that, and he kept coming, so I shot him in the heart."

Robert Pete said he fled for home then and declares that the two officers who apprehended him there lied when they said he resisted arrest. Their testimony hurt him, as did that of another at the scene of the shooting who took the knife out of the hand of the man he had shot and threw it away. Robert Pete sighed. "The jury sent me up for my natural life," he said.

He had not done badly at Angola, where his skill as a dairyman had soon earned him respect on the prison farm. And then one day: "The captain tell me to get down on that guitar and pick those blues." With that, Robert Pete went over to the seat near the door where he had left the guitar. He took it up, sat down, and started picking an intricate line, as if in demonstration of what he had played there for the captain the day that the folklorist Harry Oster came to Angola.

He sat and played for several minutes there by the door without singing a line. He just looked out the front door of his house and listened to the sounds of the late Louisiana afternoon. But more than the sounds I remember the smell. There was a thick smell of mud and wet emanating from the line of trees across the field we were facing. It was almost as though we were smelling the country right down to the roots.

"There was not a lot who played and sang there at Angola," he explained. "The onliest ones were Hogman Maxey and Guitar Welch and me. Us three met up there and made the music there. And that Dr. Oster was there to record us. And he handed me a twelve-string guitar, and I never seen no twelve-string guitar before, but I played it for them, and they say to me, 'Can you make up a talkin' blues about your family?' And so that was what I did for them."

And this was how he got out of jail. They made him a guard shortly after that, handed him a gun, and told him to shoot any prisoner who stepped over the line. He was in the guard tower quite alone one night he says, when suddenly a voice behind him—"no voice I knew"—said, "Don't worry. You'll be home for Christmas with your family." He looked around and found nobody there, and he told himself, "God is talking to me." He said a prayer right then and there, kneeling as he held onto his gun.

"And then three days later my parole came through. A man came for me and took me to Denham Springs, where I met Hattie."

He had stopped playing momentarily, but he had now come to the end of the story, more or less, and so he resumed his playing once again, and he began to chord softly through a walking blues, singing as he played.

It's a mean old world, mean, mean, mean
Been livin' awful alone by myself
This is a mean old world, woman. . . .
You know the way the world run, woman,
Sometimes I wish I was dead and gone.
The way the world run, mama,
I wish I was dead and gone.

That's the blues. These casual improvisations of Robert Pete Williams that he calls "air music" conform to no established definition, yet in context they seem to capture the very essence of the music. The operative phrase here is "in context," for what I have tried to do in providing as many details as I have is to convey something of the quality of his life. Because it is out of the totality of his experiences, beliefs, and fears that he creates his music. He may, of course, have created more impressively on other occasions than he did that afternoon I spent with him at his home in Rosedale. Some of his records have some very interesting material, and I commend them to you, but listening to them over and over again, as I have since, they seem to lack the immediacy and impact of Robert Pete in his living room. Which isn't really surprising. Hear him in live performance, and you will perceive the difference, too, I think.

And if Robert Pete Williams has created his blues out of the whole of his life, so has every other bluesman worthy of the name. Disappointment in love is cited by him and so many others as the purest sort of blues experience, yet Bukka White put it to me with that special sort of wry eloquence of his that "the blues was born behind a mule." Don't forget, in other words, that life isn't all how-I-miss-you-baby and mean-mistreatin'-mama; most of it is spent behind a mule, or washing dishes, or working on the line in some factory—if you're lucky enough to have a job at all. This is what I mean about the blues coming from the *totality* of a man's experience. In Robert Pete Williams' case, his imprisonment and subsequent parole were the shaping experiences of his life. That is why so much of his music seems to express a kind of nameless and absolute loneliness, a sense of isolation that is distinctive in the music created by American bluesmen.

CHAPTER THREE

THE BIRTH OF THE BLUES

THE DIFFICULTY in talking about the origins of the blues is that so much of what anyone might say on the subject must necessarily be guesswork—and this, of course, includes what I might have to say, as well. Not that this has discouraged debate. They keep right on telling us how it all began in tones that seem increasingly louder and more strident. Theories have been tossed up as though they were facts, and a good deal of instant erudition has been used to shore them up before the structures collapse. Actually, much of what has gone down as scholarship in this area in the past is really not much more than foggy second- and third-hand pedantry meant not so much to inform as to choke off further discussion.

The big problem is Africa. Clearly, blues and jazz and the whole world of popular music that they have produced all find their source in the American Negro and his culture. Since he came from Africa and must have brought his music with him, reason seems to dictate that we have only to go back to Africa, or to those parts of Africa from which the slaves were shipped, and listen closely to hear the roots of the music that came to bloom over here. As a result, nearly every book on blues and jazz—particularly jazz—has had its obligatory first chapter on African origins. *Shining Trumpets,* by Rudi Blesh, a very thorough book on early jazz, was one of the first to go into this at length and in detail. Marshall Stearns' *The Story of Jazz* has a good three chapters to what he calls "The Prehistory of Jazz," taking the music from Africa to the New World by way of the West Indies. And a recent book, *Black Music in America,* by John Rublowsky, a much less imposing volume than its title would indicate, devotes fully a third of its 150 pages to the music of West Africa.

This music of West Africa—specifically that from Dahomey, Ghana, Guinea, and even from down in Nigeria—was distinguished for the sophistication of its rhythm. It is essentially percussion music in which melodies are done for the most part in leader-chorus, call-and-response style. Since jazz is rhythmically different from European music, it was easy and convenient to cite Africa as the source for this new rhythm. Appropriate passages were quoted by jazz historians reminding readers of Congo Square in Old New Orleans, where slaves spent their days off, listening to the drums and the chants and dancing to them with all the energy and abandon they might have shown if they were back in Africa. And they managed to suggest that a straight line could be drawn from eighteenth-century Dahomey, that would pass through Congo Square and lead right to Warren "Baby" Dodds, the best and most inventive of all the old New Orleans drummers.

Well, fine. Surely the subtle and impressive percussive effects of the native African drummers must have had some sort of ethnic or perhaps even genetic influence on the black innovators of jazz. But a couple of things—objections, if we must call them that—should be mentioned before conceding the point. First of all, rhythm does not serve at all the same function in West African music that it does in jazz. Percussion is much more prominent in native African music and more complex, too. Not only might there be four or five percussion instruments going at any given moment, but these five will probably all be playing in as many different rhythmic patterns. The subtle blending that Westerners think of as characteristic of advanced music is there in African music, all right, but it is in the rhythm rather than the harmony.

Jazz, by contrast, developed through much simpler and more strictly defined use of rhythms. Except for the occasional wild, go-go-go drum solo, the rhythm section has traditionally restricted its activities to time-keeping. In this, jazz is somewhat closer to its European than its African roots. In fact, time signatures in jazz are adapted from those used in European music, the chief differences lying in syncopation, the contrasting use of strong accents, and the "flow" of the rhythm. As a result of all this, American music and African music clearly sound quite different. They are not the same music at all; a much more profound and complete metamorphosis took place here in America during the nineteenth century (perhaps starting even before then), producing a music that was more singular in nature than the historians of jazz and American popular music are willing to allow. Latin-American music—and particularly that of Brazil—is much closer to pure West African music than is our own.

The English blues critic and historian Paul Oliver recently raised another objection in his little book *Savannah Syncopators,* which he subtitles "African Retentions in the Blues." He notes, as I have above, the usual line of the jazz historians that associates jazz rhythms with the percussion music of West Africa. But what may or may not be true for jazz, which is largely instrumental music, he says, is almost certainly not true for the blues.

> Largely a vocal music, it is also one which was, in its formative years, created by solo artists, or by pairs of musicians. The "blues band" is seldom of more than four or five pieces at any event, and even when it is as large as this it is dominated by stringed instruments. . . . When blues instrumentation, improvisation, rhythm and use of vocals are compared with the music of the rain forest [West African] drum orchestras they seem even further removed than jazz from the African tradition.

Because he had been troubled by this difficulty for a while, Oliver became quite excited when, on a visit to Africa, he came upon a pair of native musicians in the village of Nangodi, in Ghana, considerably inland from the West African coastal belt that has traditionally been designated as the root source of jazz. This was savannah land, the long plain that gives way to the north and east to the Sahara Desert. And just as the country was different, so also was the music played there. The two Oliver heard in Nangodi were professional, traveling singer-musicians (a class he says is largely unknown among the tribes outside the savannah regions); they played stringed instruments and sang plaintive songs that seemed—to his ear, at least —to bear some rudimentary resemblance to the American blues he knows so well.

> For here was the combination of vocal, rhythm and stringed instrument which hinted at a link with the blues; here, too, I heard in person for the first time an African music which could be said to "swing" in the jazz sense, where the singer and his accompanist seemed free to improvise and where the combination of instruments had a certain feeling of syncopation.

Paul Oliver builds on this and further experiences listening to the "savannah syncopators" a fairly convincing case for these native musicians—*griots,* as they are called—as the African ancestors of American music. (To anticipate your question: Yes, slaves were taken from the sub-Saharan plain, as well as from the west coast of Africa.) And in this, Oliver has one terrific advantage over others who have written with great authority in this area: He has actually been to Africa; so many others have not.

Yet firsthand experience alone does not make an expert. And while Oliver knows his blues, he admits he is an amateur on African music. There is a bona-fide expert in this area, however, one whom Oliver acknowledges and quotes on at least one point in his short book. His name is Richard A. Waterman (not to be confused with Dick Waterman, whom we shall meet later on), and he is an ethnomusicologist with a wide and detailed knowledge of African music; he also knows a good deal about related Latin-American music, and something of Afro-American music as well. The paper that he wrote in 1952, *African Influences on the Music of the Americas,* has, yet to be superseded.

Dr. Waterman was interviewed in the magazine *Living Blues* not long ago. And because the Oliver thesis on the savannah music and the blues had just recently appeared, the interviewer questioned him closely on it. What he had to say must have given very little comfort to Paul Oliver and those to whom his thesis on the African origins of the blues made good sense. Waterman is quite devastating. Let me give a few specific examples selected from his responses.

> There are no African retentions, as such, in the blues. But undoubtedly influence was great in determining the form the blues was to take. Just how far we can go in specifying the extent of this influence is a question still open to debate. . . .
>
> . . . I don't think the savannah music bears particular resemblance to blues.
>
> . . . I think there's just as much of the roots of this blues stuff in the traditional African thing on the coast, as in Senegal and Gambia, which is where he [Oliver] is talking about. I think you probably find more of the materials that went into the blues on the coast. Although superficially the fact that you do something plunking like a guitar makes it sound a little bit like it, I think his hunch is wrong.

And so on. Yet what should probably be emphasized here since I have quoted Dr. Waterman in rebuttal, is that while he is certainly an expert on African music, Paul Oliver is no less an expert on American music—or on the blues, at least. There is —at least at the moment—no single "right" answer to be chosen from these opinions.

I am not sure that all this says much more than that the question of African origins of the blues, jazz, and American popular music is one on which reasonable men—and reasonably well-informed men—may differ. And that may indeed be all that should be said about it.* There is no better way to emphasize this than to cite an interview of guitarist Buddy Guy in another issue of that same magazine, *Living Blues.* He had just been on an African tour and had come back vaguely disappointed. He kept asking to hear some "real true African music," and then they would play imitation Buddy Guy for him, for this

*I cannot resist adding at this point, in support of Paul Oliver, that the bottleneck guitar sound, so popular among Delta blues performers, has no equivalent in the Western musical tradition and must surely be an attempt to duplicate an African sound resting in the racial memory.

was what the Africans were most enthusiastic about. But he kept insisting, and so at last they gave him some records and tapes. The interviewer then asks him, "Do you see any relation between African music and blues?" He says:

> No, don't start me to lyin', because I don't. Not of what I've heard yet. No, I mean, I met some people there and they told me that this is where it all came from, you know, and I haven't found anything yet. I mean, they playin' this South American beat, and the blues is a different thing, man. I mean, ain't no sense of me lyin', 'cause you know better. The blues is, you know, a feelin'. You got to feel it to play it.

What is lurking just beneath the surface here is Buddy Guy's suspicion that because his music is different from that of the blacks whom he encountered in Africa, he might well be different from them, too. It must indeed be a shocking realization, yet it is one experienced by hundreds, perhaps even thousands, of American Negroes who go to Africa each year. Many have come back to comment on it, often dismayed and disappointed to discover that they seem American rather then simply black to Africans. And perhaps they are also secretly surprised to learn that their acculturation has been so complete: They never knew quite how American they were until they went to Africa. (A common-enough discovery—sort of the immigrant son's equivalent of "You can't go home again.")

IN THE INTRODUCTION to another book of his, *Blues Fell This Morning,* Paul Oliver has a nice neutral statement on the blues as the music of the American Negro. Let me quote it.

> . . . If there is one simple common denominator in all these aspects of the music it is that the blues is a folk form of expression that is by superficial appearance the product of a racial group, the Negro in America; although the Negro stock has been so reduced through intermarriage and miscegenation during the centuries that it is doubtful if pure African blood can be found to any great extent in the United States, and the features of African cultural origin have been so modified and altered during that passage of time, ousted by compulsory and later voluntary absorption of a new culture, that their remains—if they exist—are vestigal.

I think that statement is notable for what it does not—indeed, what it refuses to—say. It does not say, to underline the point, that the blues is absolutely and only the expression of the American Negro. Nor does it say that its origins are exclusively, or even especially, African.

But I would like us to take that "softer," more neutral, expression of the relation of the blues to the American Negro as a starting point in this discussion of how the blues came to be here in America. This way we can begin a little more lightly. We won't find ourselves quite so weighted down with the assumptions, conclusions, and prejudices of Paul Oliver and others as we try to sort out the influences that helped shape this distinctive music.

I believe, as I said earlier, that the blues is the fundamental American music. This makes it something more than merely the music of the American Negro, though I believe it was through and because of him that that music came to be. He was the agent of change, working continually from as early as the eighteenth century upon the music that he heard around him, shaping and reshaping it, giving it back to the culture as something ever more distinct. When he began on it, there was nothing unique about that music; it was simply that which colonists and emigrants had brought over with them from various corners of Europe—though chiefly, of course, from the British Isles. By the turn of the century, however, when the Negro brought blues, ragtime, and jazz into flower, the foundation of the new idiom—American music—was complete.

And so, far from being an expression of the cultural isolation of the American Negro, the music that he produced gave him the opportunity to participate in that culture and subsequently to play a dominant role in it. From very early on, long before the Civil War was fought and the slaves were freed, the blacks in America had begun to exert a subtle but very powerful influence on the Anglo-Saxon majority culture by their very presence. A sort of symbiotic relationship grew up between the two, one which nourished both more than they would ever know or recognize. I would go so far as to say that the influence of the American blacks has been the most profound of any minority on the American culture and character: It is the Negro who has given form to the Anglo-Saxon matter and created that new

Adam they talk about in the American Studies books. To the extent that we are American, we are all part black. It's what makes us what we are.

Why? Why has the *American* Negro had this distinct identity and this strong shaping influence on the majority culture? Melville Herskovits, one of the earliest and best-informed students of American Negro culture, points out that contact between American Negroes and whites from the earliest days in the slavery period was much closer than in the West Indies and South America. As a result, Africanisms persisted in both areas in a purer form—in music, certainly, and in other areas as well. "In the earliest days," Herskovits writes of America, "the number of slaves in proportion to their masters was extremely small, and though as time went on thousands and tens of thousands of slaves were brought to satisfy the demands of southern plantations, nonetheless the Negroes lived in constant association with whites to a degree not found anywhere else in the New World." It was in LeRoi Jones' book *Blues People* that I first found Melville Herskovits cited. And it is worth noting that the militant Mr. Jones not only accepts Herskovits' authority in this, but goes on to add:

> Some of this "constant association" between the white masters and the black slaves that took place in this country can be explained by comparing the circumstances of the slaves' "employment" in America with the circumstances of their employment in the rest of the New World. It was only in the United States that slaves were used on the smaller farms. Such a person as the "poor white" was a strictly American phenomenon.

The acculturation of the Negro in America, that first stage of the symbiosis between the races, was accomplished by the poor white. He was the dirt farmer in Tennessee or Kentucky or frontier Mississippi who went out and sweated in the field alongside the black man, who unbent to talk and laugh with him and who first began to sing with him. And those first songs were very likely Isaac Watts hymns or those of the Wesleys, for the first real cultural contact of the black with the white world came through religion. This—the late eighteenth and early nineteenth centuries—was the time of the Great Revival in America. The evangelical spirit of the Baptists and Methodists, which was particularly strong in the frontier West and South, knew few limits—certainly not, to their credit, those of race. It was their enthusiasm and fervor that overcame the objections of the large plantation owners (most of whom were Episcopal, Presbyterian, or—less often—Catholic) and saw to it that the good news of the Gospel was passed on to the Africans in their midst.

That old-time religion made an immediate and a lasting impression on the blacks to whom it was preached. To this day, and in spite of the proliferation of Pentacostal and fundamentalist sects, more American Negroes are members of the Baptist and Methodist churches than of all other denominations. And of all hymns and gospel songs, the favorite of blacks is still probably that familiar one from the early nineteenth century, sung by Baptists and Methodists alike in the South, "Amazing Grace."

But no matter how enthusiastically the slaves may have sung that hymn and all the others, and no matter how profoundly they may have welcomed the instruction of the missionaries who preached to them, the chief cultural importance of all this was that it soon gave them their first opportunity to work on the material of the white man's religion and begin reshaping it, just as they have reshaped, to a greater or lesser extent, other institutions here in America. For the blacks were left more or less on their own soon enough in matters of religion, and instruction fell to black preachers—the "nigger preachers" of jokes and folklore. Were they truly such figures of fun? No, for most had been given at least a fundamental education and some could lay a claim to eloquence and were the natural leaders of their slave communities—Nat Turner was such a one.

Most knew enough, in any case, to let the natural preference of their congregations for sacred music carry the burden of teaching and testifying. By most accounts, hymn-singing played an even greater part in black Baptist and Methodist church services than in the white. And soon black Christians had their *own* hymns—and what hymns they were!

Were you there when they crucified my Lord?
Were you there when they crucified my Lord?
Oh! Sometimes it causes me to tremble, tremble,
tremble!
Were you there when they crucified my Lord?

There are a number of remarkable and curious things about these Negro spirituals, as they came to be known. The first is that they came into being so early. Well before the Civil War, the black church and its music were well known in the South and were known, at least as a phenomenon, in the North and in England, too. Since the ministry to the slaves did not really get under way until fairly late in the eighteenth century, it seems to have taken the blacks no more than about fifty years to master the style of the white man's hymns, alter it, and develop a whole body of their own sacred music.

Secondly, it was *their* music—that is to say, it was quite proper and accurate to speak of these as Negro spirituals, and not the spirituals of the Negroes in one particular section of the South or another, much less to speak of them as the spirituals of the slaves on a specific plantation. No, these hymns were spread from farm to farm and state to state so thoroughly that we must revise our notions of the isolation of groups of slaves, one from the other. Communication, at least in the form of music, seems to have been complete and fairly common among them.

It might well be that there was a special sense of urgency in the way these hymns were passed from one black congregation to another, owing to what they said, the "secret" message of protest they contained. For it has come to be rather generally recognized that when the slaves sang, "Let my people go," they were thinking less of the Israelites in captivity in Egypt than of themselves in captivity in America. A black theologian, James H. Cone, has put it quite directly in his book, *The Spirituals and the Blues*.

> The basic idea of the spirituals is that slavery contradicts God; it is a denial of his will. To be enslaved is to be declared *nobody,* and that form of existence contradicts God's creation of people to be his children. Because black people believed that they were God's children, they affirmed their *somebodiness,* refusing to reconcile their servitude with divine revelation.

With this firmly in mind, it is really rather remarkable how frequently this theme of protest against slavery and the yearning for freedom does recur in the old spirituals. Here is an example:

My Lord delivered Daniel,
My Lord delivered Daniel,
My Lord delivered Daniel,
Why can't He deliver me?

And another:

We'll soon be free,
We'll soon be free,
We'll soon be free,
When de Lord will call us home.

If you know lines and verses from the old spirituals—and it is interesting how widely they are known, even today—you can probably supply more examples from your own memory.

And finally, what must be commented on is the remarkable quality of the spirituals. Nobody who heard them could ignore them. Their emotional appeal was almost palpable in its intensity. And as music, they were something different—in ways, like the old Isaac Watts hymns from which they derived, yet with qualities of their own that suggested the forms that were to follow. There were blue notes in the spirituals, swinging tempos, and some syncopation, all of which anticipated blues, jazz, and especially gospel singing. But there were differences, too. The spirituals were ceremonial in nature, as is most African music (most *West* African music, anyway). It was choral music, too, in which a leader might sing a line and ask for a response, but in which the soloist, as such, was quite unknown. And finally, along this same line, it was also the sort of music in which the role of the individual was subjugated almost totally to that of the group—the congregation. It was "we," not "I," music.

So were the work songs, chants, and field hollers that the slaves sang. These are often cited by historians and anthropologists as sources for the blues. And at least one bluesman—Son House—agrees. He is quoted in Samuel Charters' *The Bluesmen* as supporting this notion when he says, "People keep asking me where the blues started and all I can say is that when I was a boy we always was singing in the fields. Not real singing, you know, just hollerin', but we made up our songs about things that was happening to us at that time, and I think that's where the blues started. . . ."

This is, in a way, rather convincing testimony, certainly enough to sell blues historians and scholars who seem eager to discount the importance of the spirituals as a source for the blues. Why this prejudice? It may be a sort of vague Marxist bias, a grudge against the old Negro church and the quietism that it stood for during the many decades when it served as the opium of the black people. Or it may be simply a matter of taste: remembered nausea from early exposure to the Hall Johnson Choir or a memory of Marian Anderson singing "Swing Low, Sweet Chariot." It was actually rather insidious the way that the spirituals were used *against* black people back in the thirties and forties, promoting an image of black submission that was even less accurate than when the hymns were created in the days of slavery. Among whites, it encouraged a complacency and an attitude of self-satisfied paternalism toward the blacks that prevailed until by some sort of rough justice that mood was shattered by a black churchman, Martin Luther King, Jr., in the middle fifties.

But what about those old field hollers? What relation have they to the blues? Not a very direct one, I think. I'm talking now about those wordless moans, trilling cries, and brief comments and messages that were given out in a kind of black style close to plainchant. When whites first became aware of all this back in the nineteenth century, they referred to it as Negro yodeling. Blacks themselves simply called it loud-mouthing, whooping, or just plain hollering. But it all seems to have less to do with the music that followed than with that which went before. In their rawest form, the field hollers seem a genuine and fairly pure survival from the African tradition. Harold Courlander, a widely traveled folklorist, has described in his *Negro Folk Music, U.S.A.* how he heard what seemed about the same cries in Nigeria, Haiti, and Matanzas Province, Cuba, as he had heard earlier in the American South. Probably so, but they are not heard here much today. Even a generation ago, you had to go pretty deep into the country to catch those haunting, pleasantly weird sounds, most of which were sung in modal scales. The closest most of us ever came was hearing the similar cries of the black peddlers and street merchants. New Orleans and Charleston are famous for these street cries even now, but they could be heard as far north as Chicago before the war.

Work songs are something else again. They are the rhythmic,

sometimes highly syncopated melodies and chants that are sung to provide the proper work beat for a gang of men as it toils together. The lead singer—usually the work-gang leader—in this way controls the pace of their labor. Now, there is nothing new about work songs of this sort. They probably go back to the building of the pyramids or the Babylonian temples, or before; whenever men have had to pull or strike together, songs in one style or another have helped them do it right. Nor is there anything peculiarly African about the work songs sung in America by black laborers. Many of them, in fact, sound as though they may have been derived from Irish sources, for indeed the blacks and the Irish worked side by side in the beginning on railroad and river-boat gangs even before the Civil War. In his 1876 sketch, "Levee Life," Lafcadio Hearn gives a fascinating account of the musical subculture of the black and white roustabouts who worked the Cincinnati river front, and he remarks in passing: "One fact worth mentioning about these Negro singers is, that they can mimic the Irish accent to a degree of perfection which an American, Englishman, or German could not hope to acquire." He goes on to tell of "a very dark mulatto," who sang for them "The hat me fahther worrre," and was joined by another black on the chorus:

'Tis the raylics of ould decency,
The hat me fahther wor-r-re.

And at least one of the many work songs that Hearn has transcribed from the stevedores working on the dock has a rollicking and distinctly Irish quality:

Molly was a good gal and a bad gal, too.
Oh Molly, row , gal.
Molly was a good gal and a bad gal, too,
Oh Molly, row, gal.

I'll row dis boat and I'll row no more,
Row, Molly, row gal.
I'll row dis boat, and I'll go on shore,
Row, Molly, row gal.

Captain on the biler deck a-heaving of the lead,
Oh Molly, row, gal.
Calling to the pilot to give her "Turn ahead,"
Row, Molly, row, gal.

But even among those ditties and work songs quoted in "Levee Life," you can discern a kind of black style emerging—Hearn, a good reporter, notes this at the time. And it became more and more distinct in the decades that followed—more complex in its rhythms, closer and closer to true syncopation. A few of these songs—"Grizzly Bear," "Take This Hammer," and "Told My Captain"—are still remembered and are in the repertoire of just about every folkie who has ever twanged a guitar. Another, probably the best known of them all, is not so much a work song as a work ballad. The ubiquitous "John Henry" may not even be of black origin, but it was enthusiastically taken up and sung by the black steel drivers and gandy dancers who worked the railroads throughout the South. It tells, of course, of the giant steel-driving champion (traditionally, a Negro) who takes on a steam-driven pile driver in a competition, wins over it handily, proving "A man ain't nothin' but a man." Yet in winning, he overtaxes his poor heart and dies at the moment of his triumph.

The tradition of ballad-making, which was so strong among the English-, Scotch-, and Irish-Americans, was taken up by the American Negroes in the latter part of the nineteenth century, probably sometime in the seventies or eighties. It is significant, though not really surprising, that the first of these black ballads should have come in the bad-man ballad tradition. There were plenty of white ballads describing the deeds of desperadoes, such as "Jesse James," "Sam Bass," and "Tom Dooley." There was also at least one, "John Hardy," which was a white ballad about a black murderer. But it wasn't long before the blacks themselves began telling stories in song of their own bad men, such as "Stackerlee," the Memphis gambler who shot down poor Billy Lyons in a senseless dispute over a Stetson hat. And then, of course, there were "Frankie and Albert," those ill-starred St. Louis lovers, whose tragic story became one of the best known in America (though in the bargain was changed somehow to the tale of "Frankie and Johnnie").

The underworld milieu of gamblers, gunmen, and whores that produced "Stackerlee" and "Frankie and Albert" is the same one that brought forth the earliest urban blues in cities up and down the Mississippi. Anyone who doubts the origins of blues and jazz in the world of vice has only to look at a few of the frank memoirs of the period—Louis Armstrong's *Satchmo: My Life in New Orleans* and Pops Foster's *The Autobiography of a New Orleans Jazzman* tell the story quite graphically—to find out what things were really like in Storyville. One of the denizens of that district, Jelly Roll Morton made a series of recordings for the Library of Congress in his later years under the direction of Alan Lomax, who was then Folk Music Curator. He talked and sang his way through a series of reminiscences of life in the Storyville district of New Orleans, and among the songs he recorded was an interesting one about a New Orleans bad man of the 1900s named Aaron Harris. He did not claim to have written it (which alone is remarkable, for he claimed to have written and even copyrighted many that he stole from others), but it is the sort of ballad a bluesman might write. In fact, it is a sort of merger of the two—a bad-man ballad in classic twelve-bar blues form.

Aaron Harris was a bad bad man. (twice)
He was the baddest man who ever was in this land.

He killed his sweet little sister and his
brother-in-law. (twice)
About a cup of coffee he killed his sister and his
brother-in-law.

He got out of jail every time he would make a kill.
(twice)
He had a hoodoo woman—all he had to do was pay
the bill.

All the policemen on the beat, they had him to fear.
(twice)
You could always tell when Aaron Harris was near.

He pawned his pistol one night to play in a
gambling game. (twice)
Well, old Four-Horn shot him—that blotted out his
name.

There were a number of songs that were first heard in the 1890s and 1900s in which blues and ballad elements were mixed. "Betty and Dupree" was one, a murder ballad somewhat in the "Frankie and Albert" vein that is told in three-line couplet blues stanzas. "Boll Weevil" was another, the ballad about that little bug who came up from Mexico, "just lookin' for a home, just lookin' for a home." In addition, there were songs like the old New Orleans parade classic, "Didn't He Ramble," and the blues W. C. Handy claimed, "Careless Love," which had their origins in English folk songs. And the one that Big Bill Broonzy called the first blues, "Joe Turner Blues," dated in 1890 on the advice of his uncle (Big Bill himself was born in 1893), a haunting story-song about a white man who goes about helping the blacks, in which the refrain is repeated:

They tell me Joe Turner been here and gone
Lord, they tell me Joe Turner been here and gone
They tell me Joe Turner been here and gone

In all of these and others, as well, the elements merge and mix so that it is difficult to tell quite where the ballads left off and the blues began.

In case you don't recognize it as such, that last sentence—with its implication that the blues derive directly from certain ballad sources—would qualify as the rankest sort of heresy in many circles. For those who believe intensely in the segregation of black music from white will never allow that both races continued their musical commerce right up to and including the time, just about the turn of the century, when the creation of the new musical idiom had been finally and certainly accomplished. Some adhere almost fanatically to the notion of parallel musical streams moving along through the decades right up to the present. In reality, however, while the streams certainly did originate from separate sources—Europe and Africa—they crossed and recrossed again and again, meandering tortuously, until at last they flowed together into that wide mainstream sound that we all now recognize instinctively as American.

YOU HAVE ONLY to listen to someone like John Jackson to realize of what little moment are the fine musical distinctions on which blues scholars stake their reputations. He is by classification a songster and not a bluesman, although he will play and sing more blues on a good night's parlor concert than some Delta bluesmen may have known in a lifetime. The difference is that except for an occasional extra verse or two, or new words to an old song, John Jackson doesn't write music, he collects it.

He, of course, doesn't think of himself as either a collector *or* a songster, but simply as a guitar player and country singer who happens to know a lot of songs. That is his reputation in Fairfax, Virginia, in the suburbs of Washington, D.C., where he has lived with his family since 1949.

The funny thing is that by the time you get out there just beyond Fairfax it doesn't seem like suburbs at all: it seems like country. It may have been owing to the time of year that I drove out—early spring—but there wasn't much traffic on the road. And the deep, heavy humus smell that I sniffed as soon as I stepped out of my car was a country smell. It had been raining recently, and there was a damp chill in the air, so that the effect was a little like having driven far to the west, out to the Blue Ridge country, where John Jackson had been born and where, even then, there was still snow on the mountaintops.

Met at the door by one of his children, I was ushered into the house quickly and seated in the living room by John's wife, Cora. I had been misinformed about her. Someone who should have known better told me that she was a white woman. She is not—at least not in the sense that this is generally meant. But it is worth reflecting, on meeting someone like Cora Jackson, just how little these designations of race really mean. Although her hair is auburn and her face a ruddy pink, she was born and raised a Negro in rural Virginia. And is proud of it.

She told me that Johnny had been called out to do a little job. He expected to be back by the time I arrived. "But he shouldn't be long now, because he only has one grave to dig." One of the many ways John Jackson keeps busy and supports his family is as a gravedigger in Fairfax. He has also worked as an agricultural laborer, has done a little farming himself, has pumped gas, and has a good reputation as a handyman in his neighborhood.

He provides very well for his family. They live in a comfortable single-story house of cinder-block construction on a good-sized plot of land that lies just off the highway. As Cora Jackson excused herself to go back to the kitchen—"I'm baking, and the bread won't wait once it's in the pan"—I looked over the living room and noticed a kind of antique country-parlor look to it that I liked. There were two portraits, both of them old etchings, over the fireplace. One I recognized instantly as George Washington, but the bearded face next to his called for a closer look—it was Robert E. Lee. The fire in the fireplace felt good. Warming my hands and listening to Cora Jackson sing in the kitchen as she worked the bread, I happened to notice the eighteenth-century andirons that supported the blazing logs. They were cast in the shape of coachmen, complete with tricorn hats, breeches, and cutaway coats—white coachmen.

John Jackson came in apologizing. Not just for being late, he said, "but because there's a whole bunch of boys following me down from the cemetery." They were coming to hear him play and sing a little, and I got the idea that this was a regular thing on Sundays. He wasted no time hauling out his guitar, and by the time he was tuned up, the boys had arrived and had taken places around the living room. Introductions were quite informal, but I found out that one of the visitors—two of them white and two black—was John's brother Freddy.

"Well," John Jackson said with a smile, "what would y'all like to hear?"

" 'Wildwood Flower,' " called out one of his visitors.

John nodded pleasantly, just to show he understood, but promptly launched into another song, "Rattlesnakin' Daddy," one that he has recorded and sings with a lot of verve and spirit. And he sings it in a voice that might confuse the casual listener, for he sounds "white." Most of us are so used to hearing black Southerners talk and sing in that Deep South accent that when we hear something else from them it confuses us just a little.

And John Jackson talks the way everybody does up in the mountains of Virginia. He is from Rappahannock County, up in the mountain country, hard by the West Virginia line. He is the son of a tenant farmer and one of thirteen children. He tells of how he started guitar under his father's instruction but then got a real education on the instrument when a fancy guitar player came through on a chain gang. It was from him, he will tell you, that he really learned how to play.

And you don't have to listen to him long on the guitar to realize that he is really an accomplished musician. "A real country picker," as they say down there. He can play those double lines on guitar, and make it sound almost like a piano. These were improvisations and variations that he interpolated between verses in a style that was something between early jazz and country music. He was having fun with it, you could tell. He finished with a smile on his face. He smiles a lot. He has a good time.

"Those at the end were my own verses," he explained. "I write my own verses sometimes. I heard the song off Blind Boy Fuller's record that my Daddy had, but I added to it."

I asked if he had learned most of his songs that way, from records, and he said that he had, and then went on to tell how his father had come to buy a record player in the first place. It seems a couple of salesmen for whom his father had little use came by one day with something in a big box to show him. His father told them in no uncertain terms that they were to get out, with which they drove up on the hill overlooking the Jackson place, wound up the box, and music began to issue forth from it. "Gawd a'mighty," said his father, and he beckoned them down from the hill. He and the family listened to it on the front porch for the better part of the afternoon and decided to buy it.

"We'd get the small records for ten cents then or the big ones for twenty-five. We must have had about 500 of them when we moved to Fairfax, but most of them got broke. But I'd learned them all by then."

"Blues, too?" I asked.

"Oh, sure. Blind Boy Fuller and Blind Lemon Jefferson, all of them fellas. Jimmie Rodgers, too."

"The hillbilly singer?"

"Jimmie Rodgers sang blues!" John Jackson declared. He seemed slightly vexed at the way I had so quickly classified the Singing Brakeman from Meridian, Mississippi, as a "hillbilly." "He's the onliest man I ever did hear singing the 'TB Blues,' and that was a good blues. He used to sing this one, too—" And he launched into the traditional "T for Texas, T for Tennessee," with its refrain, "I'm gonna drink muddy water, sleep in a hollow log." But only about a chorus of that—just enough to show which one he meant. "Jimmie Rodgers got that from Lemon Jefferson. He learned a lot of songs from him and some others when he used to work through Texas and Louisiana on the railroad."

"Play 'Wildwood Flower,' Jack." It was one of the men who had come in with Freddy Jackson who kept asking for "Wildwood Flower." He was white and about half-drunk.

"Please call me John," he answered mildly in reproof.

"Yeah," Freddy Jackson urged the man. "Call him John or Johnny. Jack isn't his name."

Cora came out from the kitchen. "Y'all gonna play together?" she asked, meaning the two Jackson brothers.

"Well, we just might do that," said John, obviously pleased at the idea. Freddy ran into another room and came out with a guitar which he had tuned in a moment. They sat down together, began picking around, and seeming to know just where they were headed, they began "Nobody's Business." This is a song he has recorded, and he does a fine version of it, but one much different from the one he did that day with his brother. Freddy played and sang the lead, John playing backup guitar and coming in on the choruses. The two like singing together, you can tell. Freddy's voice is thinner but a little more "black" in timbre. The two finished the song, nodded their mutual approval, and went right into the old hymn, "When the Roll Is Called Up Yonder." John harmonized on this, and everybody in the room joined in on the refrain, Cora Jackson carrying the high notes. It sounded nice, very nice, the way we all imagine it might have sounded in a living room like this a hundred years ago.

As soon as they finished, there was a general murmur of approval through the room, and the white man produced his bottle and started it around. They sang another hymn then—"one of those *old* hymns," said Freddy—called "Farther Along." And then, ready to swing a bit once more, John said, "Let's play 'Step It Up,' " and to me, in explanation, "That's kind of a ragtime song."

"You take the lead," said Freddy.

John did more than sing it. He did some real swinging on it. And what he had called "kind of a ragtime" turned out to be a highly syncopated blend of country and jazz styles that would demand a lot of any guitar player. He had it to give, though, and had the knack of keeping good time for himself on the bass line as he improvised some good licks on the treble. After a little of this Freddy just put down his own guitar and listened.

"Play another one, Johnny," his brother urged as soon as he had finished.

"Okay, how about this 'Guitar Rag'? I know a little bit of that."

And he took off once again, delivering a solid walking bass. It was just about the old "trucking" tempo, and Freddy found it irresistible. In a moment he was up, hopping around from foot to foot, shaking his finger in the air. Everybody laughed and applauded—everybody, that is, except the "Wildwood Flower" man. He was suddenly and very loudly asleep.

"Cora, you and Fred do a dance," said John. "Do the 'Flat-foot.' " He explained to me: "This is one of my songs I used to do at dances." The two of them started side by side through a kind of tap-and-clog routine that seemed to go over pretty well.

"Come on, Freddy!" somebody shouted.

"Well, I'm gettin' old." And then, cutting a particular caper, he cried out, "I'm from Rappahannock County. You can't mess with me!"

Through it all, John beat a pleasant, light rhythm on his guitar and kept things moving along just as though he were a whole rhythm section. "I love to play dances," he declared when he finished, "and I used to play a lot of them, too. But it was playing a dance that quit me playing music altogether." I asked him to explain, and he told me about playing a date in Slate Mill, Virginia, one night when a drunk came along in an evil mood. He sat down and didn't say a word for fifteen minutes, just glowered at John, who was playing the guitar. "Finally," said John, "he jumped up and said, 'You stole my guitar. Now give it here.' He was determined to fight me, but I sure wasn't going to let him have that guitar. So I just told him no, I didn't steal his guitar, and I took Cora and the kids and we headed out the door. Just as we hit outside he threw this jug at us he'd been carrying, and it hit a tree just ahead of us and broke into a hundred pieces. But we made the car and got out of there. Oh, I didn't like that at all, neither did Cora." It wasn't long before they moved to Fairfax, and because of that incident, he just decided to give up music for a while. "I really didn't play any more until 1964 or 1965."

Nobody said anything for a moment, and it may have seemed to John that things had gone a bit too solemn, for he suddenly said, "How about this?" And without further introduction, he set his guitar flat on his lap, Hawaiian-guitar style, produced a pocketknife, and did a real virtuoso slide-guitar performance of "The Wabash Cannonball."

"Hey! I know that one!" shouted the drunken sleeper, now suddenly awake. "That's the 'Wabash Cannonball.' Ain't it?"

John nodded as he continued to chord idly on the guitar.

"Now play 'Wildwood Flower.' "

"Oh, I played that one," said John with a wink to me. "Didn't you hear?"

"No, doggone it. I was asleep. I guess I slept right through it."

"Maybe next time."

Everybody laughed, but the guy never figured out why.

IT MIGHT be possible, and even desirable, to separate very precisely those elements that have shaped American music if it were dead, fixed, something in the past. But it is alive. The whole tradition lives in a good country picker like John Jackson. He will play an old hymn, such as "When the Roll Is Called Up Yonder," do a good old blues, and then cap the set with something like "Blue Suède Shoes." He knows them all. They are all real to him. They seem to him almost like pieces of the same long song.

Maybe they are.

SKIP JAMES *Ann Charters*

BESSIE SMITH *Frank Driggs Collection*

MANCE LIPSCOMB *Chris Strachwitz/Arhoolie Records*

BUKKA WHITE *Samuel Charters*

FRED McDOWELL *Chris Strachwitz/Arhoolie Records*

ROBERT PETE WILLIAMS *Ann Charters*

PART
TWO

CHAPTER FOUR

THERE IS one generalization that has been made about relations between blacks and whites in America that seems to me just about as valid today as it did when I first came across it late in the fifties. I remember reading it in an essay by S. I. Hayakawa; he offered it as a bit of folk wisdom that he felt summed up the situation pretty well: In the South (goes the analysis), they don't care how close a nigger gets as long as he doesn't get too high. In the North, they don't care how high a Negro gets as long as he doesn't get too close.

I recall with some slight chagrin that at the time I thought the North won on points in this sort of comparison. I no longer think that. I have seen too much in the intervening years of the going style of administering racial justice at arm's length from the White House, Gracie Mansion, and other Northern centers of power and influence. It has soured me a little on the liberal passion for the abstract—that de-personalizing, anyplace-but-here method of dealing with human problems of every sort: by appropriate programs, funded by sufficient money, and run by competent professionals.

That's not the South. It might well be argued that a bit more of this approach early in the game might have saved Southern whites much of the pain they experienced during the past decade in the process of being dragged into the twentieth century. But nevertheless a change has been worked, and is being worked still, down there in that region where change once seemed impossible. And it is even more profound because, in those towns and small cities where the Southern experience is shaped daily, the change is being worked on a personal level. The South is a more personal place. That is its misery and its glory; it may ultimately be its damnation or its salvation. Injustice, when it comes there (which is still far too frequently), is not so often attributable to some abstract entity such as the System or the Man, but more likely to that damn peckerwood cracker down the road. Let a man know his antagonist, give him some focus for his rage, and he may not be able to overcome, but at least he can hold onto his sanity.

A black man named Albert Murray described his own long voyage home in a fine book called *South to a Very Old Place.* In it, he remarks, "Somebody once declared that when you come right down to intimate personal contacts, the Southerner is likely to be lying when he says he is a racist and the Northerner is likely to be lying when he professes not to be one." Which is a kind of restatement of the theme with which we began this discussion.

But what is the point of this discussion, after all? Where is it leading us? To the South, on this blues trip, down to the deepest, darkest part of it, the Mississippi Delta, down where the blues was born. But I think you should know that you'll be traveling in the company of one—myself—who has had only limited experience of the region. I tend to be suspicious of knowledge that does not have some basis in firsthand experience. Mine was gained on reporting trips, visits, and a couple of tours gathering information for this book. I was more certain what the South was and what I thought of it before I had been there than I am today. I seem to have fewer and fewer preconceptions each time I go down.

What do *I* know about the South? I know, as I have said, that it is a very personal place. I also know, with a nod to Albert Murray, who framed the quality well in the title of his book, that the South is a very old place. You sense that even as you drive along the sterile Interstate routes that everywhere else tend to obscure the qualities of the country through which they pass, rather than reveal them. Here, something of the land shows through. It is there in the somber green of the rolling countryside, and in the shacks that seem to pop up each mile or so on the horizon. Travel in the winter, as I did down through the Delta land, and you will be struck by the odd quality of the daylight filtering down through the pearly skies, enough like Ireland or Scotland at that time of year so that you might unconsciously begin to look for castle ruins and flocks of sheep along the way. Take a turn off the Interstate, however, and drive into one of the little towns along the way—Como, Askew, or Itta Bena—and then get out and walk around. As that raw Mississippi wind whips through you, any romantic memories you may have had of Ireland or Scotland will be blown away in an instant. No, this is down-home country, all right, the American South—but even so, the "old" quality of the country hereabouts should be immediately apparent as you walk through one of these Delta towns, for it is like taking a stroll back into the last century. The pace is altogether slower. No building in the center of town seems to have gone up since 1900. Everything is so specific, there is such a quality of place here, that you may have the feeling that you have wandered by mistake onto some elaborately constructed and perfectly authentic Hollywood set, one that might have been kept ready on the back lot as the "Turn-of-the-Century Southern Street." *Or whatever.*

Where is the Delta country? In his book *Country Blues,* Samuel Charters quotes some anonymous source to the effect that it "begins at the lobby of the Peabody Hotel in Memphis, Tenn.," and goes all the way down to Natchez, or "just about as far south as you want it to go." A less generous, though probably more precise measure would take in everything between the Yazoo and the Mississippi rivers. Since the Yazoo flows into the Mississippi at Vicksburg, that gives us a precise southern limit. Fixing the northern limits of the Delta is not quite so easy, for the Tallahatchie flows into the Yazoo up near Greenwood, and tradition puts most of the country watered by the Tallahatchie within the realm—Clarksdale, certainly, and Cleveland, Mississippi, off straight to the west, are pure Delta.

YES, ANY MAP of the blues country of Mississippi must include Cleveland, for it was just outside there on the Dockery Plantation that Charley Patton grew up, the first of the Delta bluesmen to emerge from the anonymity of the folk blues tradition. He was born farther south, just east of Vicksburg, in the little town of Edwards, in about 1885. A small man of frail physique, he was not really built for the back-breaking work in the fields, and he managed to escape it through most of his life because of his skill with a guitar, his deep, strong voice, and his remarkable ability to make original songs from the raw material of the life he saw around him.

If not unique, he was at least unusual because of the indelible stamp of authorship he put on so many of his blues. They belonged to him and not to some vague tradition. You knew they were Charley Patton's songs because specific references abounded in them to himself, his friends, their adventures and mishaps, and the local disasters they lived through together. In this, it is interesting that the first Delta bluesman of reputation worked in a kind of transitional idiom. His songs were much more closely related to the ballads than were those of the bluesmen who followed him. More often than not, they told a story or announced an event. In "High Water Everywhere," for example, he presents the drama of the Mississippi flood of 1927, marking the progress of the rising water town by town as it moves on down the river. The song is as effective a piece of *reporting* as you will find in all of the blues, but in a way it is closer to Woody Guthrie's ballads of the dust bowl disaster than to the work of any other black blues writer.

Using that simple three-line couplet, Charley Patton could tell a pretty good story, too. His "High Sheriff Blues" tells a tale that is obviously his own, naming names and locating it very specifically in the town of Belzoni, Mississippi. But it is not really a ballad because it lacks the objectivity of a ballad. The blues spirit is there, the emotion, for it is a story told from the inside.

When the trial's in Belzoni ain't no use in screaming
and crying (twice)
Mister Webb will take you back to Belzoni jailhouse
flying.

Let me tell you folkses how he treated me (twice)
And he put me in a cell there it was dark as it could be.

It was late one evening Mr. Purvis was standing 'round (twice)
Mr. Purvis told Mr. Webb to let poor Charlie down.

It takes boozey booze, Lord, to carry me through (twice)
Thirty days seem like years in a jailhouse where there is no booze.

I got up one morning feeling mighty bad (twice)
And it must not of been them Belzoni jail blues I had

While I was in trouble ain't no use a-screaming and crying (twice)
Mr. Purvis on his mansion he doesn't pay no mind.

In addition to the ballad-related blues that he wrote, he recorded a number of straight ballads—a version of the old Boll Weevil song, which he called "Mississippi Boll Weevil Blues," and "Frankie and Albert" among them.

Yes, he recorded a good deal before his death in 1934. In just five years, beginning in 1929, he cut something like sixty sides for Paramount and Vocalion; about half were blues and the rest were ballads and religious songs. He would only be a legend today if it were not for this recorded legacy he left behind. He barely strayed from his native Delta country except to make these trips north to Richmond, Indiana, Chicago and New York to record. Otherwise his life was the sort of endless round of nights spent at country dances and juke joints, and days at weekend picnics and fish fries, that was the pattern for all the itinerant bluesmen of the region.

And if Charlie Patton is important as an innovator with a direct relationship to the kinds of music that preceded the blues—to the ballads and the ur-blues that came out of the work songs and field hollers—he is just as important as a link to the music that followed. He traveled with the younger Son House, tutored a youngster named Chester Burnett who later made it big as Howlin' Wolf, and inspired Bukka White, who as a kid used to follow him around their hometown of Cleveland. Although it would be wrong to call him the originator of the Delta blues style, Patton was the earliest practitioner to send it via recordings outside the region.

IF ROBERT JOHNSON had not existed, they would have to have invented him. His is the most potent legend in all the blues—that of the gifted young artist, driven by his hunger for life and his passion for music to excesses that killed him at the age of twenty-four. Yet he left behind him a treasure of blues recordings that have inspired collectors and musicians alike for decades since. He is the Shelley, Keats, and Rimbaud of the blues all rolled into one. If any bluesman is assured of immortality it is this little drifter-with-a-guitar who may never have left the South.

Nobody seems to know where or precisely when he was born, but by subtraction, the date comes out to sometime in 1914, and the place was probably in the vicinity of Robinsonville, Mississippi, for that was where he grew up. He showed up there, just a kid in short pants, with a harmonica, one night at a juke joint where Son House and Willie Brown were playing and asked if he could join them. He was pretty good with the harp, but it turned out that what he really wanted was to have them teach him guitar. Before they could settle down to that, though, Son and Willie moved on to another town down the river. It was six months later when they got back. They found that Robert Johnson had not only taught himself how to play guitar in the interim, but, still only a boy, he had become a bluesman of some reputation in the area.

But he didn't stay around there long. In the next few years, he was constantly on the move through the South. It must have started for him as a kind of hegira to the great cities—he got to Memphis and St. Louis early—but soon he was rambling just to ramble—Helena, Arkansas, Itta Bena, Mississippi, and on down through the Delta to Louisiana, and then west to Texas. "I got to keep moving," he sang in one song, and in another he told them,

You may bury my body, ooh, down by the highway side,
So my old evil spirit can get a Greyhound bus and ride.

Sometime during this period of wandering Robert Johnson was heard by a local record salesman of the American Record Corporation (the kind who used to fill up the car trunk with "Race" records and go out to the crossroads in black communities to peddle them). He was recommended to A.R.C.'s Don Law, who had come south to record local artists for the Vocalion label. The sessions that Johnson recorded for Law in November, 1936, and June, 1937, are among the richest in the history of the blues. Not only did they leave a permanent record of his skill with a guitar and his extremely subtle and flexible vocal style, but they also established a fund of original blues material on which the younger generation has drawn liberally ever since. For example, Cream recorded his "Crossroads Blues" as "Crossroads," Paul Butterfield adapted his "Walking Blues," The Rolling Stones included "Love in Vain" on their *Let It Bleed* album, and Taj Mahal recently cut a fine version of Johnson's "Sweet Home Chicago."

What sort of man was he? He had a reputation as a hellion, and Don Law's experiences with Johnson on their first session in San Antonio, Texas, prove the point. (I've stooped to quoting liner notes here, but the story is too good to pass up.) Frank Driggs, who produced a Columbia reissue of Johnson material, tells it this way:

> . . . A country boy in a moderately big town, Johnson found trouble within hours after he arrived. Don Law considered himself responsible for Johnson, found him a room in a boarding house and told him to get some sleep so he would be ready to begin the recording at ten the following morning. Law then joined his wife and some friends for dinner at the Gunter Hotel. He had scarcely begun dinner when he was summoned to the phone. A policeman was calling from the city jail. Johnson had been picked up on a vagrancy charge. Law rushed down to the jail, found Johnson beaten up, his guitar smashed; the cops had not only picked him up but had worked him over. With some difficulty, Law managed to get Johnson freed in his custody, whisked him back to the boarding house, gave him forty-five cents for breakfast, and told him to stay in the house and not go out for the rest of the evening. Law returned to the hotel, only to be called to the phone again. This time it was Johnson. Fearing the worst, Law asked, "What's the matter now?" Johnson replied, "I'm lonesome." Puzzled, Law said,

> "You're lonesome? What do you mean, you're lonesome?" Johnson replied, "I'm lonesome and there's a lady here. She wants fifty cents and I lacks a nickel. . . ."

He was a man of contradictions. Perhaps if he had lived longer he might have reconciled some of them and settled down to a longer, steadier, more productive career. Instead, he settled for genius. On the one hand, he was shy. Law tells of asking him to show his stuff on guitar to a group of Mexican musicians and seeing Johnson so overcome with embarrassment that he was only able to play after he had turned away from them. On the other hand, he could be bold to the point of foolhardiness. Son House says he was surprised that Johnson lived as long as he did because of the young bluesman's way of moving in on any woman who caught his eye, whether or not a husband or a boy friend were in sight. In the end, it seems to have been jealousy that did him in. He died mysteriously and violently. Some say he was stabbed and some say he was poisoned. He died, in any case, early in 1938.

Because Robert Johnson was such a complex and ultimately mysterious personality, I decided to seek out the one man left who remembers him well and can comment with authority on him. His name is Johnny Shines. He met Johnson sometime in the middle thirties in Helena, Arkansas. At that time, Shines had the beginning of a reputation himself. They were calling him "Little Wolf," because one night he had picked up Howlin' Wolf's guitar and started playing his stuff. "Suddenly everything Wolf was doing fell into place, and so I started laying it out. When he got back, the joint was rocking." And so, when Johnny Shines met Robert Johnson they were more or less on even terms—and that was how they traveled together off and on over a period of a couple of years. They are no longer on even terms, though, for while Shines could hold his own with Johnson the man, he can't compete with the legend—and I sense he has grown tired of trying.

After nearly thirty years in Chicago, he has returned to the South and lives comfortably in a suburb of Tuscaloosa, Alabama. He is a sensitive, intelligent man, somewhat disenchanted with his long career as a bluesman. If not wasted, the time he gave to it (he seems to feel) was misspent. Although he looks younger, he is now in his fifties. He is trying to make sense of his life, as a man will at that age, and is engaged in the writing of his autobiography.

"Then when I finish that," he told me, "I got another book I want to write, and the name of it is *Success Was My Downfall.* What's it about? Well, it's about all of us who want success and maybe get a little of it and are not able to cope with it."

Who and what does he have in mind? "Well, that Robert Johnson, the boy I played along with so long. If I'd been a success like him I might not have been able to handle it any better than he could. He couldn't stand the success—it was his downfall. They talk about liquor and women, but that wasn't it. It was the success did him in."

Still, Johnny Shines isn't bitter. He has a good band going now—the best in his part of the South—and a decent life for himself, his wife, and the houseful of grandchildren who are with them. If he hasn't made it big, as have Muddy Waters and Howlin' Wolf and one or two others, nevertheless he has a respectable reputation with blues aficionados around the country and plays the festivals and the blues clubs on the two coasts.

It's just that after all these years he seems haunted by the memory of his old blues buddy. This happened, no doubt, partly because writers, researchers, and the merely curious keep annoying him with questions about Robert Johnson (I plead guity on all counts) and won't let him forget. But only partly because whenever he speaks of him he seems truly baffled by this episode. Even after this lapse of years, he seems to regard his time with Johnson as his encounter with genius. Robert, as he calls him, is still a mystery to Johnny Shines.

I asked him what Johnson was like, and he took it that I meant physically. "Oh, he was a good-looking-enough fellow, but little, no size to him at all. It's what made him look like a kid to everyone."

"Was he about my height?"

"Might be, but you'd make two of him across." (I'm about five-nine, 160.)

"What kind of person was he?"

"That was just it. You couldn't figure him. Now, I mean we were together off and on a long time and did a lot of traveling together, but he never would say much except what do you think of this guitar man or that girl over there, stuff like that. And you might be playing with him someplace, and he'll say, hey, I'm gonna go out and take a leak—then that would be the last you'd see of him for two weeks until he'd show up again looking like he'd really been through it." Johnny Shines shook his head, remembering.

"But Robert was good, really good. If you want to take rock-and-roll, he was the beginning of it. When he was playing guitar he never left his tonic so far he couldn't get back, but he was so inventive that he would play with variety just within these limits. I don't think he knew one chord from another. But still, he had this great talent, he could take a broken chord and make a natural chord out of it. He was just a man who was born to do this thing of playing and singing, and he did it well."

I asked if Shines had taught him anything on the guitar, and he smiled and shook his head. "You know," he said, "I hear other guys talk about when Robert learned to play the guitar, but I don't think he ever learned. He was *doing* it when they thought he was learning. They don't talk about a duck learning to swim, do they?"

TALK ABOUT GENIUSES of the Delta blues and you must mention Nehemiah "Skip" James. He was born in the heart of the Delta country, Bentonia, Mississippi, on June 9, 1902. The son of a preacher, he attended four years of high school in Yazoo City and got a musical education by hook or by crook from local musicians. He played good guitar but wanted most to learn how to play the piano. As a young man, he traveled as far west as Texas, taking any sort of day labor he could get, and then wound up working in a sawmill job in a little Mississippi town just south of Memphis. There, he met up with an old-time barrelhouse piano player named Will Crabtree who taught him what he knew. Later he came to know Little Brother Montgomery, perhaps the best of all the blues pianists, who also became a kind of mentor to him; Skip even learned Little Brother's signature tune, "Special Rider," and adapted it for guitar. And although this was about the extent of his musical education—a little guitar picked up at home and some piano learned out on the road—it was far more than most had—and what he did with it must have surprised even him.

While staying in Jackson, Mississippi, he came to the attention of one H. C. Spears, a music-store proprietor who doubled as a talent scout for the Paramount Record Company of Grafton, Wisconsin. He sent Skip north, where he recorded some twenty-six sides for the label in about two days during February, 1931. Only seventeen were finally released, but they were among the most distinctive ever done by any blues performer during the twenties and thirties. His knowledge of the piano and his adventurous spirit led him to experiment in scales in which nobody before had ever tried to play the blues. These old Paramount sides are only partly successful—"Devil Got My Woman" and "22–20" are quite good—but nobody before had ever recorded anything like them. Hear his weird falsetto vocal style once, and you will never forget it. The voice and the far-out harmonies together must have been a little too much for the conservative blues-record-buying public. None of the Paramount records cut by Skip James sold exceptionally well. He was never invited back to record in Grafton again, and he swore later that he only made forty dollars from the two-day session.

He became discouraged, quit thinking of himself as a bluesman at all, and turned a year or two later to gospel music. He moved to Dallas, where his father had a church, and organized a quartet, the Dallas Texas Jubilee Singers. He toured with this group for about ten years, working at various jobs on the side, and was finally ordained a minister himself. He had been out of music for about twenty years when three enterprising young bluesologists—Bill Barth and guitarists John Fahey and Henry Vestine (the latter now lead guitarist with Canned Heat)—tracked him down in a hospital in Tunica, Mississippi. They convinced him that it was time to end his retirement and arranged for him to appear at the 1964 Newport Folk Festival.

His was one of the great personal triumphs in the Newport year that was probably the greatest ever for blues. Son House, Mississippi John Hurt, and Robert Pete Williams were all there, but Skip James came close to stealing the show. Although he remained active in music during the five years he had left to live, he never again achieved the sort of popular success he did that year at Newport. There were a couple of reasons for this. The first is simple: He was a sick man. They found him in a hospital with a respiratory ailment. He left it to play at the Folk Festival. And in a short time he was back in the hospital again, this time in Washington, D.C.; this last stay provided the inspiration for one of the finest of his latter-day blues, "Washington D.C. Hospital Center Blues."

The second reason is much more complicated; it is, in fact, a whole complex of reasons that add up to Skip James' unique personality. I once had an interesting conversation about this with Dick Waterman, who had served as Skip's manager during his last years and had seen to it that he was well recorded during that final period. I remember asking Waterman, innocently enough, what it was like working with Skip James then, and getting more than I bargained for in the way of an answer.

"He was a true genius, and he knew it," said Waterman. "He had a manner toward everyone that was aloof, condescending, and patronizing. And a *strong* mind. He would make demands, personal demands on people—on me. I would draw his baths for him, carry his guitar, hold the doors, everything. I know it was silly, but I felt sorry for him because by this time he had alienated a lot of people, and I felt, 'Well, I'm one of the few friends he's got.' And that was true, but he had this sort of control over a great many people."

Waterman remembered how he would appear for an engagement at a club or coffeehouse and there might be only forty or fifty people present. But to Skip James it might as well have been a concert at Carnegie Hall. He would appear in a tuxedo —not quite the picture of the Delta bluesman—and carefully shoot his cuffs before settling down on a stool and accepting his guitar from his assistant—who was Dick Waterman, of course. The trouble was that he was just as condescending toward the audience. He would lecture them on his music and its complexities.

"And that," said Waterman, "never worked, either, because Skip would use a lot of musical terms, but I always had the impression he was dropping them from a book he had read once. Very often he would refer to himself in the third person, and he would say, 'Mr. James will not play in triplicates,' and what he would play would be far out, but it wouldn't be triplets.

"And he'd play kitsch, too. I have tapes of him doing Hoagy Carmichael's 'Lazy Bones,' with all this shut-my-mouth stuff on it—but also a very interesting rolling left hand on piano that was not quite stride-style but was something all its own. But when he did material like this, he would send blues purists into agonies.

"He was a genius, all right," concluded Dick Waterman, "but he was strictly a *natural* genius."

The best kind.

FOR YEARS, Waterman was also associated with another Mississippi bluesman, Fred McDowell, who was as easygoing and unassuming as Skip James was haughty and cantankerous. Mississippi Fred McDowell, as he was known, was probably also the greatest living bottle-neck guitarist. But now he is no longer living. He died as this was being written, and the time he spent talking with me in a Batesville, Mississippi, hospital —"I got one of them ulcers," he told me—may well have been the last he was able to give to any of us who would pursue him so eagerly with pencils poised and cassettes running.

He was a pushover for note-takers such as myself because he was by nature cooperative and was quite generous with his time. At nearly every festival and concert at which he appeared he seemed to trail a wake of questioners and eavesdroppers whenever he was offstage. That was one of the reasons he was so popular with the young crowds he played for: He made himself so completely available. And the other, of course, was the glorious thing he did onstage. He would sit out there in front of the microphone, just Fred and his guitar, and with that length of copper conduit glinting on the little finger of his fret hand, he would do the most amazing things with his instrument, extracting whines and twangs from it that Andrés Segovia would never have dreamed were there. Bottle-neck guitar is its own strange sort of art. It's not just bending and sustaining those thirds and sevenths to make blue notes out of them; it's also putting it all together with the right licks and laying it down with a good steady beat. Fred McDowell played amazingly subtle music; the variety of his fillips and phrases was endless, it seemed. To be frank, many bluesmen are indifferent guitarists at best, repetitious, dull, and uninventive, and often without much sense of rhythm. But not Fred McDowell. He did it all as it was supposed to be done, giving audiences who would listen some sense of the blues guitar as it could and should be played.

And he could sing, too. He had the sort of hushed, slightly

nasal style that was just right for the sort of Delta blues material he sang. Not much of it was his, so technically he was a songster, a collector of songs. Some of the blues and sacred songs he did were his own, but most were learned—from itinerant singers (Fred stayed put for forty years) and from phonograph records.

It was after I had heard him one night at a blues festival that I made a date to talk to him. I told him I was going south on a trip and would like to look in on him if I could. He was insistent: by all means, I *had* to come by. He gave me a phone number and very precise directions to his home in Como, Mississippi (I still have them tucked away in a notebook somewhere). But when the time came, some months later, to leave on that trip, I had not received an answer to the letter I had sent him telling him when I would be coming. So, from Memphis, I called the number in Como he had given me and found out that he was in the hospital in Batesville and that I could visit him there.

Not knowing quite what to expect, I went to see him there. Batesville is one of those sleepy Delta towns, a bit bigger than most and the only one with a hospital of any size in Panola County. It is white-run and not segregated, as near as I could tell. The morning I went to visit Fred McDowell, they told me where I could find him, and a nurse even went half the distance down the hall with me to point out his room.

He seemed pretty well, and he said he was, too. Just an ulcer. They were taking care of it pretty good here, he declared, and he would be up and around soon. I asked how old he was, and he said he was sixty-eight. That surprised me, for he looked a good fifteen years younger. There were only a few gray hairs on his head, and the black pencil mustache that he maintained so carefully seemed to belong on a much younger man. Occasionally, as we talked, he seemed to be in some pain, but he kept right on talking, apparently glad to have some company.

I remember asking him if he had been born in the Delta. "No," he said, "I was born and raised east of Memphis, in Rossville, Tennessee, there in Fayette County. My father and mother didn't raise me. My uncle raised me, and to tell you the truth, I didn't ever know much about my father."

Did he learn to play guitar there? "Yes, but that wasn't anything exceptional. You take a man in my home, youngsters or old people, there wasn't hardly any seen who couldn't play guitar. There were some who were pretty good, though—Van D. McKenna, and Raymond Payne, and Jake Owens. They're all dead now. I'm about the onliest one of those Fayette County players still alive. That Raymond Payne, he was the one who taught me. It's too bad he didn't have time to record.

"Yeah, I stayed in Rossville, Tennessee, until I was grown, just farming then—that's what I did all my life. But after my uncle passed on, I had a sister who was married here in Mississippi, and so I came down here to live around her. That was around Lamar, Mississippi, and when I got down to there I found out there was a few guitars in the neighborhood, and I got acquainted with them. I remember I went to a dance one night, and there were two brothers playing, a violin and a guitar. I sat down and played, and I pulled the people away from them. I got their fans from them, and that's how I got to know them. That was kind of like one night in Cleveland, Mississippi, when Bukka White was playing for them, and then I started playing and the crowd commenced applauding me. And Bukka, he came up to me real tough, and he said, 'I don't need no goddam help from you here.' He was real tough then, but I get along pretty good with him now.

"I played a lot of dances in the country back then. I had the knack of the guitar, and everybody wanted to have me play for them. Sure, we used to play a lot of what they call blues now, only when we played it they didn't call it the blues—they called it 'the reel.' But when Blind Lemon and Charley Patton started recording, they started calling it the blues. I remember I was in Cleveland, Mississippi, in 1928 when Charley Patton put out that song "Pea-Vine Railroad." That was the first song he put out, and I remember I sure thought it was something."

When I asked Fred McDowell what occasions he played for, he carefully reminded me that times were different then from what they are today. "You want to remember," he said, "that back in the twenties and thirties, they didn't have nothin' to do but farm and nowhere to go on a Saturday night but to what you'd call a fish fry. There was no picture show or TV or nothin', just nowhere else to go. Of course, it ain't the case today. People down here got other things to do, and it's the ones from outside who come looking for the blues players in the Delta."

Did he do any traveling? "Oh, some. Just right around here to play those old juke houses in the Delta. They had to have some entertainment in them because they didn't have no record player or anything. We'd just play and they would dance. That was Eli Green and me. We did a lot of playing all around the Delta together—in Cleveland and Rosedale, towns like that. But I never did any real far traveling. I never did much hoboing. I tried it, but I didn't like it. I was scared of it."

He paused, then added with evident pride, "Of course, I've done a lot of traveling lately. The first tour I ever went on I went to Europe and I went to Germany, Denmark, and Switzerland. The blues gets through to all different kinds of people. Then I play the colleges and the clubs. I like colleges best. I even play Ole Miss around here. All this started happening after I did my first recording, though."

I asked him how that came about.

"Well, that was after I came down here to Como from Lamar in 1940. It was a good long time after that. You could check the dates on the records I made and find out for sure. [I did, and it was 1959.] Alan Lomax recorded me for the first time. I remember he was at the Pretcher brothers' house doing some recording, and somebody sent for me and said I should bring my guitar along. I did come by and played a little for Lomax, and he asked, could he come to my house on Saturday night to record, and I said, sure. So come that Saturday night the house is just full of people come to hear me recording and wanting to record, too. But right away Lomax said, 'I'm not interested in nobody but Fred.' And that discouraged a lot of them, and they left. The few of them that stayed didn't stay the whole time because he kept me going from eight o'clock in the evening to seven o'clock on Sunday morning. He'd say, 'Let me hear that one one more time.' Or, 'Do you know any songs about a mule?' He made me sing every song I knew. I played all that night, and I didn't get a motherfucking dime. Well, I did get seventy-five dollars from him later on, and then seventy dollars another time.

"I remember I was in Newport when I met him there next. He got me to come, sent me a little expenses and all. Then he said, 'All right, you all give me your address, and I'm going to mail you a check.' I ain't seen a check yet. He did the same thing with the Sea Island Singers. That Lomax, you'd think he was a millionaire the way he wear these big, rich-looking suits down here. But at those workshops at Newport, he wore these old clothes, overalls and all."

Fred McDowell broke off momentarily, shook his head in disgust, and lit up a cigarette. He had smoked more or less steadily through the hour or so I had been with him. It didn't seem to hurt him, but I wondered if it was the right thing to do with an ulcer.

"You take Chris and Dick, though," he continued, referring to Chris Strachwitz (of Arhoolie Records) and Dick Waterman. "They're the best somebodies I ever worked with. Dick has brought me to where I am now—why, I was still farming until I hooked up with him. Every time he sends for me I'm willing to go. Matter of fact, you going to be talking to him soon?"

I said I expected I would be.

"Well, I want you to tell Dick I'll be ready to go. I'll be out of the hospital soon, and I'll be ready next job he has for me. See, I can't get a job—a regular working job—now because of my age. But it works out pretty good now, because both Chris and Dick stick right with you and see you get your money."

About that time his wife and other members of his family showed up at the door to his hospital room, and I started to say my goodbye. He reiterated that he would like me to tell Dick that I had seen him and that he was all right now and ready to go. He was so insistent that I did call Waterman while I was still out on the road and found that he had not known that Fred McDowell was in the hospital; he had tried to reach him at Como a couple of times and had had no luck. I gave him Fred's message, told him it was supposed to be an ulcer, and that he seemed pretty well.

And that was the last I heard about it for a couple of months, when I got a call from Waterman who was changing planes in Washington; he had been down to help Fred McDowell settle his affairs. It was stomach cancer, he explained, and just a matter of time.

Mississippi Fred McDowell died in Baptist Hospital, in Memphis, on July 3, 1972, less than five months after I talked with him.

CHAPTER FIVE

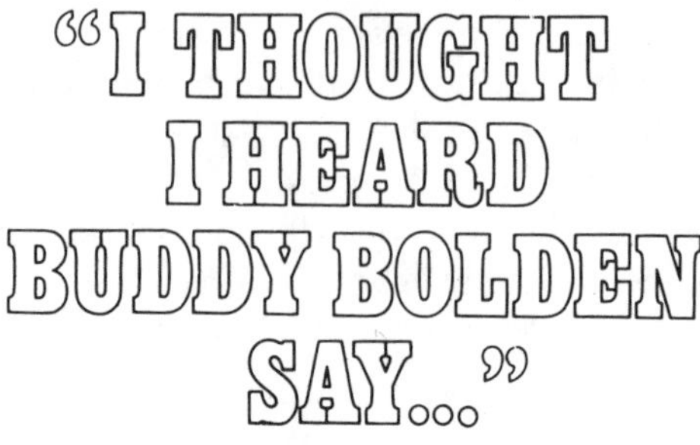

"I THOUGHT I HEARD BUDDY BOLDEN SAY..."

From about 1900 on, there were three types of bands around New Orleans. You had bands that played ragtime, ones that played sweet music, and the ones that played nothin' but blues. A band like John Robichaux's played nothin' but sweet music and played the dicty affairs. On a Saturday night Frankie Dusen's Eagle Band would play the Masonic Hall because he played a whole lot of blues. A band like the Magnolia Band would play ragtime and work the District. They'd play *Bag of Rags, Frog Leg Rag, Maple Leaf Rag, Champagne Rag,* and ones like that; they were all dance numbers. All the bands around New Orleans would play quadrilles starting about midnight. When you did that nice people would know it was time to go home because things got rough after that. The rough guys would come about midnight. They were pimps, whores, hustlers, and that bunch. They'd dance with no coats on and their suspenders down. They'd jump around and have a bunch of fun. They wanted you to play slow blues and dirty songs so they could dance rough and dirty.

The speaker here is George "Pops" Foster, the New Orleans bassist. Born in 1892, he began playing more or less professionally around town in 1906 and had one of the longest playing careers in jazz. It ended only with his death in 1969. I'm calling him as an expert witness here because his classification of the three kinds of music played in New Orleans at the time jazz was taking shape has a lot to say about the part played by the blues in its development.

Although elsewhere in his autobiography Pops Foster draws the line of development from New Orleans ragtime to jazz ("What's called jazz today was called ragtime back then . . ."), in that passage just quoted he makes a point of mentioning Frankie Dusen's Eagle Band as the one that played the blues during that seminal period. And the Eagle Band had been taken over by Dusen from the legendary Charles "Buddy" Bolden, the New Orleans cornetist who is invariably cited as the first real jazz player, if not the man who started it all. The history of jazz goes back no further than Buddy Bolden.

The New Orleans barber, who was born in 1868, put together a six-piece band in 1895 to play in a dance pavilion at a private park. He was an immediate sensation. Everyone seems to agree that he could not read a note of music and had only the crudest sort of technique on his instrument, but the spirit was there—and the power. Yes, on that they are unanimous: Buddy Bolden was just about the *strongest* hornman who ever put mouthpiece to lip. Jelly Roll Morton called him that and said that when Buddy Bolden played a dance it was unnecessary to advertise it; all he had to do was point his cornet up at the sky and let loose a few well-chosen licks and he could be heard for ten miles around. And Louis Armstrong had something to say about Bolden's power, too. In his unghosted autobiography, *Satchmo: My Life in New Orleans,* he tells of living down the street as a kid from the Funky Butt Hall, where this first jazzman held forth nightly. "Old Buddy Bolden blew so hard that I used to wonder if I would ever have enough lung power to fill one of those cornets. All in all Buddy Bolden was a great musician, but I think he blew too hard. I will even go so far as to say that he did not blow correctly. In any case he finally went crazy. You can figure that out for yourself."

It's true, Buddy Bolden went crazy. That happened in 1907. He was playing a street parade with Allen's Brass Band when he suddenly flew into a berserk rage, broke ranks, and began to wield his cornet as a weapon, striking out wildly at bystanders and fellow bandsmen. When they overcame him, he was carted off to jail, pronounced insane, and shipped off to the East Louisiana State Hospital at Angola. There his illness was diagnosed as "dementia praecox, paranoid type," and, showing no signs of recovery, he died in the asylum in 1931.

It had been a long time coming. He was notorious as a heavy drinker and when, early on, he would become abusive and quarrelsome with people around the bandstand, and generally erratic in his behavior, people assumed he was drunk. His paranoid mutterings may well have inspired that strange blues about him, with its odd refrain:

I thought I heard Buddy Bolden say,
'Dirty, nasty stinky butt, take it away.'

After a while—this would have been around 1900—he was unable to get along even with the members of his own band, and one night he walked off the stand in a fury. That was when the Buddy Bolden Band became Frankie Dusen's Eagle Band. Dusen was his trombone player, just as funky as Bolden, but a lot more dependable. He hired another cornet player, Joe Howard, to take his place, then let Buddy come back when he promised to be good. That was how the Eagle Band happened to have *two* cornetists, the first of the New Orleans bands to double the lead.

What kind of music did this mad first king of jazz play? Although Buddy Bolden never recorded, Martin Williams, in his book *Jazz Masters of New Orleans,* has come up with a few titles that go a long way toward suggesting the peculiar sweaty, low-down quality of it. Buddy Bolden's Greatest Hits? How about "If You Don't Like My Potatoes Why Do You Dig So Deep," "All the Whores Like the Way I Ride," and "Make Me a Pallet on Your Floor." You get the idea, I'm sure. It was rough, tough music of a particular sort. And just what sort that was, Pops Foster makes most clear in his autobiography. He writes, "I only saw Buddy Bolden's band play once at Johnson's Park. That's where the rough people went. I knew all the guys in the band and later on played with them. Buddy played very good for the style of stuff he was doing. He played nothing but blues and all that stink music, and he played it very loud."

Blues is the point: ". . . nothing but blues and all that stink music . . ." The musician who is generally credited with putting together the first jazz band, and was acclaimed the first "king" of jazz (King Bolden became his nickname), was essentially a bluesman. No single fact that I have come across makes quite so clear the debt of jazz to the blues. Blues must have been there in some crude shape before Buddy Bolden picked it up and started blowing it on his horn. And to the extent that he influenced other musicians in New Orleans—and they all agree he was a moving force there in the music—jazz derived from the blues. The roots of jazz are stuck deep in that older, cruder, more basic music.

And what about ragtime? What influence had it? Probably a great deal, for this lively, complex, and subtle music was sweeping the country at just about that time. It was originally, and remained largely, the creation of itinerant black piano men. In the 1890s, one of them, Scott Joplin, got musical learning enough to begin to set down on paper what had by then become the prevailing style in St. Louis and on down the river. When his "Maple Leaf Rag" was published in 1899, the new music was formally launched, and Joplin himself became, for a while at least, a kind of celebrity.

Fundamentally, ragtime was a strong two-handed piano style in which the left hand beat out a steady 2/4 rhythm while the right hand executed a highly-syncopated eight beats to the bar. There were about as many variations of this as there were ragtime tunes, but this at least was the point from which most of the variations began. In the hands of men like Tom Turpin and Eubie Blake, who were skilled improvisers, the style began to shade subtly into jazz. But even early on, in the compositions of Scott Joplin, you could hear echoes of the blues. Just catch them* in his early composition (1902), "The Entertainer," which, to me at least, is the most beautiful and haunting of them all.

Given the nature of ragtime, it was almost inevitable that the New Orleans musicians would be drawn to it, for its basic 2/4 rhythm was march tempo, and the brass band tradition among

*An excellent selection of Scott Joplin compositions is available in two volumes on Nonesuch Records, beautifully recorded by a classical pianist named Joshua Rifkin, who is largely responsible for the recent revival of interest in Joplin and his music.

blacks in that city went far back into the nineteenth century. (Some say there were colored parade bands there well before the Civil War; New Orleans had the largest free black and mixed population of any Southern city during slavery days.) The challenge for groups like the Magnolia Band, mentioned by Pops Foster earlier, was to adapt a music that was essentially pianistic—ragtime—to the instrumentation and style of a brass band. They managed it well, if we are to judge from all reports of the music that evolved from that experiment. But, in his own way, Buddy Bolden was engaged in a similar experiment, for he was adapting what was essentially string and vocal music—the blues—to the brass band style. Eventually—or perhaps, more accurately, immediately—there began a pattern of borrowing back and forth, and the process of musical amalgamation began, so that by the time jazz came to be known as jazz (in 1917—fairly late in the game), there were elements of parade music, ragtime, and blues in it.

One peculiarity of those early New Orleans bands—including the Bolden Band, the Eagle Band, the Magnolia Band, and most of the rest—is that they did not carry piano players. It wasn't because they were trying especially to maintain the brass band instrumentation; all of them were hybrid organizations that used at least some stringed instruments—bass and guitar were the usual thing, but violins were also known. Why no piano, then? One very logical and simple explanation has been offered for this: None of the piano men who were good enough to play that early jazz wanted or needed to play with the bands because they could make far more playing in the big brothels in the Storyville District. These whorehouse "professors" of infamous legend were skillful, all right—Tony Jackson and Jelly Roll Morton were among the best of them—and they played a lot of blues and ragtime, if we are to judge from the repertoire that Jelly Roll carried with him into the recording era.

Ferdinand "Jelly Roll" Morton was, in almost every way, a remarkable man. What was most remarkable about him, however, is that with all the other things he was—pimp, con man, and pathological liar among them—he was nevertheless also a considerable musician. Jelly Roll could play a mean piano; he has left recorded evidence of that. He could sing. He could lead a band. He did not, however, "invent jazz," as he told Alan Lomax at a Library of Congress recording session once. Neither was he much of an influence in New Orleans jazz, for he left the city far too early for that. He began traveling as early as 1904, when he was only nineteen, but he would return from time to time, catch up on what was happening musically, and throw his weight around a bit. But he began to see more and more of the world, and his returns to New Orleans became more infrequent and brief. He traveled up to St. Louis and made friends among the ragtime players there, he cut quite a figure himself down in Memphis, and he became one of the first to bring jazz and the blues out to the West Coast. He saw more of the country in those few years as an itinerant piano player than any contemporary Delta bluesman would have seen in his whole lifetime. Yet he had not much more to show for it all than that famous gold tooth he sported with the diamond mounted in it. It was not until later, when he was in Chicago during the twenties, that he made the records that assured him his niche in jazz history.

Jelly Roll never lost his feeling for the blues. It is the essential element that is constant in nearly all his best recorded work. It provided the emotional basis and the source—as Martin Williams suggests—for his music. He borrowed freely from folk sources and occasionally he stole—but always to good purpose. For that quality of giddy, jittery euphoria that makes so much of the music of the so-called "Jazz Age" sound silly today was, for the most part, blessedly absent from the music of Jelly Roll Morton. There was substance and depth to it, which came from the blues sources from which so much of it was directly derived.

Pops Foster talked about another brand of music that was dished out regularly in New Orleans—not blues and not ragtime. He cited John Robichaux's band as an example of the sort that "played nothin' but sweet music and played the dicty affairs." Robichaux himself was a light Negro, a Creole, who was well schooled in music and insisted that all those who played with him be able to read his arrangements note for note. Some jazzmen played jobs with the band—Pops Foster was one—and most of the material they played was jazz or ragtime in style. But Robichaux's band played a music apart, for it was carefully orchestrated and had to be played with a precision that utterly throttled spontaneity. Whitney Balliett speaks of jazz as "the sound of surprise"—and that inspired phrase defines the difference between real jazz and the kind of music that John Robichaux's band played. In that brand of sweet music there were no surprises.

I may seem here to be trying to pass myself off rather shamelessly as an expert on the music of a band long gone and little recorded. Yet I'll confess that my impressions of the band are based on secondhand evidence—of a most intriguing sort. A contemporary group that calls itself the New Orleans Ragtime Orchestra has recently recorded whole albums precisely in the manner of the old Robichaux band. They were able to do it because the complete Robichaux repertoire—its "book" of arrangements—had been discovered not long ago and was donated to the Archive of New Orleans Jazz at Tulane University, in New Orleans. A young man named Lars Edegran, who works as a researcher there, came across the Robichaux arrangements, realized their value, and got permission to have them copied. With these in hand, he organized the New Orleans Ragtime Orchestra to play them. It proved worthwhile. The band has been in existence since 1967, and it has made a couple of records on the Pearl and Arhoolie labels. Chiefly because of them, the New Orleans Ragtime Orchestra has been invited to play at a couple of New Orleans jazz festivals and in 1970 journeyed north to the Newport Jazz Festival. It has been very well received wherever it has played, for if the group lacks something in fire—these are, after all, society band arrangements, which are played note for note here—it does offer a lot in nostalgia. The thin, treble sound of its violin-trumpet-clarinet lead gives a kind of wistful quality to the music. It is dated, even rather corny, but that somehow is its special charm. It is a valid re-creation of the popular style of another era.

WHEN I CAME to New Orleans, I had with me a kind of informal introduction to Lars Ivar Edegran, the leader of the New Orleans Ragtime Orchestra. He turned out to be a quiet and precise young man, with a conservative mien, a clean jaw, and a short haircut. We went off together to a nearby restaurant for coffee. There we talked about how and why he had come over, and it turned out that his father had been a musician in Sweden, and that Lars had gotten started listening to jazz at home —mostly records. He got started playing in Sweden, and one year he came to New Orleans to listen and stayed on to play. "In the beginning it was with string bands and jug bands, and so on," he told me, "but I got to know the local musicians better, and soon I was sitting in with them. It didn't take long, really."

He began asking me questions. He wanted to know what I was looking for in New Orleans, whom I wanted to hear, and so on. He told me then what everyone else I talked to in New Orleans would later confirm: that there really is not much blues to be heard in the town. Never was. "Oh," he added with a shrug, "there's Babe Stovall, but he's—well, you can decide for yourself about him."

What Edegran had hesitated to say about Babe Stovall was that he is an evident alcoholic. Over in nearby Jackson Square we found him, a tall, loose man who looked to be in his fifties (but, born in 1907, he was well into his sixties). He was standing at a junction of walks in the park whanging away at a steel-bodied guitar and singing sacred songs, with no one around but us to listen. He was sweating hard and blinking painfully in the bright sun, but he kept right on singing. It was "Do, Lord, Remember Me" when we walked up. Then, sensing us there, he began to run through a few tricks for us; almost mechanically he twisted the guitar around behind his back and began to strum it that way—the rankest sort of old-time showboating. His voice came out a querulous cry, squawking on almost tunelessly until at last the song ground to a halt. He mumbled something to Edegran that I couldn't understand—and he did so without quite looking at him; Stovall just kept blinking those watery, red-rimmed eyes as though they wouldn't focus. Then he launched into "May the Circle Be Unbroken."

Edegran pulled me a couple of steps back and said into my ear that this was no time to talk to Babe Stovall. "When he drinks, the booze goes to his brain. He's not bad when he's sober. But the drunker he gets, the more commerical he is—that picking the guitar behind his back, it's stupid isn't it?"

I shrugged, and asked if he thought it would be better to come back tomorrow. Would Stovall be here then?

"Sunday? Always. It's the big day here in the park. He'll be in better shape to talk then." Edegran suggested we walk around a little, and so we left Babe Stovall, still blinking. I dropped some money into the peaked cap by his foot.

Circulating around the curving walks of Jackson Square, we encountered an old banjo picker, who Edegran said was Ernest Roubleau, and listened to him do "Sweet Georgia Brown" and "Mississippi Mud" before we went on. We also met a friend of Lars', an English trumpet player named Clive Davis, whose story was quite similar; his love of New Orleans jazz had brought him to the city and he had stayed on to make a little of it himself. We didn't get much beyond this when Lars asked him how his lip was, and Davis said he thought he would be able to play again soon. I noticed the jagged scar on Davis' lip then, and when we left him, I asked Edegran what that was about.

He explained that Davis had been following one of those traditional New Orleans funeral parades through a black district of New Orleans when suddenly, and for no reason, someone heaved a brick at him, and it hit him squarely in the mouth; the damage it did to his lips had kept him from playing his trumpet for well over a month. "That was near the Lucianne Avenue Project, where they had all that trouble with the Panthers—the shoot-out, you remember? There's been a lot of trouble here. At that same parade, an Irish couple who had just come to New Orleans to hear the music were beaten with chains by blacks. And not long after that, a friend of mine from Sweden was on the Magazine Avenue Bus—the only white—and they took his glasses away from him and broke them and threatened his life." Lars hesitated, then blurted out suddenly, as though it were something that had been eating at him a long while, "What's the matter with those people anyway? They must know people who come out to listen like that are not racists, or they wouldn't be there. What's the matter with them?"

We wound up the afternoon at Lars Edegran's very nice and comfortable loft apartment on Charter Street. He played records from his extensive collection of blues and jazz, and, as I remember, Lee Collins, the trumpet player, was on one of them. It was an LP of European issue, and it was about the only time I had heard that skilled second-generation New Orleans trumpeter recorded to good advantage. I mentioned to Edegran that I had heard Collins once as a kid (at that concert in Chicago I described earlier), and he was interested in that. I told him about the session, as I recalled it, and I added that another New Orleans musician had been there—Tony Parenti, the clarinet player. He made a face at the mention of his name. What was the matter with Tony Parenti? I wanted to know. (I happened to think he was pretty good.) "Typical white musician," Edegran said, with a dismissive flick of his hand. "He lacked the *true* feeling." Then he added, by way of general explanation, "Most Europeans like only Negro music. I don't know why this is—not for racial reasons. We respond to it better, though. I wonder why." And that was about all, except that he added later in the afternoon—I forget the context exactly—"Some Europeans may hate everything about America except the Negroes and the Negro music." I got the idea that Lars Edegran considered himself one of these Europeans.

That night I went out and listened to jazz in New Orleans, such as it is. The reality is bound to disappoint, for it must contend with wild expectations conjured up by our fantasy. We know what New Orleans jazz *should* sound like; it should sound like King Oliver, Alphonse Picou, Kid Ory, Louis Armstrong, and all the rest from that pantheon of pioneers. And it isn't like that at all.

It is by now a fairly slick commercial routine, a product offered to satisfy the expectations of tourists and drinking residents. On any given night, wandering up and down Bourbon Street, you are likely to hear "When the Saints Go Marching In," "High Society," and "The Birth of the Blues," each about a dozen times. Neither the repertoire, the ensemble style, nor even the solos seem to vary much from place to place. The band that Lars Edegran was with at the Paddock Club was just about the best of them. Between sets he shrugged off my praise and said it was just a gig, but that I should be sure to hear his friend and fellow countryman Orange Kellin, up the street at the Hurricane. I did, and it was worth the visit. Kellin himself is a fine, fluent clarinetist who sounded a lot like Tony Parenti to me; the band was good enough, too—at least it didn't hold him back.

Finally, I ended the evening at Preservation Hall, which has become more or less the official sanctuary for traditional jazz in the city. The title it carries makes it sound a grander spot than it is. The place is on a French Quarter side street, a narrow little ground-floor room through which tourists are shunted at quick-step to squat on the floor and listen to a crew of grizzled old-timers push and grunt their way through a two- or three-tune set (which must necessarily include the ubiquitous "When the Saints Go Marching In"). The eager all-white crowd reacted with wild applause when occasional flashes of competence would pierce the dismal air of mediocrity that smothered the proceedings. But no more of that. Enough. About the music played at Preservation Hall, the less said the better.

The next day, sometime early in the afternoon, I started for Jackson Square, and walking through the Quarter I chanced to meet Lars Edegran and a young lady he introduced as his girl friend. They were standing at the corner of St. Peter and Royal listening to a street gospel trio preaching away at a song:

Ninety-nine-and-a-half won't do!
Lord, I'm prayin' and tryin' to make a hundred
Ninety-nine-and-a-half won't do. . . .

I asked who they were, and Edegran said the woman playing the guitar with the broken strings was Idelle Williams. When I started to ask something more, he said, "Ssshhh. Don't talk too loud. I've got a cassette going." He indicated the wrapped package in his hand from which protruded an amorphous dark shape that had to be a microphone; I would never have guessed.

For some reason, that bothered me a little. I stood around a few moments more, then indicated with gestures I was going on to Jackson Square. Lars Edegran waved me on my way with a quick motion of his free hand and gave me an abstracted smile.

It was easy to find Babe Stovall, even though the park was teeming with Sunday loungers and dotted with sidewalk entertainers of one kind or another. Stovall was right there in the middle of a big crowd, sounding a lot better than he had the day before but still indulging in the same sort of horseplay. He picked the guitar upside down, and then twisted it behind his back to play it. And again those sacred songs he had done before —"Do, Lord, Remember Me," "May the Circle Be Unbroken," and "When the Saints Go Marching In"—but he was in better voice and seemed generally healthier: alert, and none of that troublesome blinking.

Babe Stovall has recorded once. A session for Verve was arranged by local jazz enthusiasts, and an LP of traditional blues and folk material came out of it which bears listening to. It is difficult to praise him, though, for there is so little variety and subtlety to his performances that the best one can call them is spirited. Words are bawled out street-corner style, so that he is seldom, if ever, on pitch.

He is, however, a better guitar player than I had at first thought. I gradually became aware of the good things he was doing as I listened to him that Sunday in Jackson Square picking with some precision through "See, See Rider" and "It Takes a Worried Man," and I later confirmed it listening to his record. Yes, the licks are there, all right. He plays a kind of ragtime style that is highly syncopated and that, on that National guitar of his, gives a real banjo sound to his music.

Later, when I talked with him, I asked him why he played that steel-bodied guitar. They are as rare as can be now, and he must have been tempted many times to sell his and buy one of the standard wooden sort. "Oh, yeah," he told me, "that's right. You can't buy them no more. Why do I like it? That's because it gives me a sound 'twixt a guitar and a banjo." If that is what he is trying for, that is what he is getting, all right.

He kept right on playing through the afternoon, carelessly mixing the sacred songs with the most secular material—from "Jesus Is the Captain" to "Salty Dog." And as he serenaded the crowd around him, two or three white guys, hard cases all, circulated through the audience first asking, then demanding, money. They were out to get as much for Babe Stovall's efforts as they could. They were his bottle gang, drinking buddies who would share the bottles of wine that his concert would buy. Stovall has ten kids.

As the sun slanted down and dusk began to fall, the park custodians called out that they would be closing the gates soon. Babe Stovall began to pack up, and I stepped forward—rather aggressively, I'm afraid—and started to ask him questions.

He told me he was from Tylertown, Mississippi, "way down between McComb and Columbia," and that he had come to New Orleans in 1964.

I asked him how many songs he knew—none of his material seemed to be original—and he said he didn't know how many exactly, but it was a gang of them. "I just pick up anything I hear. If I like it, I learn it and start playin' it."

Was that the way it had been for him here in New Orleans? How many had he learned here? He looked at me kind of funny then, shook his head, and said, "No, I brought all my songs with me from Mississippi. I never learned none of them here in New Orleans. Ain't none of them here to learn."

I hesitated, and Babe Stovall asked, "You done now? My buddies is calling me. They want me to come with them."

IF, AS Babe Stovall says, there were no songs to learn there, how did the blues ever get to New Orleans in the first place? How did Buddy Bolden happen to learn them? Pops Foster answers colorfully, "Most of the guys you heard singing down there [in New Orleans] were guys who came out of the woods somewhere with a guitar playing and singing the blues." Guys, in other words, not much different from Stovall himself, who may have found their way into the city from the surrounding provinces bearing with them the heavy message of the blues. They unburdened themselves on street corners from Storyville to the Irish Channel.

But there were a few who themselves emerged from the alleys and back streets of New Orleans, bluesmen who were among the first to translate the urban experience into twelve-bar terms. The best of them, and the only real first-rank interpreter of the blues to come out of New Orleans, was Lonnie Johnson, of whom I spoke earlier. But I knew there were others, and to find out who they were and something about them I traveled out to the Archive of New Orleans Jazz at Tulane University, and with the help of the Archive director, Richard B. Allen, I managed to learn a little about a couple.

Lemon (born Lemoine) Nash, who died in 1969 without ever having recorded, was born in upcountry Lakeland, Louisiana, in 1898, but he lived in New Orleans from the time he was two months old. In his time he saw a bit of the world—hoboing, working the medicine shows and circuses, and even putting in a wartime stretch in the merchant marine. But what he was, for the most part, was a musician, a singer, a serenader. There were string bands of these so-called serenaders who used to roam the streets, playing the bars and the brothels one by one as they came to them and even holding forth on the street corners if that was where the action was. You had to play a lot of different instruments to be a serenader, and in his time Nash had played guitar, mandolin, ukelele, and even a little banjo. But he liked ukelele best, believe it or not, and from all reports he was about as skilled as one could be on the instrument. Was Lemon Nash a bluesman? Well, he knew a lot of blues, and by definition would probably have qualified as a songster, but he must have thought of himself chiefly as a performer. What he did with his material was terribly important to him. He knew medicine show routines, vaudeville routines, and lines of patter that he stuck between all the songs he did. It was show business of the neighborhood, down-home sort. All Lemon knew was that his audience sure did dig those blues, so that was what he played.

Richard "Rabbit" Brown was an altogether different sort. Allen played for me one of the two records he had made and showed me an early article by Abbe Niles from a 1928 issue of *The Bookman,* which contained a review of the record and some additional information on the artist. It was, Allen said, just about the first *serious* attention ever given to a bluesman in a national magazine. Niles told in the article how Rabbit Brown, when not out singing on the street corners, would hire himself as a kind of New Orleans singing gondolier, offering a rowboat ride into Lake Ponchartrain for a fee, during which he would haul out his guitar and give his passenger a short blues concert.

Lemon Nash had little use for Rabbit Brown. The two came from the same neighborhood, a particularly tough part of town known as the Battleground (Louis Armstrong grew up there, too). Nash had played with him a couple of times and claims that Brown knew only three chords on the guitar. According to Nash, Rabbit "would just hit the guitar and yell. He was what you call a clown man." But "clown man" or no, Rabbit Brown used to sing the blues, and on that recording session he had in 1927, just ten years before his death, he did the "James Alley Blues," a song about his street in the Battleground. It begins,

Times ain't now, nothing like they used to be,
(twice)
And I'm telling you all the truth, oh, take it from me.

And if he could sing that then about New Orleans, he would shout it at the top of his voice if he were to see the old town today.

CHAPTER SIX

"T FOR TEXAS"

HUDDIE LEDBETTER was the first bluesman of note to show up in Texas, and he came there from Louisiana in 1909. This is not to say he brought the blues with him. The music was already there, existing in a sort of state of potential, because, after all, the blacks who worked the cotton fields of east Texas were essentially the same blacks who picked cotton and corn in the Mississippi Delta and jived all night long in the juke joints; and they were ethnically the same as those who were at that moment creating a new kind of music in New Orleans that would later come to be known as jazz. The same music was there in east Texas, too, in the form of ballads, breakdowns, and early barrelhouse music, all of which were popular even then in the region. The blues was taking shape about this time in this westernmost sector of the old South, and it was following the same, if slightly retarded, pattern of development. It grew out of local circumstances. For some reason, the music of the Texas jails and chain gangs—such songs as "Ain't No More Cane on This Brazos," "Another Man Done Gone," and "The Midnight Special," for example—were especially rich and were certainly the kind of music that deepened and helped extend the blues tradition in Texas.

Huddie Ledbetter himself is credited by some with "The Midnight Special." It may well be that Leadbelly wrote the song, too, for he served time twice in Texas, on the first occasion for assault on a woman said to be a prostitute, and on the second for murder. He had always been a violent man, quick to anger and eager to punish, and there seems no doubt that he killed a man in the Texas town of New Boston during a quarrel. He was sentenced to thirty-five years and wound up at Sugar Land, a work camp outside Houston that was located alongside tracks of the Southern Pacific Railroad. There was a superstition among the Sugar Land inmates that if the light of the Midnight Special, the fast train to Houston, were to shine its light on an inmate, he could expect to be released in a short time. This is the sense of the song's plea, then, that the Midnight Special should shine its "ever-lovin' light on me." If Leadbelly didn't write it, he certainly sang it often, and he may even have included it in his program at that most famous concert of his, the one before the governor of Texas, Patrick Morris Neff, in 1924, during which he sang his way to a pardon. The Governor was so impressed with Leadbelly's sincerity and his progress in rehabilitation that he declared him sufficiently punished for the offense committed and set him free in January, 1925.

Within a short time, he was back in Mooringsport, Louisiana, near Shreveport, where he came from, and within three years he was up before a judge again for murder. Again it was in a brawl, and again there seems little doubt that Huddie Ledbetter actually committed homicide; the only real question was whether he had or had not started the fight. He was given a sentence of from six to ten years at hard labor at the Angola, Louisiana, prison farm. In 1933, when Leadbelly had been there five years, two men—John Lomax and his teen-age son, Alan—showed up with permission to record songs by the inmates for the Library of Congress. Not many could or would record for them, but Leadbelly, of course, was eager to perform from the moment he heard about their project. He saw a chance to repeat his previous feat of singing his way to a pardon. And that, in effect, is what he did. For he not only impressed the Lomaxes with his songs, he also laid down a steady barrage of entreaties, pleading that they do what they could to help him get out. In fact, they did just that. John

Lomax interceded in his behalf with Governor O. K. Allen of Louisiana, and Huddie Ledbetter was granted a commutation of sentence in 1934.

In effect, Leadbelly was paroled in the custody of Lomax, for he was taken north to Washington, D.C., by him, and then to New York. There he was unveiled to the public, presented at cocktail parties, brought around to play at a few colleges and universities, and finally recorded. He became a kind of trained bear for the Lomaxes, performing in convict stripes before their friends, running through his routine on command. Just how original some of his material may have been is, as I suggested earlier, open to doubt. Although he claimed to have written a good many songs, including one or two that he almost certainly did *not* write ("See, See Rider" and "Black Snake Moan") and a few others that are doubtful ("Goodnight Irene" and "Midnight Special"), there are some, nearly as good ("Mister Tom Hughes Town," for one), that Leadbelly very probably did write, for they tally with what we know of his personal experience. Paul Oliver indicates he was not an original bluesman and says flatly, "Leadbelly was a songster, and he had the songster's pride in the breadth of his repertoire."

He wasn't much of a musician, either. We have this on testimony from bassist Pops Foster, who recorded with him a number of times. "Willie [the Lion Smith] and I used to play with Leadbelly. I think we were the only two guys who could play with him. Leadbelly didn't know which key he was going to play in. He'd play in all naturals and sharps. We'd have to listen to him, then search around to find the key. Then when we found it, we'd take off. . . . When Leadbelly would get mad, he'd just sit and grit his teeth. One time I told him he'd have to play a chord up on his guitar or we couldn't make no record. He just set and started gritting his teeth. I told him he could grit his teeth all day, but if he didn't play the chord, we couldn't play with him. He finally played it."

What sort of singer was he? One whose virtues and limitations seemed to match those of the whole man almost perfectly. He had an enormously powerful voice, one to go with his immense physical strength. Yet there was no subtlety to it, just a kind of direct bellow that seemed an expression of the rage he carried with him always. He seemed to exercise as little control in phrasing and modulation over that voice as he did in keeping his physical strength in check when he lost his temper.

If his claims as a songwriter are open to dispute, if he lacked even rudimentary skill as a musician, and hadn't much to offer as a singer, then why is Huddie Ledbetter such an important figure in American music? What claim has he on our attention? He was the first backwoods black music maker to gain national prominence. Before Leadbelly, blacks who gained the attention of whites with their music were all professional enough to at least put a show-business shine on their presentation; they were sophisticated enough to choose material they thought might please this different audience. But not Leadbelly. He went at it like the country man he was, shouting out the songs just as he had on Shreveport's rough Fannin Street, hollering the blues in the same rough tones he had used on Dallas street corners. His introduction to the white intellectual community of the thirties by the Lomaxes marked the beginning of widespread serious interest in the black ethnic underpinnings of American music. He gave white intellectuals their first shot of the real hard stuff.

During the years Leadbelly was on the loose in Texas, he played and sang through the streets of Dallas with a bluesman ten years his junior named Lemon Jefferson, a better bluesman in nearly every way. Jefferson was born blind in 1897 near Wortham, Texas—hence, *Blind* Lemon Jefferson, as this widely-traveled singer came to be known all through the South. He made it one of the most famous names in the blues, working through that tough street-corner apprenticeship and going north to Chicago with a recording contract in 1925. There he became the most prolific of all early blues recording artists. Before he died in 1929, he had recorded seventy-nine pieces for the Paramount label and two for OKeh. He even managed to make some money at it, but except for a car he bought and a chauffeur he kept on salary during the last years of his life, he squandered nearly all of it on liquor and women.

And liquor and women were what he sang about in so many of his blues. A lot of the blues he recorded were not especially original—a tune borrowed, lines cribbed here and there—and many of them were derived from that rich repertoire of Texas prison songs, though Blind Lemon had never done time as

Leadbelly had. But the best of them clearly came from his own experience. If you've ever wondered, for example, what a blind street singer feels out there on the corner all day, it's right here in his "Tin Cup Blues":

I was down and I cried, my suitcase was down the line (twice)
Ain't it tough to see a man go to wreck and almost fall and die

I stood on the corner and almost bust my head (twice)
I couldn't earn enough money to buy me a loaf of bread

Baby, times is so hard I almost call it tough (twice)
I can't earn money to buy no bread and you know I can't buy my snuff

My gal's a house maid and she earns a dollar a week (twice)
I'm so hungry on payday I can't hardly speak

Now gather 'round me people and let me tell you a true fact (twice)
That tough luck has sunk me and the rats is getting in my hat.

The very specific details of that song ("My gal's a house maid and she earns a dollar a week" and "the rats is getting in my hat") are the source of its real power. This is so with so many of Blind Lemon Jefferson's songs that it may seem somewhat ironic that his most famous blues, "Black Snake Moan," is noted for its sexual symbolism. The moan is precisely that—a kind of extended groan with which he begins the first lines of every chorus. But the black snake of the title seems rather more Freudian than real.

Ummmmh oh ain't got no mama now (twice)
She told me last night you don't need no mama no how

Mmmmmm mmmm black snake crawling in my room (twice)
And some pretty mama had better come and get this black snake soon

Ummmmuh that must have been a bed bug baby, a chinch can't bite that hard (twice)
Asked my baby for fifty cent she said, Lemon, ain't a dime in the yard

Mmmmama that's all right, mama that's all right for you (twice)
Say baby, that's all right most any old way you do

Mmmmmm mmmm honey, what's the matter now? (twice)
Tell me what's the matter, baby. Don't like no black snake no how
Mmmmmmm mmmm wonder where is my black snake gone (twice)
Black snake, mama, done run my darling home.

But a transcription of the text does no justice to it, for "Black Snake Moan" is, after all, a song. What cannot be conveyed on paper is the eloquence of Blind Lemon Jefferson's strong but surprisingly light voice and the deft figures that he interpolates on his guitar. His was one of the great primitive talents in the blues, but only by searching out and listening to his recordings, many of which are still available in reissue, can you begin to realize just how great that talent was.

Recording was his life. All that was best in him is on those eighty-one sides he cut. In fact, he died just after his last recording session in Chicago in the dead of winter. He left the studio intending to go to a party. He was to be picked up by his car, but somehow the driver just didn't show up, and so Lemon started out into the snow, convinced that he could make it alone. He didn't. They found him the next morning frozen to death in the gutter. Paramount Records shipped his body home, and Blind Lemon Jefferson was buried under the warm Texas sun.

Another bluesman of note who emerged from Texas in the twenties was Alger "Texas" Alexander. He is about the only male blues singer of note, except for the modern pop blues phenomenon Bobby Bland, who played no instrument. That being the case, he owes at least some of his early success to his accompanist, who was none other than Lonnie Johnson. When the great New Orleans guitarist set off on his rambles just after World War I, Dallas was his first stop. Johnson hooked up with

Alexander there and helped him give a little polish to a style that remained pretty rough throughout his career. And when Lonnie Johnson traveled north and started to record, Texas Alexander followed him up and began a modest recording career of his own for the OKeh label.

A Dallas piano player named Alex Moore, who was born in 1899 and is still alive today, gained some reputation around town as a soloist and accompanist. The shrill whistling that he did when playing solo earned him the nickname "Whistlin'" Alex Moore, and it was under it that he did all his recording—not much—during the twenties and thirties. He was recently rediscovered and recorded, however, on the Arhoolie label.

Alex Moore is worthy of note as one of the few surviving members of a whole school of piano playing that had quite an influence both on jazz and the blues. The Texas "barrelhouse" piano style was an intricate blend of blues and ragtime delivered with a strong left hand, which anticipated boogie-woogie by about a decade. Among those remembered as barrelhouse men are Robert Shaw, who has also been recorded by Arhoolie, Frank Ridge, and R. L. McNeer. Pete Johnson, a traveling Kansas City pianist, is the direct link between these Texas players and exponents of the boogie-woogie style that he himself helped perfect.

Most of these musicians and singers seem to have been located in or near Dallas, but in Texas today Houston is the big blues town. Musicians and singers break in there every year, but one of the top performers among those who stay on permanently is Eddie "Cleanhead" Vinson, the blues-singing alto-saxist whom I used to listen to out on the South Side of Chicago. He has set the level of competition there in town, uncomfortably high for many of the country boys coming off the farms in east Texas hoping to find fame and fortune with their guitars. Vinson, who was not only a good singer but also a competent soloist by big band jazz standards (he spent years with trumpeter Cootie Williams' orchestra), could certainly work outside Houston again if he chose to, but he has decided he likes it where he is.

Sam "Lightning" Hopkins was for years the real boss in Houston, though. It was probably because of his continued presence there that it became the blues town it is. Samuel

Charters calls him the last of the old country bluesmen, and that seems about right, for although he has had a world of experience, Lightning remains as rough and unsophisticated in his style as when he first began. He has the old country intensity in his voice: While it may at first sound casual, there are subtle tensions in it and tricks with dynamics that would be remarkable in a singer of any sort. The total effect is a style that is personal and confidential, a tone that is almost insinuating in quality.

As a writer of blues, he produces work that is extremely spotty. He can come up with good lines and occasionally a whole song—"Black and Evil" is, in its rough way, very powerful—but too often he falls back on the old traditional lines and verses that seldom follow in logical sequence. He has recorded something like 600 times; no bluesman has that much original material in him—or not Lightning Hopkins, at any rate. His musicianship is also rather slapdash. He plays a little piano—*very* little, as the old joke goes—but guitar is his instrument. And characteristically, we see in his playing style the triumph of the instinctive musician over the unskilled instrumentalist. For his choruses are sometimes of uneven length, and in improvising he gets into such weird harmonies that one can only conclude he has hit a wrong note or two and is trying to work his way out of it as best he can. But working on familiar material, he can play licks and get effects that would be the envy of much better guitarists. The resonant, dramatic single-string style that he uses is actually beyond him technically, but he pulls it off somehow and gives the general impression that he is a much better guitarist than he really is.

Perhaps he has always had his troubles with the guitar. Samuel Charters tells a story in *The Country Blues* about the time Lightning drove with his father from his hometown of Centerville, Texas (he was born there in 1912), to nearby Buffalo for a picnic. Although just a boy, Lightning had his guitar with him, and so he headed quite naturally for the musician who was holding forth before a good-sized crowd; he was a fat blind man who turned out to be Blind Lemon Jefferson. Never one to hang back, Lightning came up behind him and began to pick along, annoying Lemon greatly, who assumed someone was moving in on his territory. Lemon shouted out critically, "Boy, you got to play it right." Young Lightning said something back, and Lemon realized he was just a boy and let him stay and play.

Lightning Hopkins' first professional experience came a few years later, during the thirties, with another established blues singer, Texas Alexander, who happened to be his cousin. Alexander had established himself by then, gone North and recorded, and come back to Texas; he was a little down on his luck by the time the two got together. As Lightning tells it, Alexander was so desperate for an accompanist (remember, he played no instrument) that he used to carry a guitar in a case around with him on the off-chance that he might meet up with someone who could play it for him. Lightning, of course, turned out to be that someone. They began traveling together and even made it to Houston. But this was the Depression era, and times were especially tough in the Southwest. Lightning decided to return to the farm.

He didn't try Houston again until just after the war, and this time it went fairly well for him. He hooked up temporarily with a barrelhouse piano man named "Thunder" Smith, and the two caught the attention of a scout from Aladdin, a West Coast label, now defunct. The two recorded as a duo, and that was when Sam Hopkins became Lightning (Thunder Smith and Lightning Hopkins), the name under which he has recorded ever since. As I indicated earlier, he has recorded a phenomenal number of sides, many of them for small blues labels such as Gold Star in Houston, TNT in Harlem, and Ace in New York.

Lately, however, he has been most active playing dates for the blues collector labels, such as Arhoolie. The finest introduction to this unusual singer, who is indeed sort of a survivor from an earlier era, is avilable on Poppy Records. The two-record album was produced by Arhoolie's Chris Strachwitz, and it offers Lightning at his relaxed best. He frequently plays concerts at colleges and universities, too, and sometimes dismays his audiences by being as irascible, cantankerous, and downright mean onstage as he is known to be off.

THE SONGSTER TRADITION has also been very strong in Texas—perhaps partly because a good many Texas bluesmen were secret songsters. A lot of what they claimed as original material was actually borrowed or adapted. But why not? No great store was put on private property among bluesmen, copyrights were virtually unknown, and singers were expected to know a lot of songs. At least one well-known Texas singer—Henry "Rambling" Thomas—laid no claims to originality. He was a songster with a vast repertoire, and he recorded only a bare fraction of it on the Vocalion label when he went north to Chicago in the twenties.

Mance Lipscomb is the leading representative of the Texas songster tradition today. He knows and sings many blues, but he is also fond of ballads, sacred songs, and even old popular songs from his youth. He is a walking mountain of folklore material and has been interviewed, pumped, and taken through his repertoire so often that it is remarkable that he remains so easygoing and cheerful when questions are put to him. Once he was asked how many songs he actually knew, and Mance replied, giving a very specific number in the hundreds, then explained: "That's how many Paul Oliver said I know." Mance's implication was that the English blues historian would know more about that than an old sharecropper from Navasota, Texas.

That's where he is from, a little town in the southeastern part of the state, seventy-two miles north of Houston and 200 miles south of Dallas. Born in 1895, he farmed around Navasota for most of his life, worked hard, and gained a reputation for steadiness and reliability that he is proud of today. "Ain't paid a fine in my life," he will tell you. "The first thing you hear in Navasota is that Mance don't drink. I take a little sniff of it now and again, but I don't get drunk." He was a sharecropper, and as hard as it is to survive under that damnable system, Mance Lipscomb actually prospered most years by working harder than anyone else; he is proud of that. In 1956, at the age of sixty, he suffered an accident that brought him a modest insurance settlement. And because his legs had been troubling him with varicose veins, he decided simply to retire. He took his settlement, bought a small piece of land, and built a two-room house on it.

That might be all there is to tell about him if it were not for his music. He came by it naturally, growing up a member of a big musical family (there were eleven children). His father was an old country fiddler who used to play at breakdowns and taught Mance how to play, too. Then, some years after he quit fiddling, "I took up the guitar," he remembers. "That was along about 1918, when everybody started getting guitars. They were getting these old pine guitars back then."

It was about that time, too—he places it at about 1917, although he is not entirely reliable on dates—that he encountered Blind Lemon Jefferson on the streets of Dallas. Until he was well into his sixties, that was the farthest he had ever traveled from home. He was there to pick cotton, and he remembers coming into Dallas on a Saturday and hearing a blind man on a corner playing something powerful. Was that the first blues he heard? "Oh, well, you know the blues was around a long time before that. People been playing blues or something like it from pretty far back."

Once Mance took up the guitar he began playing country dances and picnics, picking up songs everywhere. He had soon committed to memory just about everything anyone in town knew. "Then I learned songs off records, too," he adds. "You know that old Bessie Smith song?"—he half hums, half sings a little of it ("This house is so haunted, I can't move"; it is "Haunted House Blues")—"I learned that song off the Victrola. I used to lay down in the cotton patch and listen to Bessie Smith on records." And did he learn any songs from singers who traveled through Navasota? "Oh, yes, some. There was this fella Blind Willie Johnson. He was a songster, but not much of a guitar player until I tuned his guitar for him. I remember I learned 'Motherless Children' and 'God Moves on the Water' off of him when I tuned his guitar." He sums up: "Oh, I just learned my songs from all over."

Well, wherever he learned them, and no matter how many he knows, Mance Lipscomb certainly sings his songs well. There is nothing flashy—or even, in the usual way, very professional—about his presentation. He simply sits down in front of the microphone, wearing his hat, as he always seems to do, and plays his guitar and sings in a kind of reedy, high baritone. Nothing extraordinary about that at all, until you begin to notice that he really is getting around the guitar awfully well for such an old man, and there is something in his voice, a kind of sober dignity, that seems altogether distinctive and has the effect of elevating some of the rather ordinary popular song material that he includes in nearly every set he sings. When, for instance, I listened to him launch into "You Are My Sunshine" one afternoon before a Midwest college audience, I heard a few sounds of annoyance around me. "Come *on!*" somebody groaned out loud. Mance followed that up with "I Ain't Got Nobody" and "Alabama Jubilee," and just when he seemed to have his young blues audience pushed to the point of exasperation with this little Hit Parade medley, he cut loose with some of the good stuff: "Can't Do Nothing for Me," "Baby, Please Don't Go," "Truckin'," "See, See Rider," "T for Texas," "You'll Be Sorry That You Done Me Wrong." But then came a rendition of that hoary superauthentic folk blues, "Shine on, Harvest Moon." Well, that really upset the audience; a few got up and left, and those who stayed began shifting noisily in their seats. A shame, really, for those who walked out missed the really first-class work he did on "Motherless Children" (complete with bottle-neck guitar effects) and "When the Saints Go Marching In."

Such a set is typical of Mance and characteristic of the entire songster tradition. You never know quite what you are going to hear when a songster sits down to strum. Nevertheless, those who can appreciate the range of musical interest and enthusiasm that goes into such a performance are themselves a long way toward understanding how the many loose ends in our music may be tied into some sort of comprehensive knot.

I had made a date to talk with Mance following his set. It was easy to arrange. He was eminently approachable. In fact, I had almost bumped into him coming through a door, recognized him instantly, and put out my hand to shake. "Howdy doo," he said to me. "Mance Lipscomb's the name." Just like that. When I asked about talking with him afterward, he nodded vigorously and said, "Oh, sure. I'm getting rid of my bad habits as I grow older, but interviews—that's a good habit to get into." He was openly pleased by this sort of attention.

Something struck me in that first moment of meeting with Mance, and it stayed with me as I listened to him up on the stage and later settled down to talk with him. It is worth mentioning only because it made me feel somewhat more personally close toward him: He reminds me of my grandfather, whose name, should it matter, was Elmer Moon and who was also a farmer or a farm laborer nearly all his life. There is a distinct physical resemblance between the two and also a similarity in their personalities: a kind of upright, hard-necked quality that comes, I think, from a certain feeling of self-satisfaction in a life spent at hard physical labor. That old phrase from a country and western song says it: "Pride in what I am."

"You can't just pick up a song and talk it," he told me when I asked him about what he had been singing a little while before. "You got to think how it was when it was written, got to think what it means. Yes, I make up my own songs, too. I read people's appearance and fix my mind on them, and then I make up the words to fit." Some, he indicated, were verses and stanzas added to the songs he regularly sang, but others are his alone. " 'What You Gonna Do When Death Comes Creepin' at Your Room'—that's mine. I sold that song for $500."

I asked about the sort of playing and singing he did around Navasota before he began recording and going around the country to play at colleges and universities. He shrugged deprecatingly as if to indicate that it didn't amount to much and said it was "Saturday night parties mostly." But then he went on to describe them: "They were something, though. People had a lot of fun at them. You could buy yourself some lemonade and dance and tromp all night. I played parties and breakdowns where they'd kill a hog and serve it up with beans and people would dance all night. They had a custom then, you paid five cents to dance with a partner. If you was a good dancer you'd fill up a handkerchief with nickels. And even fifty cents would buy a lot in those days.

"That's how Arhoolie found me, from those old dances I used to play. It was a surprise. Mack McCormick and Chris Strachwitz, they didn't know who they was lookin' for when they set out from Houston, but they was lookin' for anyone who could sing and play music. They got my reputation around Navasota and quite naturally they came to me. They recorded me the same night. That was the number one time I recorded."

Was he surprised when they showed up so unexpectedly? "Oh, you bet I was. I didn't like it. I came in one evening, and they made themselves known by their truck in my yard. I didn't know what these two men on my porch were up to. They ask me, 'Can I play?' And I say, 'A little bit.' And then they asked would I play a little for them now, and I said I would if they'd let me go in there and clean up, take the grease off me. I said, 'You're blockin' the way. I can't get aroun' y'all.' So I came out on the porch with my guitar, and I played the worst one I could think of just to get rid of them. And then they said to me, 'Play us one of those old blues like you play in the country.' And so I did, and they carried on like they liked it a real lot. They said they'd be back in an hour or two, and then they left.

"Now, what they did was go after the recording equipment, only I didn't know. I thought they were trying to run a trick on me. So I think to myself, 'I can whip that little one, and maybe I can knock the big one down with a chair.' But when they got back, they had all this equipment, so I guessed that they was all right. I sat down and played about an hour for them, and they took the best of that and gave me fifty dollars for my work. That was more money than I ever got. But my wife, she was still suspicious. She thought maybe there was something wrong about making money that easy. She lay across the bed chewing me out, saying she was sorry she ever married a guitar-picker. Then I got a long letter from Chris with $300 in it telling me to come on out to Berkeley and record some more. She changed her mind after that."

Mance Lipscomb's circumstances have changed quite a lot since then. For a man who had never gone farther from his home than Dallas, 200 miles away, he has adapted remarkably well to a life that calls for him to travel great distances across the country, often on a rather tight schedule. But he is obviously enjoying himself. "That's what I've been doing ever since that first time, just traveling and recording, and going to play for people at shows like this. Two weeks out of the month I'm out, it seems like. My wife never has gone anyplace with me. I think she's afraid to travel, but I kind of like it myself. I like to get with people and let them know what I'm doing, then we can communicate. You've got to combine yourself with people some kind of way."

He now owns a six-room house in Navasota, where he lives with his wife and one of his grandchildren. Apparently referring to the white people in that Texas farm town, Mance remarks wryly, "It's funny. They didn't know me in my own hometown for sixty or seventy years, until the publicity started. Now they all do."

Traveling around, playing at festivals and colleges, Mance has met a lot of songsters and bluesmen, and has become well known himself. He cheerfully gives estimates of any and all. Of Sam Hopkins, who now lives about a hundred and fifty miles away, in Centerville, he says, with a shake of his head, "I can't get along with Lightning. Very few people can. You have to handle him like a soft-boiled egg. And that Howlin' Wolf, he's another one. He's got that mean look. He talks mean, too."

But the one he likes to talk about most is Mississippi John Hurt, the great old songster who died in 1966. "I met him at Newport in 1965. Everybody was saying to me, 'You ought to hear that John Hurt. He sounds a lot like you.' He came on right after I left the stage, so I walked right around and leaned up against a tree and listened to him. He played 'Candy Man'—you ask me, that's one of his best songs, that and 'Stagolee'—and ooooh, he sounded good. We were big friends from then on, him and me. He was about my biggest fan. Course, he died a couple of years ago."

Mance got to talking again about all the traveling he had done in the past few years, and I remember suggesting he must be the most widely traveled seventy-six-year-old man in the state of Texas. He allowed that that might be so, and then went on to say something that summed up his last ten years rather eloquently. "Yes," he said, "here I was an old farmer with his head down, given up on things, and these people come along and gave me a whole new life with my music."

CHAPTER SEVEN

HERE'S FURRY. A little man nestled on top of his bed and hunched over his guitar. He spends a lot of time on that bed, which, oddly enough, is stuck up against the wall next to the front door of his house on Mosby Street in Memphis. He keeps his bed in the living room because he finds it a little hard to get around now. He lost a leg in a railway accident over fify years ago. It didn't bother him too much for most of his life—in fact, he got around on his artificial leg well enough to work as a street cleaner for the city for forty-four years. But now he's seventy-eight, and he spends most of the day with the leg off, hopping around the room when he has to, and waving the stump about without embarrassment.

Furry Lewis is whipping that old guitar of his, not artfully perhaps, but very enthusiastically. Sitting on the bed, he can reach over and open the door for the visitors that stream in to listen. Every morning there is a little party at Furry's house that may last into afternoon, depending on whether or not somebody has brought a bottle along. Today somebody has.

"Don't forget to put in your book that this is the first time old Furry ever see whiskey," he says as he gulps down another slug.

"Don't forget to put in he can lie, too!" hoots one of his guests.

He is a mailman, as are a couple of others there that day. For some reason Furry's house is a gathering place for the men in gray in that section of town. I get the idea that they rush through their routes and then go over to Furry's to hide out. A couple of ladies are there, too. Modishly dressed and self-possessed. They laugh a lot at Furry and seem to regard him with indulgence.

Furry delivers a rather broad wink and says for their benefit, "A lady asked me two weeks ago, she say to me, 'As long as you been around, Furry, you never took a wife. How come?' And I say to her, 'What do I need with a wife as long as the man next door got one?' " He gives a great cackle at that, and the mailmen take it up.

And in between he sings. Blues mostly. Something he calls "Furry's Blues"—the idea being that he has a woman for every day in the week, a recitation of what he does with his Monday woman, and his Tuesday woman, and so on. It's one those bold, bragging songs that a Muddy Waters or a Howlin' Wolf might be able to pull off but not little Furry Lewis. Somehow he seems to know this, too, and he tries to distract our attention by playing little tricks with his guitar, elbowing his fretboard—"I'm just a crazy man," he calls out to nobody in particular—and beating on the body of his guitar as if it were a tom-tom. This goes over pretty well with the crowd in Furry's living room. They laugh, nod, do everything but applaud. And Furry cackles again, delighted with himself. He is the consummate entertainer; he lives for an audience.

"I'm gonna pick you some blues again," he announces, and he begins to tune up. He has a little trick with this. Like most guitarists, he has a little tune-up tune; his is "Taps." And then, just so he can be sure that we appreciate what he was up to, he picks "Reveille" for us very carefully. "Okay now, here we go. Here's a blues that I wrote."

Well, there's one kind favor I ask of you,
One kind favor I ask of you,
Lord, there's one kind favor I ask of you,
Please see that my grave is kept clean.

Lord, it's two white horses in a line,
It's two white horses in a line,

Lord, it's two white horses in a line
To take me to the burial ground.

Oh, dig my grave with a silver spade,
Dig my grave with a silver spade,
Yes, dig my grave with a silver spade.
Just let me down with a golden chain.

It is a good song—haunting and ominous in its overtones, dark and tragic in outlook—but it is Blind Lemon Jefferson's song and not Furry Lewis'. He seemed willing to claim just about anything he played or sang that day. He went on to do "Brownsville Blues," which has been credited to Willie Newbern but is more likely the work of Sleepy John Estes—and is not, in any case, that of Furry Lewis, as he claimed it to be.

I doubt if his audience there that morning—which by then had become afternoon—really cared if Furry had written any of the blues he played. They were there to enjoy themselves, relaxing in the parlor of the neighborhood's most colorful character. Nobody expects too much of him in the way of variety, and that's just as well, too, for old Furry only has one performance in him. He plays and sings the same songs whenever he squats down on that bed. His audiences come and go, but Furry just keeps singing the old songs that he learned a generation or more ago.

He no longer even sings them very well. He recorded back in the twenties, and held onto a good reputation then for years. People in Memphis tell me that he could sit down and do a pretty good set of blues until not so very long ago. But age seems to have caught up with him; years of jiving and shucking have taken their toll. Furry still goes out to play now and again. He was invited down to Preservation Hall in New Orleans for a session recently. He has even gone on tour with a rock road show, the Alabama State Troupers, that features him right up there with Don Nix, Jeanie Greene, and Brenda Patterson. His audiences are seldom disappointed, for he puts on a pretty good show. It's just that he can't play or sing much any more.

Still, he has been a part of the musical history of this very musical city for more years than many better bluesmen have lived. Born in Greenwood, Mississippi, in 1893, Walter "Furry" Lewis came up to Memphis with his family in 1899. He was hardly grown, he says, before he took up the guitar and started playing with various bands around town. "I played with W. C. Handy and Will Shade and the Memphis Jug Band, too. Handy gave me a guitar, I remember. It was the best guitar I ever had, too." When was that? He frowns and shakes his head. "That's kinda hard to answer," he says. "I don't remember as good as I used to. If Will Shade was still around you could ask him. He's dead two years now, though.

"No, I don't know any of the old-time musicians today but Gus Cannon. He still plays banjo some, but he won't go out in public, and he won't talk to anybody, either. Oh, he's *old,* older than I am, probably ninety or something. But him and me, we used to play a lot together, you know. We played those doctor shows, medicine shows *you* call them. We traveled through Arkansas, Louisiana, Mississippi, all over. Sure, we was selling Jackrabbit Syrup and Corn Salve."

THAT WAS the Dr. Willie Lewis Show. At one time or another most of the top Memphis bluesmen and street singers worked the medicine shows. Among them were Jim Jackson, oldest of them all; Robert Wilkins, who subsequently became a preacher in Memphis and gave up blues singing altogether; and Gus Cannon and Will Shade. The idea was that the medicine show used the bluesmen to gather a crowd at the little crossroads in the rural South where patent medicine pitchmen like Dr. Lewis would step up while the music was still ringing in the air and sing the praises of Jackrabbit Syrup or some similar preparation that was guaranteed to cure just about everything from snakebite to acne.

That was what the bluesmen did for fun. Furry and the others considered life out on the road with the medicine shows a kind of paid vacation from the rigors of town life. Town was Memphis, and Memphis was Beale Street, and there wasn't a tougher, more swinging and wide-open street in any city in the country during the first two and a half decades of the twentieth century. Beale Street grew up around an Italian-American saloon keeper and gambler who went by the name of Pee Wee. He came to Memphis in the 1880s, gravitated to the black gambling action in town, and won consistently and heavily enough so that he was soon able to buy into a saloon. He showed he had just the sort of dubious talents it took to run a honky-tonk, and it wasn't long before he had one of his own—Pee Wee's—going full blast on Beale. His place set the tone and the pace for the entire street. The tone? Anything goes. The pace? Fast and ragged, to a heavy blues beat. Pee Wee liked the music. He knew it was good for business; it brought the crowds in to drink and gamble. The better the bands, the bigger the crowds—it was as simple as that—and so there was a lot of competition among saloon keepers up and down the street to bring in the swingingest jug bands and the howlingest bluesmen. And that was how Beale Street happened to become America's Main Street of the blues.

Walk down it today, and you will be disappointed. Urban renewal has swept away all but a block or two. And on what is left, all you will see are pawnshops and cut-rate clothing stores. Most of the blacks have moved out from that section of downtown Memphis—Furry Lewis himself lived at Beale and Fourth until a few years ago, but decided to go because there was nothing doing on Beale Street any more. But in its day it teemed with life and echoed with song. It was a good-time district, noted particularly throughout the South for its good-time women. Their praises were sung up and down the river in tones of good-natured lust:

I'm gonna stay around this town
Where the gals won't allow me to walk around
Ain't Nobody's business but mine

I'm gonna stay in Memphis, Tennessee
Where the gals in Memphis take a liking to me
Now ain't nobody's business but my own

And wherever there are women there are bound to be plenty of blues. Out on one corner of Beale Street you might hear that blind man W. C. Handy wrote about moaning "See, See Rider," "Careless Love," "Joe Turner Blues," and most of the other old standard folk blues. On the other corner, competing with him lustily, you might hear a couple of country boys from someplace like Clarksdale, Mississippi, playing something they had heard Charley Patton do the week before.

And down the street, in Pee Wee's, you might catch the Memphis Jug Band, which made quite a name for itself locally and then went on to gain national recognition recording for Victor. Will Shade, the leader of the group, was himself practically a one-man band, playing guitar, harmonica, jug, or tub bass when the occasion demanded. Mostly he sang, however, for there were always good stringmen in the group to back him up —and he specialized in little blues duets with his wife, Jennie Mae Bofors.

The Memphis Jug Band was the first of all the Beale Street string bands, and it stayed together in one shape or another until well into the thirties. But just as good was Cannon's Jug Stompers. Led by Gus Cannon, who went by the nickname of "Banjo Joe," the Jug Stompers was a trio composed of Cannon, a harmonica player named Noah Lewis, and a guitarist named Ashley Thompson. The three got together in the outlying rural area, and played country dances and picnics for a couple of years before they tried out on Beale Street. They went over big in Memphis, however, and Gus Cannon, one of the few bluesmen to play banjo, has lived there ever since.

There were other jug bands working up and down Beale at this time. Note, too, that they were *jug* bands—that is, they all honored the local preference for a bass line supplied by puffing into an empty gallon jug. It made an explosive tubalike sound that was especially effective against the strings. If, with a nod to the hype-artists at Stax Records, there really is such a thing as the "Memphis Sound," then it originated with the rhythmic rumbles that issued forth from those Beale Street jugs.

One solo performer who deserves special mention is Minnie Douglas. She was married for a while to bluesman Joe McCoy and was remembered by some (including Big Bill Broonzy) as Minnie McCoy, but she was known to the world at large as "Memphis Minnie," the name under which she recorded a number of fine blues. She was not a native of the city but was born farther south, in Algiers, Louisiana, on June 24, 1900, and grew up in a little town in Mississippi just over the line from Memphis. She early became such an accomplished performer on guitar that by the time she was fifteen she was singing on the streets of the city. She worked in and out of the saloons and up and down Beale Street, just as her brother blues singers did. In fact, she was still singing the streets when a scout for Columbia heard her, signed her up, and brought her north to Chicago to record. That was where Big Bill Broonzy met up with her and had the famous 1933 blues contest that he described in *Big Bill Blues.* What happened? He lost! When she got the joint rocking with "Me and My Chauffeur" and "Looking the World Over," Bill declares, he just didn't stand a chance with the audience or the judges (who were, incidentally, Tampa Red, Sleepy John Estes, and Richard Jones). His considered opinion: "Memphis Minnie can make a guitar cry, moan, talk, and whistle the blues." Coming from Broonzy, who was a fair guitarist himself, that's quite a tribute.

W. C. HANDY WAS once closely associated with Memphis, Beale Street, and the beginnings of the blues—far *too* closely to suit most blues historians and critics. They have been justifiably annoyed at the way he was billed as "the father of the blues." Handy, of course, was not the music's father; the most that can be said for him is that he was its rich uncle. But having been denied paternity, he has virtually been made into a nonperson: His name barely appears in the blues histories; he and the important part he played in popularizing the music have been all but ignored. Since he has lately been neglected somewhat, let us look at what he did and did not do and decide for ourselves just what sort of recognition he deserves—perhaps none at all, perhaps a little more than he has lately been allowed.

He was born into a fairly prosperous, landowning Negro family in Florence, Alabama, in 1873. He grew up there, constantly urged upward by his father, always admonished to improve himself. It was, in fact, because music was not "steady work" and not because young Handy lacked talent that his father forbade him to pursue it as a career. But he went against his father's wishes, bought a cornet, learned to play it in secret, and was well on his way before anyone was the wiser. One of the musicians with whom he played around Florence when he was little more than a boy was a violinist named Jim Turner, a drunken refugee from Beale Street. It was from him that Handy heard tales of that street that never shut down.

W. C. Handy spent his life in music and gives a fascinating account of it in his autobiography, *Father of the Blues.* Even if the title puts your teeth on edge, don't be put off by the book, for it contains, among much else that is good, a remarkable description of just what show business was like for blacks around the turn of the century. He went out on the road with Mahara's Minstrel Men, an all-black minstrel troupe that covered the entire country from top to bottom and one corner to the other. Touring with a tent show of any kind was no picnic; for blacks there was the very real danger of offending a hostile local populace in some way or other and having the show shot up or one of their number seized and lynched. It happened during Handy's years with Mahara's Minstrel Men. He paid his dues.

Handy was a legitimate musician, an excellent cornet player, and a good bandmaster. A theme running through his autobiography is the conflict in his life between strait-laced respectability, to which he was born and ultimately returned, and the keen attraction that he felt to the vulgar, the common, which the blues represented to him. He was excited by it because he was a good musician and saw the very real possibilities it offered. There is a key passage in the book in which he tells of the moment when he first realized that the music he had been hearing around him might be translated into something with wider appeal. He had been working as the leader of the local Knights of Pythias band in Clarksdale, Mississippi. Returning to the town one night, he had a long wait in the Tutwiler railroad station. He dozed off only to be awakened by a Negro next to him, who began playing a guitar and groaning out his intention: "Goin' where the Southern cross the Dog." Just a traveling song, as it turned out—nothing special, but it stuck in his mind, and Handy began wondering if music of this sort, music that he heard all around him in the Delta country, might not be written down and orchestrated for the band he led.

Well, that is just what he did, and suddenly he found his Knights of Pythias band the most popular in the region. It wasn't long until he was summoned to Memphis to take over a bigger band there. They played picnics, dances, and for special occasions up and down Beale Street, too. The Handy band was soon the toast of Memphis, playing for the white gentry at the city's Alaskan Roof Gardens, where it was billed as "The Best Band in the South." Which, remembering New Orleans down the river, was probably not true.

The great success of Handy and his band was due in large

measure to the special material that he wrote for it. He did an election song for E. H. Crump, the notorious boss of Memphis, which he titled respectfully, "Mr. Crump." After Crump's election—the issue was never in doubt—Handy decided to do something more with the tune, which had become enormously popular around town. He had it published at his own expense, but when it appeared that the sheet music was not moving he allowed himself to be persuaded to sell the rights to the song for a small figure (probably about $100). He saw it become a national hit as "The Memphis Blues"—and though he was not a cent richer, he was much, much wiser. He formed his own publishing company, and wrote and published in quick succession, "St. Louis Blues," "Yellow Dog Blues," "Joe Turner Blues," "Hesitating Blues," and "Beale Street Blues." All were hits. Blues was the new craze in popular music, and because he had written them all, he was hailed as "the father of the blues."

And yes, he *had* written them—not just taken them down, note for note, from that "blind man on the corner." As a trained musician, Handy had a grasp of what was going on musically when a Delta man sat down with his guitar and began hollering out his miseries. And nobody better than he was equipped to translate the folk idiom into something with a broader, more popular appeal. He selected, chose, and borrowed from the blues—but he never simply stole. He took the trouble, in his book *The Father of the Blues,* to make a detailed demonstration in one chapter what and how he had borrowed from folk sources. He concludes very candidly: "There are those who wish me to approach the subject of blues as though this type of music should be shrouded in mystery. Thousands have heard the material which went into the making of the blues . . . but they didn't write it down. I formed the habit of writing down ideas from watching my father." The combination of his systematic middle-class habits and the low-down black blues proved quite unbeatable.

No, you can't ignore William Christopher Handy. The job of bringing the blues and blues-based material to the vast American listening public was one that had to be done; only an anthropologist could wish that this great music be kept a secret.

In a way, Memphis has continued to be a good blues town, even though Beale Street went into a steep decline following the war years. The city is still the first stop for the boys who emerge from the Delta with guitars in their hands. An inexhaustible supply of talent seems to lie all around it in the small towns and rural areas of Mississippi, Tennessee, and Arkansas. The last real superstar the city produced first surfaced as a disc jockey —that was Riley B. King, "the Beale Street Blues Boy," who kept up a line of patter and jive between the blues records he played until he started listening to them a little closer and decided he could do better himself if he put his mind to it. He clipped his DJ tag to initials only, and began touring the South as B. B. King.

It may have been inevitable, considering all the talent from around the area, that Memphis should have become a recording center. It started with Sam Phillips, a white radio engineer from Florence, Alabama, who set up a recording studio in Memphis in 1950. Although the label that he founded, Sun Records, became best known for the rockabilly-sound white singers such as Elvis Presley, Jerry Lee Lewis, and Carl Perkins singing black material—Phillips started out by recording black singers in the Memphis and mid-South area. For its first few years, Sun was a black blues label and featured one local heavy in particular named James Cotton, who went on to make a name for himself first as Muddy Waters' harp player and then leading his own blues band.

Stax, the white-owned, black-managed Memphis recording company, is now just about the top soul label in the country. Nearly all of its top attractions come from Memphis or very nearby—including Isaac Hayes, David Porter, Carla Thomas, and the company's famous house rhythm section, Booker T. and the M.G.s. The only real blues singer on Stax is Albert King, who comes from just up the river in Osceola, Arkansas, a few miles from Johnny Cash's hometown, Dyess. Stax has made a star of King, the burly ex-bulldozer driver, and has given him a national following on the white rock circuit in addition to his loyal black audience. He had to work hard to get where he is. His success, which began when he started recording for Stax in 1966, was preceded by about twenty years of trying. But Albert King has a lot to offer, too—a good, rough, husky voice that sounds as though it belongs to a man who has experienced all the bad times the world has to offer and a style that blends country feeling with city sophistication in a rather subtle way.

On top of all this, he has one of the most distinctive electric-guitar styles in the blues: when he really gets going on a solo, he bends practically *every* note that he plays so that he makes it twang and whine through the amplifier, making it sound like an old Delta bluesman working a steel-bodied National with a length of tubing capped on the little finger of his fret hand.

If I seem suddenly quite specific, it is because I have a particular afternoon with Bukka White in mind. That was in Memphis, too, on Dunlap Street, not far from Furry Lewis' place. Bukka—the name is a corruption of Booker (he was born Booker T. Washington White in 1909)—is a tough-looking, though fairly genial, individual whose daughter calls him "big Daddy," and whose neighbors seem to give him a wide berth. They treat him as though he were a pretty tough customer, and they have good reason to, for he not only boxed professionally back in the thirties, but also did time for murder in Mississippi's notorious Parchman Prison Farm.

Bukka is probably Parchman's most famous alumnus. He had already recorded the first of his famous Vocalion sessions in 1937 when he was involved in the incident that sent him to jail. According to Paul Oliver in *The Story of the Blues,* it was a shooting fracas outside a Mississippi roadhouse. A man was killed, but there must have been extenuating circumstances, for Bukka was released in three years' time. It's no use asking him, though, for he won't talk about it, except to say, "Yeah, I cut some time down there, but I'll tell you this—I was just as innocent as you are, sittin' there right now. What was it like? Oh, it wasn't any too tough for me. I was lucky. They set me playin' instead of workin'. Just playin' for the big rich folks was all I was doin' there."

And though he would discuss the experience in terms no more specific than those, he was glad to sing his song about it to me, his famous "Parchman Farm Blues." He took a moment to set the National into rough tune, then launched into the driving, relentless, and, finally, monotonous rhythm against which he began groaning out his blues.

Judge gave me life this morning down on Parchman
Farm (twice)
I wouldn't hate it so bad, but I felt my wife in
mourn.

Oh, goodbye wife, oh you have done gone (twice)
But I hope someday you will hear my lonesome song.

Oh, listen you men, I don't mean no harm (twice)
If you wanna do good you better stay off of
Parchman Farm.

We go to work in the morning just at dawn of day
(twice)
Just at the settin' of the sun, that's when the work is
done.

I'm down on old Parchman Farm, but I wanna go
back home (twice)
But I hope some day I will overcome.

Of all the Mississippi bluesmen still singing today, Bukka's style is the most primitive, the least affected by all that has happened in music in the years since he started singing and shouting his way up from Mississippi in 1929. His intonation and his phrasing are virtually unchanged from what you will hear on those famous Vocalion blues sides that he made in 1937 and 1940. He had a way then of connecting lines and stanzas with a kind of nasal drone, and he still uses it today. This, together with the constant rhythm that he churns out monotonously as he declaims his lines, gives his performances a peculiar chanting quality.*

That rhythm he uses is especially interesting. It varies hardly a stroke from song to song, pulsing and driving along. Fundamentally, it is train rhythm; he seems to rock on and on at express tempo all afternoon. I asked him about this, and I could tell from the odd expression that came to his face that I had hit something sensitive.

He grinned almost slyly. "How you tell that?" he said. "You know, I live around trains all my life when I was a boy, so that's bound to be in my music, now ain't it?" I agreed that it was, and he went on to say, "My father, John White, was a railroad man from New York. He come down to work as a fireman. Oh, he was a huge man. He musta weighed about 286 pounds, and he

*I would speculate, purely on the basis of the striking similarity of their styles, that Richie Havens has consciously imitated and adapted mannerisms of Bukka White's.

worked all his life on the railroad—first for the M & O, and then he went to the Frisco. I got the trains from him, and I got the music from him, too. He played violin, and he gave me my first guitar. He died in 1930—that's the year I came to stay in Memphis."

I asked him if he had lived there ever since. He shrugged, not much interested in the question. "Oh, on and off, in and out, you know. I used to hobo a lot when I was young. But when I settled down, I settled down here. 'Course, there was that bad time down in Mississippi, but that's long in the past." He meant the Parchman Farm episode, of course.

How had he come to record those sides for Vocalion? Had he been discovered by someone? Gone up North to look for work?

"Oh, that was Lester Melrose come and find me. A lot of fellas they had trouble with him, but I never did. He nice to me till he die, and his daughter, she still send me money. I remember Melrose came down to Mississippi. He left the Delta and came up to the hills, and that's where he found me with my guitar in my hand. He say to me, 'This is what I been wantin'.' And he give me a railroad ticket taller than you to take me up to Chicago to play for him there. I was two weeks in Chicago that first time. He gave me a meal ticket, and I just stayed there right in the hotel. He brought whiskey to me. I wouldn't fool with it then, though. I'd just taste it then. Now I swallow it." He exploded suddenly in laughter at the little joke he had just made.

As nearly as I could remember, he did only original material. Where did he get his songs?

"I only do about three songs that ain't mine. I do St. Louis Slim's 'Please Write My Mother,' and 'Baby Please Don't Go,' by Big Joe Williams, and 'John Henry,' too. I don't know who wrote that. It's about 200 years old. Except for them, I pulled all my songs out of my brain. When I come to the point when I want to do it, then I'll do it. They just come."

Does he see any of the other old-time bluesmen around Memphis?

"Oh, sure. Some. You know. I see little old Furry. He lives pretty close here. And I see Memphis Minnie sometimes, too. She's in a nursing home now, and I went with a white boy from Washington to see her not so long ago. You know, she got fat as a butterball, that woman did, and all she do is sit in her wheelchair and cry and cry. But in her time she was really something. She was about the best thing goin' in the woman line. And then my cousin, of course."

His cousin?

"B.B! B. B. King. He ain't no real *old-time* bluesman, but he's pretty good at the blues, ain't he? He's my first cousin, and I give him some tips every once in a while. He was startin' to play too loud, too, like that band the Grateful Dead in San Francisco. So I just told B.B. to cut it out because he was putting more racket in it than solid music. And he just said, 'Okay, cuz, you know best.'

"B.B.'s okay. They all are. I met some pretty good people in this business to tell you the truth. And I think I did pretty good in it, too. I been blessed. I never run up again too many bad people to take advantage of me and all.

"And that's more than most can say."

CHAPTER EIGHT

"GOIN' TO CHICAGO— SORRY BUT I CAN'T TAKE YOU"

CHICAGO IS the home of the blues today. It is its own dark place and has its own wild style. They started out calling that style urban blues to distinguish it from the more primitive old country blues that was played in the juke joints of the South. But now they call it *Chicago* blues, because that's where the urban blues is at today: just plain Chicago. And how did it get there? Because that's where the blues was recorded. When Blind Lemon came north to record, it was to Chicago he came. When Sleepy John Estes and Hammie Nixon hoboed north to cut for Decca, they found the freight trains stopped at suburban Markham, Illinois, and they hitchhiked in from there. And when McKinley Morganfield came up from Stovall, Mississippi, looking for fame and fortune, he found it as Muddy Waters at the end of a phonograph needle out on the South Side of Chicago.

This story begins, as all too many Chicago stories do, in New York. It was there in February, 1920, that a plump *café au lait* contralto named Mamie Smith recorded a couple of songs, "That Thing Called Love" and "You Can't Keep a Good Man Down." They were neither blues nor jazz, but vaguely "jazzy" numbers with a kind of old-time show-business bounce to them. And Mamie Smith wasn't a blues singer, either—just a girl who had paid her dues in vaudeville. She did the job, though—and that was to break the color ban in recording. For over a year a little Harlem hustler named Perry Bradford had been pitching all the New York recording companies on that vast, untapped Negro phonograph-record market out there. "There's fourteen million Negroes in our great country," he told them, "and they will buy records if they are recorded by one of their own." Well, nobody paid much attention to him until he went to OKeh, then an aggressive independent company that was a bit more willing to take chances. They recorded Mamie Smith early in 1920, and then had a few months of misgivings before they finally released her record in August of that year. And although she was not advertised as black, Negro newspapers let out the news, and the record took off and sold an estimated 75,000 copies. The lesson was not lost on OKeh: they got Mamie Smith into a recording studio immediately, cut another record, and released it, this time proclaiming her as black in advertisements. It went over even better than they had hoped—and all of a sudden the "Race" race was on.

There was suddenly terrific competition among record companies to sign and record black artists—blues singers they were called, whether they sang blues or not. Few of them did. But as the black audience became more discriminating, the record companies, which with one exception (Black Swan) were white-owned and run, had to come up with real down-home funky blues singers doing real black blues. It wasn't long until it took such as Alberta Hunter, Bessie Smith, Clara Smith (no relation to Bessie), Ida Cox, Ma Rainey, Blind Lemon Jefferson, and Lonnie Johnson to satisfy them.

They were listed in the catalogs as "Race" artists, meaning, simply, Negro. (It was a term used by blacks themselves at the time and in the twenties had a great vogue in the black press.) No matter what they were called, their records sold phenomenally. Perry Bradford, who subsequently did well for himself as a songwriter and entrepreneur, had been proven right. There *was* a black audience out there, and they were willing to pay plenty. Those first records by Mamie Smith on the OKeh label, for example, cost a dollar each. Bessie Smith records on Columbia toward the end of the twenties went at seventy-five cents each and sold better than 20,000 each.

(But careful. Don't jump to conclusions. In his book *Screening the Blues,* Paul Oliver does just that when he observes,

> Five or six million Race records sold annually at a time when the total Negro population in the United States was only double that amount meant that a very large proportion of the Negro world must have been hearing the music; a single record could be familiar in the lives of half a dozen people and many a young Negro grew up with the phonograph blues always in his ears. The colossal output indicates irrefutably the important part played by the gramophone in the spread of Negro musical culture and gives some indication of its potential strength in directing and forming Negro taste.

Most of which is true enough, but Oliver does seem to assume rather blindly here that *all* Race records were bought by blacks —and this was simply not the case. Records by Negro jazzmen were also listed in the Race category, and these included artists such as Louis Armstrong, Duke Ellington, Fats Waller, and others who were nationally popular with whites; of the blues singers, Bessie Smith, at least, and probably Ida Cox, too, had plenty of white record-buying fans. Taste is not and was not ever as neatly segregated in America as all that.)

From early on, Chicago had a big piece of the recording action. Paramount, especially, with a big mail-order and "drummer" trade in the South, was eager to record authentic black music that the country audience would buy. The man in charge of the company's Race recording operations in Chicago was J. Mayo Williams, himself a Negro; he brought Blind Lemon Jefferson up from Texas to cut records as early as 1926. After a brief and unsuccessful venture on his own, Williams joined Vocalion as a talent scout and began recording everyone from the old Memphis bluesman Jim Jackson (his "Kansas City Blues" was a big hit) to Tampa Red (Hudson Whittaker) and Georgia Tom (Thomas Dorsey). And later, when English Decca opened an American office in Chicago in 1934, they engaged J. Mayo Williams as scout, and he built up an impressive roster of black talent in a year's time.

Not surprisingly, the Depression hit the record industry hard, and that part of it supplying black music was hit hardest of all. Paramount folded. Field trips to various sectors of the South for on-the-spot recording, which had become standard procedure for some companies, were discontinued in the interest of belt-tightening. But somehow Chicago held on—perhaps because by this time there was in the city a kind of resident blues nucleus, some of them bluesmen who had come or been brought up north to record for one label or another and had simply stayed on to play at some of the many South Side bars as they waited for their next recording date to come up. It was in those South Side clubs that the country blues style of the Deep South was metamorphosed into what they would soon call urban blues. How was it different? It was music to be performed, music to dance to, music that had to compete with the jazz bands that were then so popular with blacks and whites alike in Chicago. And in competing, it became more than a little like jazz in the bargain—a little less personal and a little more structured. Johnny Shines, who started out country and wound up urban, explains the difference this way: "You take a man playing the country blues, he plays just what he feels because he's playing the country blues, he plays just what he feels because he's playing all by himself nine times out of ten, and he don't have to cooperate with nobody. But you take Chicago blues style, when you get up there with a band, you have to play together real tight just like it was any other arrangement. It was different, of course, with country blues, because there wasn't any arrangement. If your bluesman felt like holding a note for nine beats, he held it for nine. He didn't know nothin' about any one-two-three-four."

One of the originators of this urban style in Chicago was a William Lee Conley Broonzy, nicknamed "Big Bill," who was born in Scott, Mississippi, on June 26, 1893. He came to Chicago on his own, he says in his autobiography, *Big Bill Blues,* in 1920, and started playing for chicken and chittlin's at those Saturday-night rent parties. It took him a while, however, to convince somebody that he was ready to record—and that somebody was J. Mayo Williams, who was running things at Paramount. Bill did indifferently well. Of the four sides he cut, only one—"House Rent Stomp"—was released, and that after a delay of some months, in 1927. But he was available—very much on the scene in Chicago—and so he continued to record, usually in solo but sometimes backing up other singers. Although he was not above lifting material, most of what he recorded was his own, or at least freely adapted.

Most of his early recorded work shows him to be playing country blues of more or less the old sort. But gradually, in the early thirties, a change became perceptible. Perhaps influenced by the popular LeRoy Carr-Scrapper Blackwell duo, or swayed by the things that Tampa Red was doing with Georgia Tom Dorsey, Big Bill teamed up with a piano player named Joshua Altheimer, added rhythm and a saxophone-clarinetist named Buster Bennett—and out came Big Bill Broonzy's Memphis Five. What they played was a kind of good-time style that mixed blues with dance music. Through the thirties, as he began warming up to that Memphis Five band of his, he became more and more proficient as a guitarist. He could hold a good, steady beat as a rhythm guitarist, and as a soloist he was fluent, if not always very imaginative. It was largely because of his skill on the instrument and because of his wide contacts among Chicago bluesmen and black musicians that he became associated with Lester Melrose, a white blues entrepreneur on the order of an independent producer who worked with both Vocalion and Bluebird. He seems to have had a much freer hand and been more active for the Bluebird label. Bill recorded for both labels under Melrose's auspices, but for Bluebird he became a sort of house guitarist, putting together backup groups to record behind such favorites as Washboard Sam (whose real name was Robert Brown and who was actually Big Bill's half-brother), and later with a first-rate female vocalist named Lil Green who sang a lot of blues.

By and large, the Chicago blues sound began with these Bluebird sessions of the thirties and early forties. The talent on them was impressive. In addition to those already named, Bluebird artists included Lonnie Johnson, Tampa Red, and blues harp blower and shouter John Lee "Sonny Boy" Williamson (the *original* Sonny Boy, and not Rice Miller, who later took his name). It wasn't just the emphasis on groups—on blues bands and the bigger sound for dancing—that made the urban blues what it was; it was because it was about those *Chicago* miseries —and the lyrics complained of Depression unemployment, tough cops, and freezing cold, and sang their longing for the South, not because it was better but just because it was home. By and large, at least during this early period, it was a blues of exile made by exiles from the blues country.

Blues recording divides sharply into prewar and postwar periods. Wartime shellac restrictions went into force early in 1942, and the cutback hit blues record production hardest of all. And if things weren't bad enough, James C. Petrillo, president of the American Federation of Musicians, became disturbed at about this time about the impact of jukeboxes on the employment of musicians for live entertainment, and he called for a strike. It took two years to hammer out an arrangement on royalties, and during that time—from 1942 to 1944—no recording was done by AFM musicians. And although not all bluesmen were union musicians, the effect of the recording ban was to shut off what little wartime activity there was left. When the ban ended, there was some effort to revive Race recording activity within the limitations imposed by the shellac restrictions. But nothing much happened, because they brought back the old prewar favorites. And by that time, there was a new cast on the Chicago scene. A new era had begun.

NINETEEN FORTY-TWO was also the year that Albert Luandrew came north to Chicago to stay. He had been up once before. "Yeah, I came to Chicago first time in 1933. I was like everybody else in the country during the Depression, running around without no job. I took a look around up here and figured it would be easier to get by in the country, so I went back. That was my first try at Chicago."

Like so many Chicago bluesmen, Luandrew, who is known universally as "Sunnyland Slim," is a country boy from the Mississippi Delta. He was born in Vance, Mississippi, in 1907, grew up and learned to play the piano there. He went rambling then, sitting down at any place along the way that offered a piano and a stool. He played and shouted the blues in jukes, levee and highway camps, and sawmills. He played the good-time towns like West Helena, Arkansas, and became one of the mainstays on old Beale Street in Memphis. Along the way, he jammed with the legendary Robert Johnson and told the kid to mind the beat. And he saw his competitors among all those down-home piano men, Little Brother Montgomery and Roosevelt Sykes, go up North to Chicago and make it pretty big. He traveled up for that look-around in the Depression that he mentioned, got cold feet, and took the next train back to Memphis.

What happened then? "Oh, you know. I played those little old jobs in the country from around Vance and Longstreet. They got a lot of piano men from around there but I'm tops among them. Come right down to it, me and Roosevelt Sykes and Little Brother, we're the only ones living of that whole bunch of piano players and we're all up here in Chicago."

We were talking together in Slim's living room on East Seventy-ninth Street in Chicago. It is a small, comfortable apartment, a walk-up over a cleaning shop. It shows his wife's hand: The place is spotlessly clean, even *smells* clean—or is that the cleaning-fluid odor from downstairs? Bric-a-brac and figurines cover all available surfaces, and pictures crowd the walls. The television is on—one of those morning game shows. Slim ignores it, but his wife watches from a chair close by in rapt concentration.

He explains to me that when he came up in 1942 there was plenty happening in the music line but no recording because of the ban. He didn't like that, because it was in hopes of cutting some records that he had come up North. Everybody else he ever knew down there in the Delta had gone to Chicago and gotten a record contract, so why not him? Well, eventually he did—but not until 1947, when he cut some sides as "Dr. Clayton's Buddy." Who was Dr. Clayton? An old Delta blues singer-comedian who had cut quite a figure when Slim traveled with him on the chittlin' circuit—but that was years before, and here he was still just Dr. Clayton's Buddy.

What bands was he playing with during this time? Did he have his own group? "Naw, I didn't have my own group. I was just doing, you know, backup work. I was able to get Wolf and Muddy jobs pretty regular. They came up about this same time I did, and we always got along pretty good, I guess. That Muddy, I'll tell you, he's a good person. Always was. He's the goodest person you could meet."

He was playing with Howlin' Wolf's band the last time I had seen him, and that had not been long ago. Was he still? He nods. "Yeah," he says, "but I'm not going stay with Wolf. People come up to me and they say, 'Man, I'm surprised to see you with Wolf.' Nobody in his band doing anything but Hubert [Sumlin] and me. See, I do it a little different from Wolf personally. I don't do no slow four-five stuff. I lay it down *hard* on the piano. The way I do it I get a person to tap his foot just like a Baptist preacher."

Sunnyland Slim still has hopes of getting his own group together and playing the colleges and the festivals the way that Muddy and Buddy Guy and Junior Wells are doing—and he may make it yet. Nobody deserves it more than Slim, for nobody has worked harder than he has in the dives of the West Side and South Side of Chicago in bands headed by this guitar man or that harp blower. He is a sideman. He has recorded plenty for one label or another, but nearly all that he has done has been in a backup capacity. He sings well enough and he plays good piano—all he lacks is . . . what? A certain authority, perhaps, or the kind of personal magnetism that today passes for charisma. But Slim still makes plans for that band he's going to have—musicians, instrumentation, and the kind of material they will play—and in the meantime he keeps on taking those jobs with Wolf and may do a little session work with Willie Dixon to pay the rent.

His affairs are in a mess. He brings out a handful of letters and documents, spreads them out on the sofa between us, and begins a long, complicated, and somewhat rambling explanation of his problems. He has written songs, others have recorded them, and he feels he has not been paid as he should have been. Ideas, he says, have been stolen from him. In general, he seems to feel a sense of frustration and depletion as he sifts through the papers, and at one point he explains, "That's what my whole life is," and sweeps a big hand forward and back as though it were all laid out between us. "After fifty years of playing I ain't got nothin' to show for it. I mean, if anybody ought to be gettin' money in this business it's Brother, Sykes, and me."

And then, perhaps thinking to make his case stronger by repetition, he starts through it all once again, but breaks off suddenly. "I don't know," he says. "Maybe I messed up a little, I don't know. Some damn thing sure went wrong, though." Albert Luandrew, a.k.a. Sunnyland Slim, shakes his head and groans eloquently.

THE CHEAP BLUEBIRD LABEL on which the early urban blues came to be heard back in the thirties was dropped by Victor in 1950. Nobody really noticed, for by that time about all that appeared on it were reissues from earlier, livelier times. Robert Brown, who as Washboard Sam had been Bluebird's top star for nearly a decade, had by this time dropped out of the music business entirely and become a Chicago policeman.

With the war over and the blues business in full swing, records of the new Chicago sound began to pour forth plentifully —but from the oddest sources! For the most part, the major companies got out of blues recording just as the music was going into this new phase, and so it was cut on a score or more of fly-by-night labels—marks such as Tempo Tone, Ora Nelle, Chance, Keyhole, VeeJay, and J.O.B. Many of them were "club" labels, run by the manager or maybe just the bartender of some blues club where the groups were appearing. The boys might get together on their day off for a recording session, and the record would be pressed in limited quantity and then sold across the bar along with "Slitz" and watered-down rotgut.

That was how the Aristocrat label got started. If that name doesn't ring any bells, it may help to learn that it became Chess in 1950, the year Bluebird was discontinued. Yes, it was as neat as that, for Chess became just as important as Bluebird had ever been. Just look who they recorded: Muddy Waters, Howlin' Wolf, Little Walter, Buddy Guy, and just about everybody who was anybody in Chicago blues. And in the mid-fifties, with Chuck Berry and Bo Diddley under contract, Chess was one of the first to put on records that new sound that they first called rhythm-and-blues, and then rock-and-roll.

The Chess brothers, Leonard and Phil, owned a club in Chicago called the Macambo Lounge. As night-club owners, they got into the record business more or less by accident, according to Peter Guralnick in his book *Feel Like Going Home.* A talent scout came there to check out a singer named Andrew Tibbe at their club. On the spot, they decided that if he was good enough for somebody else to record he was good enough for them to do it, too. But whether they entered by accident or not, once in, the Chess brothers stayed in the business and worked hard at it, too. Where, for instance, others who ran club labels were satisfied to sell them across the bar and at a few shops in

Bronzeville, Leonard Chess took their records out and placed them with distributors and directly in record shops, especially around the South. It paid off, too, for first Aristocrat and then Chess were more than just Chicago labels; it wasn't long before they were running a national operation.

And if there ever was a time when exciting things were happening in Chicago blues, it was in the late forties and the fifties decade, when the Chess brothers hit their peak as recorders of the music. They made more money later on. In 1963 they paid a cool million for a radio station in Chicago—and converted it into WVON, soon the top black station in all of mid-America. By the sixties, there was a clutch of separate labels under the Chess umbrella: Argo (a jazz label, later discontinued), Checker, Cadet, and, of course, Chess. By this time, too, young Marshall Chess, Leonard's son, was getting into the business with a lot of new ideas for some of the label's old talent, mixing Muddy with acid rock, and Howlin' Wolf with howling feedback—with generally disastrous results.

If Chess was in large measure responsible for getting the Chicago blues sound out for the rest of the world to hear during its most exciting period, then the Chess brothers are, of course, to be commended. They kept a lot of blues fans happy and, moving into the sixties, helped reach a whole new audience of young whites with the music. And so, admittedly, they did a lot for the blues, but what did they do for the bluesmen? Charles Keil, in his excellent sociological study *Urban Blues,* had this to say about the Chess operation in 1966:

> Standards of honesty and integrity seem to be high, considering the industry as a whole. One arrives at an appraisal of this kind with mixed emotions. Stories circulate in the Chicago blues community that are not very flattering. At the same time, most of the performers currently under contract seem to be reasonably well satisfied with the arrangement. Muddy Waters, for example, has been with the company almost from its inception in the late 1940s *without* a contract. In a sense, this mutual trust in a highly competitive field speaks well for both Waters and Leonard Chess. Yet the arrangement also smacks of the old plantation and paternalism. I suspect that Waters can go to the Chess family with big dental bills or overdue car payments and receive a sizable "advance on royalties" on the spot, with no

> questions asked. On the other hand, if Muddy were to become "uppity," it is possible that his career might be seriously disrupted. "We're just one big happy family here," say the Chess men when asked about management problems, and I am almost persuaded that they believe it.

That "almost" speaks volumes. For, yes, there have been stories about the Chess operations in the past and a good deal of grumbling about the practices of Willie Dixon, bassist, songwriter (or song copyrighter anyway), Chess A & R man, and kickback artist extraordinaire. But all that talk has now subsided to a mere whisper, for the situation there has been altered considerably in the last few years.

There is still a Chess Records, although it was bought in 1969 by the GRT Corporation, a recording-tape manufacturer, and has subsequently been moved to New York. Leonard Chess died not long ago at the age of fifty-two. His son Marshall and his brother Phil stayed on briefly with GRT, but both are now completely out of the organization. Phil Chess runs WVON, and Marshall Chess is now connected with the Rolling Stones' business organization. Willie Dixon continues as an independent producer in Chicago with occasional forays into New York and Memphis, although today he lacks the considerable clout he once had as the black knight on the Chess board.

ALTHOUGH THE BLUES recording done in Chicago is very important and, I think, offers a key to the dissemination of that blues style which has been so influential in American music of the past two decades, nevertheless none of it would have worked if there had not been an abundance of blues talent on the scene in Chicago, clubs for them to play in, and fans to come, drink, and listen. But all the elements were there. There was a big active blues scene in Chicago for many years after the war. The city became a kind of blues mecca, drawing the faithful from close by and from every corner of the South. They went to the clubs and they bought the records. It was a loyal and enthusiastic audience, just the kind of following the bluesmen needed to keep them cooking.

But gradually that audience disappeared. Blame it on television, the coming of soul music, or any of a dozen other factors, but the fact of the matter is that at the end of the fifties there were blues bars all over the South and West sides of the city—one on every block, it seemed—and through the decade that followed they began to shut down at a dismaying rate. Most of those that stayed open made do with jukeboxes. It was the end of an era, though the survivors may have thought it just a wrinkle in taste, a temporary difficulty to be endured somehow until times got better. For some of them things never really did pick up again. There have been an astonishing number of deaths among this group of bluesmen in the last decade or so—many of them young men and none of them old: Little Walter Jacobs, Magic Sam Maghett, Earl Hooker, Otis Spann, Ernest Crawford, J. B. Lenoir, and Junior Parker, to name just a few casualties of the era. As clubs shut down, competition for jobs became intense and waits between them longer and longer. But a few of those hearty enough to weather this period of adversity were finally rewarded with salvation of sorts. For beginning about 1967 that vast, young white rock audience out there discovered blues in the persons of B. B. King, Albert King, and Muddy Waters, and by 1968 most of the top Chicago blues bands were getting at least a few bookings at colleges, universities, and rock clubs. And once given a bit of exposure, a few of the lesser-known bluesmen have begun to pull and hold audiences all around the country—have become, in short, bigger names away from home than they had been back in Chicago.

J. B. Hutto is a case in point. The short-statured Chicagoan who was born in 1929 in Augusta, Georgia, has been seeing a lot of the country lately. I caught him in Los Angeles at the Ash Grove on the last night of his engagement there. We talked briefly, and he told me he would be coming East pretty soon, so why couldn't we get together then? And sure enough, in a couple of months' time he showed up at Mr. Henry's on Capitol Hill in Washington, D.C. His manager is a Washingtonian named Topper Carew, a promoter active in a number of the arts and an outspoken controversialist on a variety of issues. He has given J. B. Hutto a solid home base at Mr. Henry's, the club at which Roberta Flack held forth for a couple of years, and is getting him bookings in and out of colleges throughout the East. And all this has been accomplished without benefit of any special record successes to back J.B. up—he himself is painfully aware of this, as we shall see.

Once you see him onstage in front of a group it is easy to understand how he has managed it. A mild, shy man in conversation, he is transformed before an audience into a sort of roaring, howling Mr. Hyde, big-mouthing his blues in memorably earthy style as he plays a slide electric guitar better than anyone else has managed to do since his mentor, the great Elmore James. He is a great, driving performer who leads a band—he is always billed as "J. B. Hutto and the Hawks"—with great authority. But oddly enough, although I found J.B. the same from the Ash Grove to Mr. Henry's, the Hawks were metamorphosed utterly. It was a big black blues band in Los Angeles of about the same instrumentation as the one Muddy Waters tours with—including French harp (harmonica) and piano. But in Washington, he had three white long-haired rockers with him, all quite proficient but not one of them over twenty-two. I asked J.B. about this when I sat down to talk with him in Washington.

He explained that when he had gone to the West Coast to play that date at the Ash Grove, he had worked with local musicians. They had had some good rehearsal time beforehand, so it had gone pretty well. This new group? Yeah, they were local, too, but he liked working with them, and since he was going to be playing a lot of dates in the East for Topper, he was hoping to keep them together. "My white boys really play the blues," he concluded brightly.

We were in Topper Carew's apartment in Northwest Washington. J.B. was all alone there on a bright autumn afternoon, just waiting for the day to end so that his could begin. He asked me if I would like some tea. "That's what I usually drink," he explained. When I said yes, he went at it efficiently like a man who had had some practice at it—no "flow-thru" teabags for him.

Bands, he continued, are always a problem, even back in Chicago. "You'd get a good group together and maybe get a job out of town not too far, and one or two would say no, they didn't want to play anyplace but just in Chicago. There always seemed to be something to hinder them from traveling. But I can't be too hard on them, though, because I've had some pretty good years, and it's because I've had some good bands. I mean I been fortunate enough to play a lot with good musicians like Big Walter Horton, the harmonica man—you know him?" I nodded. "Well, so I can't complain. But I guess most of those real good bands were in the old days."

"When were the good old days in Chicago?"

"For the blues? Well, you go back to 1945 to 1960, along about in there, and there was really a lot of young talent around. Everywhere you went there was some kind of club with a band or something or other. I don't know what happened then, but things got pretty tight. All these old musicians around town started retiring, dropping out—you know. I never had to. I was lucky. I stayed with it. But it was pretty bad for a while there. People would hear you start playing the blues and they'd walk out. Right there on the South Side, too, where the blues was home!

"But I stuck it out. I hoped it would come back, and it did. Right there around 1968 and 1969 people began hiring back blues bands again. Now even the young ones are starting to enjoy the music. I would say the people are getting re-educated to the blues. The younger people are getting into it. Right now I got a good public. The fans follow you. They say, 'Oh, when you coming back?' Yeah, it's building up pretty good."

I asked him to tell me how he happened to get started in the blues life. "Me? Oh, I was just a kid, but I'd sneak in those places like Sylvio's, and I remember one night I had a long talk with old Memphis Slim, and that got me decided that playing the blues was what I wanted to do. So I took up the drums, and I fooled around with that for a while until one night I heard Elmore James someplace around in Chicago. He was just getting started and he was real heavy, you know. He played it different from anybody. Old bottle-neck guitar had died out by then, nobody played it any more. And Elmore was the first I ever heard go at an electric guitar with a bar. Well, I never heard anything like that before. So I got me a guitar and a piece of pipe, and I went to work with the two of them. And oh, yeah, I suppose I ought to say, too, that T-Bone [Walker] was around then, and I started to listening to him, too. I learned from those I was listening to at the time.

"And then I tried putting my first little band together. And that's the problem, then, getting known. You got to work all those little clubs so long and work with different people and all. But most of what we played in the beginning wasn't even clubs, it was just most of them parties—basement jumps, they call them. And somehow or other when I was playing them I started calling my band J. B. Hutto and the Hawks, just because somebody told me the group needed some kind of odd name. I just came to me—J.B. and the Hawks—and so I stuck with it.

"I mean, it wasn't always so great after that. I've had my troubles, but they weren't music troubles, they were troubles with companies. Yes, those companies have given me some *hard* problems. On records, I stayed on one man's* contract for five years. I cut records, and they were supposed to sell here, but instead they sold them overseas. You know how much I made off that contract? Two hundred and fifty dollars in five years' time. I wouldn't have known what he did with the stuff I cut at all except I got three or four letters from overseas telling me how much they liked my record."

You could tell that it troubled him just to think about it. We were sipping tea now, and he sat staring down darkly into the tea leaves at the bottom of his cup. For a moment I caught a glimpse of that angry Mr. Hyde he becomes when he steps onstage.

At last he continued: "I've got Topper working on this now. We're trying to get a contract with the *right* record company now, one that will distribute my stuff. Get it out so the people who come to hear me can buy it when they want to."

I asked him if he had ever been tempted to get out of music altogether when things got tough back in Chicago. A few of them dropped out back then. Had he ever thought of quitting?

J.B. shook his head. "No," he said, "blues is my bag. Singing the blues—let me put it this way—you get the chance to tell the public what you're thinkin' and what you're doin'. See, you catch the heart of the public with the music. One of the verses you sing might catch somebody just right, tell him about his feelings or problems. Like my song, 'Now She's Gone,' well, every man has got a woman gone on him sometime—well, I'm *talkin'* to that man. And 'Alcohol'—I had to do that three or four times at Henry's the other night. A lot of people have that kind of problem. You get with a band that's good and you got a good voice, then you can handle it. Singing the blues is always just talking to somebody. That's how I see it."

*Not Chess or any of its affiliates.

CHAPTER NINE

TRANSATLANTIC BLUES

"THE AMERICAN DARKY is the performing fool of the world today. He's demanded everywhere. If I c'n only git some a these heah panhandling fellahs together, we'll show them some real nigger music. Then I'd be sitting pretty in this heah sweet dump without worrying ovah mah wants. That's the stuff for a live nigger like me to put ovah, and no cheap playing from café to café and a handing out mah hat for a lousy sou."

These are the thoughts of one Lincoln Agrippa Daily, nicknamed "Banjo" for the instrument he carries with him from one bar to the next on the Marseilles waterfront. He picks and sings for whatever francs come his way, telling himself that he is just between berths as a merchant seaman. In the meantime, he and his multinational black buddies—Bugsy, Malty, Ginger, and Dengel—laze about the beach, scrounge food where they can, live off the generosity of the girls in the quarter, and panhandle the American tourists when all else fails.

But Banjo has a talent and a dream. And he comes close to realizing that dream when a flute player named Goosey (an American black) and a Nigerian guitarist named Taloufa show up on the same boat ready to jam. That's what they do one glorious night when Banjo takes them around to his favorite hangout, and they play and sing for the dancers for hours until a casual shooting scatters the crowd. And although it goes well that night, the three never really get it together quite the same way again. The group is riven by controversy. The two newcomers deplore Banjo's easygoing ways and bemoan his lack of racial consciousness. At one point they fall into argument, and Goosey tells him: "Banjo is bondage, It's the instrument of slavery. Banjo is Dixie. The Dixie of the land of cotton and massa and missus and black mammy. We colored have got to get away from all that in these enlightened progressive days. Let us play piano and violin, harp and flute [Goosey's instrument]. Let the white folks play the banjo if they want to keep on remembering all the Black Joes singing and the hell they made them live in." It is talk like that which splits up Banjo's little band, and all eventually go their separate ways.

If you have not recognized it already, the book I have been talking about is a novel titled *Banjo,* by Claude McKay, a Negro novelist and poet of Harlem's Black Renaissance, which was published in 1929. It is a lively and engaging book that is interesting in a number of ways. First of all, it presents a remarkable picture of life on the Marseilles waterfront—no French novel that I know of offers anything as graphic. Secondly, it discusses questions of race more frankly and honestly and in greater depth than do most black novels, even today. Finally, it is (as far as I know) the first personal account of what it is like to be an American black in Europe—and in particular, an American black musician. Even when Claude McKay wrote about it, Banjo's experience was certainly not unique. It might well have been generalized from scores who were around the Continent by the end of the twenties. They were known chiefly for their music, their song and dance. The queen of the Paris music halls just then was a twittering yellow-skinned girl named Josephine Baker, whom the French (in their confusion) regarded as a jazz singer. During the mad, manic phase of European culture that followed World War I, black music was regarded with immense enthusiasm but little understanding. Banjo was right: the American darky *was* the performing fool of the world in that particular day and age.

It wasn't so in the beginning. As closely as I have been able to ascertain, the earliest firsthand experience Europe had of black music was provided by the Fisk Jubilee Singers, a choir of four men and five women who sang a repertoire of spirituals, during their tour in the late 1870s. They did well enough. Audiences turned out in good numbers all over the Continent; they may have come out of curiosity, but they were charmed by what they heard. However, the European musical establishment was not especially impressed. A German musicologist named Richard Wallaschek dismissed the spirituals as "mere imitations of European compositions which Negroes have picked up and served up again with slight variation." And the composers themselves, who were caught in the last harmonic throes of the Romantic movement, were not about to have their attention diverted from the serious matters at hand by this musical oddity from Nashville, Tennessee.

Gradually, however, black American music did come to have some effect on European composers, if only superficial and temporary. Ragtime was what caught their fancy first. Starting in the 1890s, the compositions of Scott Joplin, Tom Turpin, and Eubie Blake began to find their way across the ocean. The lovely, lively syncopated rhythms of the music fell on the ears of modernists such as Camille Saint-Saëns and Claude Debussy and convinced them that this was just the stuff with which to mock the stuffy old Romantics—hence those novel and essentially meaningless compositions such as the ricky-ticky little *Golliwog's Cakewalk.* None of which really proved anything.

The first real inkling of jazz that Europe got came from a couple of tours by bands led by a black man whose name was, appropriately enough, James Reese Europe. The first band he brought over, which was known as the Tennessee Students, played vaudeville theaters in London, Paris, and Berlin in 1905. It was essentially a show band that specialized in big orchestral arrangements of solo ragtime material and syncopated popular songs. Traditionally, the United States Army entertaining band he brought over in 1917 has been cited as the first real jazz group to be presented on the European continent. However, because the band never recorded and boasted no soloists of special note, its credentials as a jazz organization are slightly suspect. It did catch the interest of Europe, however—particularly France—and readied the way for the real jazzmen, who began to find their way over starting just after the war.

Will Marion Cook brought a big orchestra to London in 1919

that seems to have been about the same sort of show band as the one Jim Europe had had in France—except that Cook's New York Syncopated Orchestra, as it was known, featured the clarinet of jazzman Sidney Bechet, and there is no denying that Bechet is as authentic a jazzman as New Orleans produced. There were others—enough real, if minor, jazzmen who traveled over to give Europeans a general idea of what the music was all about. By this time, too, American records were starting to get wide distribution overseas and were getting through to the relatively few listeners and musicians in France, England, and elsewhere who were deeply interested in American music and regarded it as something more than a fad.

The man who really turned Europe on, however, was Louis Armstrong. He made it over first in 1932 without a band, where he had been preceded only by a couple of white groups—who had played there years before. He was booked into the London Palladium and brought over a pickup band from Paris, mixed French and expatriate-black. He rehearsed them, played a fabulously successful two-week engagement, and sent them back to Paris (the tough British musician's union forbade them to stay longer). Then, with an English band, he started a tour of England and Scotland which, with return engagements, lasted the better part of five months. This in the bottom year of the Depression. Louis was most gratified.

According to Armstrong himself, he picked up his famous nickname over in England on that trip. Heretofore he had been known as Gatemouth or Dippermouth (Dipper for short), because of his colossally large mouth. For some reason, Percy Mathison Brooks, editor of the English publication *Melody Maker,* got the nickname wrong and greeted Armstrong as he came down the gangplank with a rousing "Hello, Satchelmouth!" Louis loved it, shortened it to "Satchmo," and kept it in the act.

It was on his second trip to England the following year that there occurred another one of those incidents that has now become one of the chief features of the Armstrong legend. It was at a command performance, again at the Palladium, and with King George V up in the royal box, Satchmo thought it might be proper to dedicate his finale to him. And so, wiping his sweating face with that omnipresent handkerchief, he grinned and said, "This one's for you, Rex."

That trip to Europe, which began in 1933, lasted a full eighteen months. It included another tour of England, a radio broadcast from the Netherlands (a rare and grand thing for a jazz performer at that time), and a continental tour that took him through Scandinavia, France, Belgium, Switzerland, and Italy. But more important than where he went was how he was received. And audiences all over Europe were wildly enthusiastic for Armstrong, the trumpet player, the groaning, bluesy singer, and most of all, for Armstrong the performer. In those eighteen months he had done more to further the cause of American music in Europe than the small army of musicians who had preceded him there. By the time he left, Duke Ellington and his Orchestra, Coleman Hawkins, and Fats Waller had all come on their first visits. But Louis paved the way for them. He made all Europe jazz-conscious.

Traffic increased. Many others made it across. Louis himself came back a time or two before World War II began. The war put an end to things temporarily, of course. Only not really, for even during the war, in Germany and Italy, where American music had been banned, there existed an underground of jazz fans and record collectors who kept up their keen interest in the music and looked forward to the day when they could get back to the things that mattered. In his book *The Story of Jazz,* Marshall W. Stearns has some funny stories about a Lieutenant Schulz-Kohn, an avid jazz fan who kept a kind of Schweikian resistance to Hitler's jazz ban. During the occupation, he managed to get himself posted to Paris, where he searched out the French jazz critic Charles Delaunay. The two worked together on the 1943 edition of Delaunay's *Hot Discographie,* and it later turned out that the Frenchman was active in the Resistance. Later he was transferred, but he surfaced again rather surprisingly during surrender negotiations at St. Nazaire. At a lull, a German lieutenant suddenly piped up and asked in English if any of the Americans there collected Benny Goodman records. It was Schulz-Kohn.

After the war it *was* different. The late forties saw an explosion of interest in all things American among Europeans, and a passion for American music in particular. Things were helped along considerably by the postwar emigration of American jazzmen to Europe. The smoke had barely settled on the Continent when Sidney Bechet grabbed a boat back. The late

Don Byas, a superior tenor saxophonist who cut a groove somewhere between Lester Young and Coleman Hawkins, was another early émigré; he married there and started a new life for himself. Many others did—clarinetists Mezz Mezzrow and Albert Nicholas, saxists Ben Webster and Phil Woods, trumpeter Art Farmer, bassist Red Mitchell, and on and on. The names are too numerous to list here; most of them came to stay more or less permanently; even those who eventually returned, such as trumpeter-arranger Quincey Jones, did so after lengthy residence, renewed as musicians.

Few came earlier and none have stayed longer than drummer Kenny Clarke. He was well established in America as the originator of the bop drumming style and was working regularly in New York with such performers as Dizzy Gillespie, Charlie Parker, and Tadd Dameron. But suddenly he decided to leave all that and showed up one day in Paris. He just gigged around the city for a while, playing jazz at the clubs and working with French show bands and recording orchestras; there was always plenty of work for American jazz musicians there. But from a quartet that Clarke put together for a 1961 date in Cologne grew the mighty Kenny Clarke-Francie Boland Big Band, possibly the best band of its kind in the world and certainly the best in Europe. The seventeen-piece organization plays concert dates and festivals all over the Continent; its presence there has helped immeasurably to keep Europeans enthusiastic for jazz. Among the most enthusiastic, of course, have been the many native Europeans who have made careers for themselves as jazz musicians—Clarke's co-leader pianist-arranger Francie Boland, German trombonist Albert Manglesdorf, French pianists René Utreger and Martial Solal, and, of course, the Scandinavian contingent—but again the list is too long.

The Clarke-Boland Band is a true European band, for their musicians are settled in cities all over the Continent; they assemble to play concerts and then disperse to their local scenes and gigs. But Paris, as you may have guessed from what has been said thus far, is the center of most of this activity. This is partly because it is such a pleasant place that it attracted many just after the war who simply stayed on. It is partly, too, because local authorites there have—at least, until recently—been far more liberal than elsewhere in permitting foreign musicians to work. It must be admitted finally that the French have long made a display of enthusiasm for jazz, and, indeed, for all American music. But I, from two army years in Europe and a few visits to France, am inclined to view such enthusiasm rather skeptically. Europeans in general, and especially the French, seem terrifically excited about our music without ever really understanding what it is about. The composer and critic Ned Rorem, who knows the French so well, seems to agree with me in this: "Rightly or wrongly the French have always condescended to cultures beyond their frontiers. Before the New Wave of 1960 they admitted to no American influence, since what, after all, beyond our 'barbarism,' did we have to offer? Surely not so-called Serious Music. Except for Gershwin's, names like Copland or Harris or Sessions were merely names when I first arrived here, and are still merely names. The 'barbarism' of jazz, which they respected (or rather were dazzled by), they quickly mistranslated into Ravel or Josephine Baker."

I like that; there is a world of wicked understanding in it.

IF IN THE last few pages I seem to have talked a lot about jazz and not much about blues, it is not because I am trying to pretend they are precisely the same, but because until fairly recently the Europeans had no firsthand experience of the music from the men who made it, the bluesmen themselves. Oh, they would hear plenty from jazzmen like Louis Armstrong; he sang a lot of blues, no mistaking, but he was chiefly a performer, a great solo musician, and certainly not a bluesman of the old sort. Except through phonograph records, the pure blues style was virtually unknown in Europe until Big Bill Broonzy made his way over in the early fifties. He did a short tour on the Continent but enjoyed his greatest success in Great Britain, where he not only played to interested and receptive (though never especially large) audiences, but also was taken up by a group of intellectuals, including the then quite young Paul Oliver, all of whom were most encouraging. They made him feel so welcome there that he stuck around long enough to do an "as-told-to" autobiography, which he called *Big Bill Blues,* with one Yannick Bruynoghe.

Ultimately, Big Bill returned to Chicago—he died there in

1958—and told a friend of his, Peter Chatman, that they sure liked listening to those old blues over in Europe. And who is Peter Chatman? He is a piano-playing bluesman who was born in Shelby County, Tennessee, in 1915—that's Memphis. And when he first began playing and singing around the South, he took the city's name as his own and began calling himself Memphis Slim. It wasn't until he came North, to Chicago, in 1937 that Slim really hit his stride, though. After he had been there a while, he hooked up with Big Bill, who encouraged him to drop the style he had developed (which Slim admits today was highly derivative of Roosevelt Sykes') and develop his own. He did, and he has done well ever since—with Broonzy, and subsequently as one of the house rhythm section for blues recording sessions on Bluebird in Chicago.

Memphis Slim did a lot of writing, too. He estimates that he must have composed about 300 songs in his lifetime, and these include a couple that would classify as classics on just about any list: "Feel Like Screamin' and Cryin'" and "Every Day I Have the Blues." In addition, he is one of the ablest of the blues pianists, right up there with that paragon of the two-handed style, Little Brother Montgomery. And he sings in good, full voice and shows an ability to phrase that not many of the older singers can match.

In other words, he was far better equipped than most of the blues practitioners in his little circle in Chicago, and when Big Bill Broonzy came back from his successful sojourn in Europe telling all about it, Slim was one of the top bluesmen in town. And although Europe sounded pretty good to him, he had too much work to consider a trip then. Just a couple of years after that, however, something called rock-and-roll blew the bottom out of things there in Chicago, and before he knew it Peter Chatman was just another bluesman looking for a gig.

More resourceful than most, Memphis Slim managed to work his way into the folk-concert-and-coffeehouse circuit. He played the Newport Festival in 1959, was picked up by Joe Glaser, Louis Armstrong's manager, and was booked the following year for a European tour.

"Yes," says Slim, "that was 1960, but I wasn't over long then —just three months, and all that was in England and Belgium and Denmark. It wasn't until 1962 that I came back and hit Paris for the first time. I haven't really left since."

And how has it been for him in Paris? "Oh, it's been fantastic. I've got more peace of mind over here. There's less discrimination, so to speak. Although you get a certain amount of prejudice all over the world, here they let me do my thing. I've found here what practically every man is looking for—a lovely wife, a darling daughter."

It was his wife, Christine, with whom I had talked on the telephone and arranged the interview. "Are you sure it will be all right?" I asked, for I had not written and asked beforehand.

"Oh, yes," she assured me. "I make these appointments for him all the time." Her English is good, but, as one might expect, she has a heavy and rather charming French accent. She is attractive, dark-haired, precise. There is something almost shrewd in her manner. It later came as no surprise to learn that Slim has given her a great deal of credit for his success in Europe, pointing to the good advice she has given him in career matters and the managing of his money.

Signs of that success are evident everywhere. The Chatman's big, plush, and beautifully furnished apartment is located in a big elevator building on the Boulevard Suchet, near the Bois de Boulogne. It is one of Paris' most luxurious districts. His Rolls-Royce Silver Cloud is parked out on the street, and her Cadillac is in the garage.

Europe paid for all this. For quite some time he held forth with great success at Les Trois Mailletz, a left-bank club, traveling out of Paris from time to time to do concert dates all over Europe. But for the past few years now the more lucrative concerts have predominated. He ranges wide across the Continent, calls himself "the ambassador of the blues," and presents a unique show which he calls *The Story of the Blues.* It's just Memphis Slim and his piano up there on the stage in a kind of lecture-concert of nearly three hours' duration. He plays and sings the songs, traces the development of the music chronologically, and strings it all together with anecdotes, personal reminiscences, and his own knowing brand of black-belt humor. Whether they understand precisely or not, audiences in just about every European country have responded warmly to him.

When one meets him in person, it is easy to understand why. For one thing, he is a very impressive man physically. About six-feet-five or six-feet-six in height, he is very dark in complexion, with what may be a birthmark patch of white in his closely-cropped black hair. As I shake hands with him, it occurs to me that mine has probably never been gripped by one quite as large. His hands are nearly twelve inches in length, but because of his long, tapering, narrow fingers, they seem almost delicate. But physical presence aside, Memphis Slim exudes a kind of confident warmth that is quite infectious.

I guess it was because of the frank, direct quality that I perceived in him that I felt encouraged to ask him the sort of personal questions that are best left to the end of any interview. I remember inquiring if he thought his lengthy stay in Europe had changed him much.

"You mean as a man? Oh, yes, I've changed quite a bit. I've stopped drinking—just mineral water and some Coke, you know. No vices to speak of now. I'm a typical family man in the way I never expected to be. But you know how it is, it's about time. I've done everything else that a man *shouldn't* do, so I guess it's time that I was decent for a change."

And as an artist? Has he changed that way, too? "I think, yes, I am different as an artist. I've learned a lot over here. I'm more relaxed and confident. I really know about audiences now. But I've worked at it, the way I never really did back home the way I should. You know, I've seen just about all my old friends at one time or another since I settled over here—either they're passing through here or I catch them on these short trips I take back to the States. And they want to know, you know, how it's done over here. How did I get all this? And I'm not sure just what I can tell them. I guess I should say it's not so easy to make it over here as it looks. Partly it's a question of being in the right place at the right time. And partly, too, it's a matter of having the right sort of character to know how to get along. One thing I found out right away, for instance, is you can't come here and tell them we do it this way back home, and so that's the way you ought to do it here. They're proud, these people, and they don't like to be told."

"You do get back to the United States every once in a while then?"

"Oh, sure. I was back and did Newport in 1965, and then the next year I did the Monterey Festival." That was in 1966. He was booked down to play in the Ash Grove in Los Angeles, and he found it quite an experience. "Oh, they liked me pretty good, but I was shocked at them—acting so goofy and dressed so funny. The girls were wearing old evening gowns and going around barefoot. I guess you'd call them early hippies."

Slim says that what he would really like to do is play concerts like the ones he does at colleges and universities across Europe. "Give my wife a chance to see America and get some idea of it. She'd really like to do that. But I know we'd go back to Paris, because this is home to us."

Bad experiences in the past have convinced him, too, that he doesn't want to get deeply involved in business dealings back in America. "Oh, man, it was a rat race, I'll tell you. Those companies I recorded for, they made so much money off of us that we never saw. It was always like that. You'd call up and try to get some kind of explanation out of them, and unless you were riding on top with a hit record just then they wouldn't even talk to you. *That's* the rat race I'm talking about. I fought this shit a long time, and then I got out of it just the way I wanted to by coming over here. I don't know if I would even have survived if I'd stayed there.

"It's entirely different here. They treat you like you're somebody. I've been on television so many times and in so many countries I can hardly keep count. This fellow, Jean-Christophe Verte, he helped introduce me with his television show. I was on it a lot—1962 and 1963, that was Memphis Slim year on French TV. But then I've been on television in all those other countries, too—Rumania, Yugoslavia, Italy, Belgium, England, Germany, Holland, Poland, Austria, Switzerland—and concerts there and other places, too. So, you see, I really keep pretty busy over here. And oh, yeah, a little movie work, too. I had a small singing part in that American movie they shot over here, *The Sergeant.* And then I did the music for this one French film, *Femme Noire, Femme Nue,* and I'm going to do another one."

"What about European audiences?" I ask. "Are they different from American"

He nodded emphatically. "Yes, I think European audiences in general are more appreciative than in America. In America, see, they think they know all about it, and they almost let it get away from them. Over here they give you the same attention they would give any classical artists. They really *study* the blues when I talk to them about it. I tell them, you know, 'The blues is not so bad. The blues is part of life.' And they're really listening to you, see.

"I don't know, they're all good, I guess. But I like playing for French audiences because they may not know what you're saying about blues being a spiritualistic thing, but they go for it anyway. I get through to them. I feel it. I know I'm getting the same reaction from them here as in the Baptist Church, where they cry and shout. Well, they don't do that here, but they understand. They may not know English, but they like the music.

"Germany? You get a good audience there, too. Jazz is quite new in Germany, and they're still learning. *Very* attentive, you know? I remember I was onstage at a concert in Germany when the news came about President Kennedy being killed. The concert ended right then. The people started crying and walked out. The Germans would come up to me then on the street, guessing I was American, and they'd say to me that it was a shame and all because Kennedy was such a president for the black people. Oh, he was loved by the people in Europe and loved here in France, I'll tell you he was.

"Then just a little while ago, when there was all that rioting and stuff, people here in Europe they'd come up to me and say, 'What's the matter? Is America falling apart?' And I'd say, 'Hell, that's how America was built.' You know how it is. Just because we're over here doesn't mean we stop being Americans. Us musicians, we talk like hell about America, but we don't want a foreigner saying anything bad about it. If they do, then we jump all over them. But I guess that's just the natural way to be."

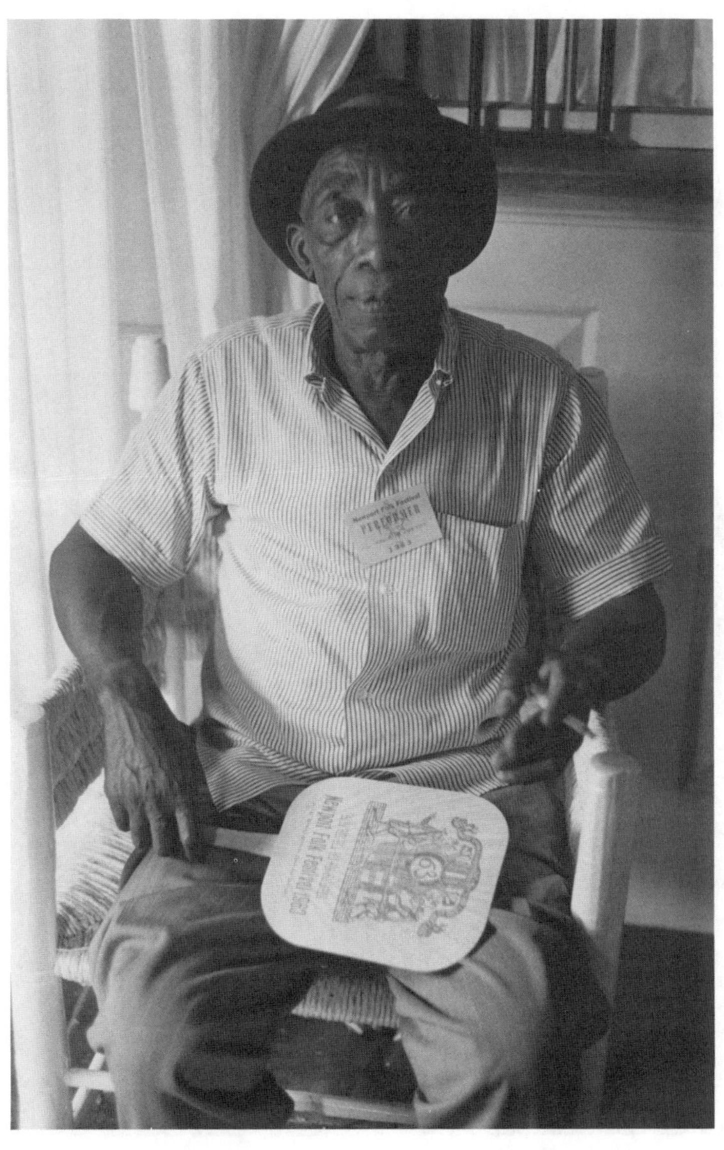

JOHN HURT *Ann Charters*

FURRY LEWIS *Ann Charters*

LIGHTNING HOPKINS *Samuel Charters*

SON HOUSE *Ann Charters*

MUDDY WATERS *Ann Charters*

B. B. KING *Frank Driggs Collection*

PART
THREE

CHAPTER TEN

"NASHVILLE STONEWALL BLUES"

HAVING GONE to such lengths earlier to try to prove mutual influence between white music and black as early as the nineteenth century, I am obliged to explain—or explain away—the determined survival of a brand of music that proponents insist is *pure* white. But "survival" is all wrong; it is far too weak a word. Right now there is no form of popular music in America that shows quite such vigor and activity as that of the Southern whites—call it hillbilly music, country and western, or anything you like, it is where a lot is happening right now.

Does this contradict my contention that the blues is the *fundamental* American music, that it has given shape and substance to all our music in the twentieth century? I don't think so. For although Merle Haggard is proud to be an Okie from Muskogee, and although all the country music cats in Nashville went for George Wallace in 1968, and although there really was a hillbilly hit a few years back by a character who called himself Johnny Rebel titled, "Nigger Hatin' Me"—nevertheless this music that has been extolled as racially pure was actually about octoroon at the outset and is now of such mingled parentage that it is a kind of miracle of musical miscegenation. The miracle is that, in spite of all evidence to the contrary given us by our ears, country and western continues to "pass" as white.

Like every other form of American music, country and western is an amalgam of styles. Musical influences from all over have come together to make the music what it is today. However, as the now widely accepted label—country and western—indicates, two strains predominate, and they survive even today, certain performers emphasizing one or the other or perhaps bringing them both together into a kind of neutral Nashville style.

Country music came first. It is probably what people mean when they talk about hillbilly music, for a lot of the first country performers came from the southern Appalachian belt and carried the old mountain balladeering and country-dance styles into the recording studios with them when, in the early twenties, the first samples of rural Southern white music were put on wax. Among many of them, too, there was a great preference for old songs—popular hits of the 1890s that perhaps had just worked their way up into the remote mountain recesses from which some of the best singers and pickers had come. This may have been why country music was never referred to as hillbilly music (a slang term with pejorative overtones) in the early record catalogues, but as "old-time music."

Just how "white" was it? Not very. The popular music of the 1890s and the first decade of the twentieth century was all ajump and aquiver with ragtime—America's first black music craze. And ragtime breaks and devices, as well as its distinctive tempo can be heard in country tunes like "Ain't Nobody's Business" and "Bully of the Town." There were also the so-called "coon songs," nearly all of which were written and sung by whites and were what was left of the old black-face minstrel tradition of the mid-nineteenth century. It may have been a poor imitation of black music, but nevertheless it *was* an imitation that was based on something real.

By the time the ballad tradition had merged into country music, it was a long way from the pure English style that the first rural settlers had brought with them. These were American ballads that were recorded by the early performers—"The Wreck of the Old 97" (Vernon Dalhart), "Buddy, Won't You Roll Down the Line" (Uncle Dave Macon), and "Wabash Cannon

Ball" (The Carter Family)—some of which were derived from Negro sources and all of which contained those subtle black rhythms, licks, and harmonies that even by the late nineteenth century had permeated nearly all American music.

And country dance? The instrument that made it what it was, that gave its distinctive ticky-ticky sound, was the banjo. They call it the only native American instrument—but how American was it, really? Musicologists trace it back in its fundamental form (strings stretched across a drumhead) to an African instrument called the *bania.* Even the white country guitar style, which expanded the player's range beyond old-fashioned strumming, was widely known as "nigger-picking," a clear nod to the black's superior technique on the instrument as source and inspiration.

But this talk of influences and sources is all pretty vague. It may give the erroneous impression that all this took place in two or three thick-walled chambers where from time to time wisps of melody managed to penetrate and were sometimes picked up. The reality was much different, of course. Music was in the air all the time. Even in medium-sized cities in the South like Atlanta, Charleston, and Richmond there would be buskers on every corner, white and black, singing out and trading songs with one another. Music was a matter of direct face-to-face encounter. You get an idea of this from what Bill Monroe told James Rooney in the latter's book, *Bossmen.* Monroe, of course, is the champion of bluegrass, which comes down to us as a direct and fairly pure survival of the old country style. The question was how he got started, and answering it, Monroe began talking about a black man back in Kentucky.

> The first time I think I ever seen Arnold Schultz . . . this square dance was at Rosine, Kentucky, and Arnold and two more colored fellows come up there and played for the dance. They had a guitar, banjo, and fiddle. Arnold played the guitar but he could play the fiddle—numbers like "Sally Goodin." People loved Arnold so well all through Kentucky there; if he was playing a guitar they'd go gang up around him till he would get tired and then maybe he'd go catch a train. . . . I used to listen to him talk and he would tell about contests that he had been in and how tough they was and how they'd play these two blues numbers and tie it up. And they had to do another number and I remember him

> saying that he played a waltz number and he won this contest. . . . There's things in my music, you know, that come from Arnold Schultz—runs that I use in a lot of my music. I don't say that I make them the same that he could make them 'cause he was powerful with it. In following a fiddle piece or a breakdown, he used a pick and he could just run from one chord to another the prettiest you've ever heard. There's no guitar picker today that could do that. I tried to keep in mind a little of it—what I could salvage to use in my music. Then he could play some blues and I wanted some blues in my music too, you see. Me and him played for a dance there one night and he played the fiddle and we started at sundown and the next morning at daylight we was still playing music—all night long—that was about the last time I ever saw him. I believe if there's ever an old gentleman that passed away and is resting in peace, it was Arnold Schultz—I really believe that.

Bear in mind that's Bill Monroe talking, foremost exponent of the style that is thought by some to be the purest "white" music played in America today.

The "western" component of the country and western label is, in some sense, a misnomer. By and large, it is that only by comparison to the "eastern" country music, which seemed to emanate originally and almost exclusively from the Southeast. All the early stars of country music were from well east of the Mississippi, but the music's first real superstar, Jimmie Rodgers, was born in Meridian, Mississippi, right in the heart of blues country, in 1897. Rodgers' mother died when he was only four years old, and his father, a gang foreman on the Mobile and Ohio Railroad, began taking the boy out on the line with him. It was a rough way to grow up, knowing no real home, sleeping in bunk cars and cheap hotels throughout the Delta country. But he saw a lot of the world that way. His father worked in and out of the cities of the mid-South, and as a boy, Jimmie Rodgers had a chance to hear every sort of music the region had to offer; and this included a liberal education in the blues. In fact, when they returned to Meridian, when he was still a boy, he began to earn money of his own by carrying water to the black work gangs there in the yards. The black men taught him songs and gave him his first lessons on guitar and banjo.

He kept right on playing and singing when he went to work for the New Orleans and Northeastern Railroad as a brakeman, carrying his guitar with him, as legend has it, learning songs up and down the line from blacks as well as whites. And at the same time he had a little combo with which he played dances, picnics, and rallies around Meridian. He loved music, but would probably have continued indefinitely as a railroad man, except that in 1925 he showed up with tuberculosis and the railroad doctors forced him to retire. Left with no livelihood, he decided to try the only other thing he knew: He joined a medicine show that was touring the area, and because of his singing style and repertoire, he did his act in blackface. While he was out on the road, however, his health deteriorated, and he decided he might be better off breathing mountain air. He moved to Asheville, North Carolina, organized a little hillbilly band, and began to make a local reputation for himself playing around town and on the local radio station.

That was what he was doing when he was discovered in 1927 by a scout for the Victor Talking Machine Company. He signed a contract and began recording immediately. On his first session he cut a ballad and an old-time popular song; when released the record did well enough to let the Victor people know they had a potential winner in Jimmie Rodgers. Before the year was out they had him up to the big studio in Camden, New Jersey, for another session—and he came well stocked, bringing a lot of original material with him to record. Among these songs was his first big hit. Here's how it went:

T for Texas, T for Tennessee (twice)
T for Thelma, that gal that made a wreck of me.

If you don't want me, mama, you sure don't have to
call (twice)
'Cause I can get more women than a passenger train
can haul.

I'm gonna buy me a pistol just as long as I'm tall
(twice)
I'm gonna shoot poor Thelma just to see her jump
and fall.

I'm goin' where the water tastes like cherry wine
(twice)
'Cause the Georgia water tastes like turpentine.

And so on. Pure blues—some trace it back to Blind Lemon Jefferson—with this difference: Between phrases, Rodgers would put his head back and wail out a yodel. This was the famous "Blue Yodel," which he was to repeat in a numbered series of blues all the way up to the thirteenth, which was known as "Jimmie Rodgers' Last Blue Yodel" and recorded just two days before his death from tuberculosis in 1933. Rodgers' yodel was something different. In intonation and phrasing it was far removed from the Swiss yodel, which was the presumed model. It was almost closer to the falsetto cry used by certain Delta bluesmen. But there was also a lot that was original in it, too, and it became Rodgers' signature as he became better and better known throughout the South.

He recorded many other blues without the yodel during the six and a half years that he had left in his career. Some of them were original and some simply cribbed from local bluesmen whom he had followed around as a boy and younger man. Although the yodel and his cowboy ways (he made his home in Texas) were what his fans remembered, his lasting contribution to country music was the blues. If ever a white man could sing them, it was Jimmie Rodgers. He introduced the raw black strain into Southern white music, and because he was its biggest star (only Hank Williams since has even come close) and an enormous, lasting influence, it has flourished there ever since. The western component in country and western, then, is essentially and most importantly the introduction of pure blues and blues elements into the music.

Inevitably, Jimmie Rodgers had imitators. Some of them, like Gene Autry, Hank Snow, and Ernest Tubb, became stars in their own right, chiefly by emphasizing the cowboy image even more strongly than had Rodgers. Although he is not quite so well remembered today as a country and western performer, Jimmie Davis was certainly the most interesting of them all. When he was at the top of his musical career, he was best known as a songwriter—his "Nobody's Darlin' but Mine" and "You Are My Sunshine" became national favorites. In fact, by the end of the thirties, Jimmie Davis was riding so high that he decided to run for governor of his home state of Louisiana. He was better qualified than you might suppose. With a B.A. from Louisiana College and an M.A. from Louisiana State University, he had taught history and social science at Dodd College before he had decided that he might, after all, be able to do better as an entertainer. Running against the tough Louisiana Long machine, he beat Huey's brother and the incumbent governor, Earl Long, in the Democratic primary of 1944 and became governor of the State of Louisiana until 1948. Beaten out by Earl then, he returned for another four years in 1960. What kind of governor was Jimmie Davis? Not bad, even by national standards. He was, of course, a Populist—since Huey Long every Deep South governor must be a Populist—but unlike some others, he was notably liberal toward his black constituents; he came as close as any for a long time to being a governor for *all* the people of Louisiana.

If he had not, he would have been an awful hypocrite, for Jimmie Davis, the country and western performer, owed southern blacks a great debt, greater perhaps than that of anyone since Jimmie Rodgers. Davis was from Shreveport, Leadbelly's stamping grounds, an old blues town that was blessedly free of Cajun, zydig, and jazz influences. The future governor grew up listening to the blues, and that was what he poured into his music time and time again, on record after record. The material he became known for first was distinctly black in tone, much of it in the blues form and nearly all of it downright bawdy: "She's a Hum Dum Dinger from Dingersville," "Triflin' Mama Blues," and "Sewing Machine Blues." Not only that, but he recorded with black musicians, a practice that was virtually unknown in the South during the thirties. And if he sought out such musical associations, it was because they were natural to him. Jimmie Davis had a keen appreciation of black music in general, and of the blues in particular.

Are there any other white singers who continue to extend the sound and spirit of the blues into country and western music? There are at least a few. First of all, there are the many who have worked their way in through rock-and-roll. Nashville called it "nigger music" when Elvis Presley first exploded out of Memphis in 1954, and wanted nothing to do with it. At that time they wouldn't even allow drums to be played on the stage of the Grand Ole Opry. But gradually the entrepreneurs of country and western were won over. There was no arguing with the fact that the kids liked the music, was there? And, well, it might not really *hurt* to have a couple of them around, like this Conway Twitty and this piano player from Louisiana—what was his name?—Jerry Lee Lewis, that was it. After all, they were all good country boys at heart, and maybe they might have a little something to offer.

Right on both counts. They were good country boys at heart —and Conway Twitty proved it by immersing himself completely in a sweet country style that has all but obliterated traces of the old rock-and-roller. And Jerry Lee? Still hangin' in like Gunga Din, he hasn't changed himself or his style to suit anybody, but he has certainly had an effect on the music. He opened up country and western, "modernized" it (though I'm not sure what that means in this context), and gave it a harder sound. He and the Elvis Presley influence (which has been terrific in the mid-South) helped pave the way for exciting young performers like Jerry Reed.

But there are also a couple of others who, like Jimmie Rodgers, seem to carry in them the old blues spirit. Do they sing the blues? Sure, every singer in country and western today has some blues or blues-derived material in his repertoire. But more important, these two have the old blues feeling—the bitter knowledge of disaster and personal misery that may be there waiting for us on this day or the next. They've been there and back; they know the score. And ask any bluesman what the blues is all about, and they'll begin, "Well, the blues is a feeling. . . ."

Merle Haggard has it. He's lived the life everyone seems to think that Johnny Cash has. He was born the son of an Oklahoma migrant in California at the end of a long trek not unlike that of the Joad family in *Grapes of Wrath.* Times were hard for them. His father died early, and Merle got in trouble—burglary and jailbreak kind of trouble—and wound up doing three years in San Quentin. That was the first time Merle Haggard ever heard Johnny Cash—at a concert when Cash drove in and drove out of the state prison on the same afternoon. It looked to Merle like a better way to make a living than the one he had tried, and so when he got out he gave it a whirl. It worked out well for him because even by then—and he was only in his mid-twenties—he had amassed enough bitter experience to make those tough songs he sang—"Lonesome Fugitive,"

"Mama Tried," "They're Tearing the Labor Camps Down," and "Hungry Eyes"—practically quiver with authenticity. It was inevitable, too, that Haggard would be drawn to Jimmie Rodgers, and he has become the old Singing Brakeman's greatest modern interpreter. The two-record album of Rodgers' songs that Haggard recorded a few years ago comes as close to being a top country and western classic as anything—well, as close as anything since Jimmie Rodgers himself died, choking on blood, just after his last recording session.

Waylon Jennings is not nearly as well known, nor has he led the sort of hard life that may be equated directly with the groaning miseries of which he sings. Oh, there were the usual troubles with the pills (as booze to bluesmen, as heroin to jazzmen, so amphetamines to country and westerners), but they were par for the course. Somehow all the disappointments, difficulties, and agonies he has ever had are right there in his voice, though, transmuted into something beyond sadness—a kind of infinite weariness that seems to say he is ready to endure anything life might have in store. Although he is not a prolific writer of songs, as is Merle Haggard, Jennings has shown excellent taste in choosing material; you don't find the usual minimum of 25 percent of sentimental trash on his albums that nearly all other country and western performers seem to carry on theirs. He has been far more venturesome in picking his songs, too. Not only has he recorded work by the top young writers in the field—Kris Kristofferson, Mickey Newbury, and Haggard, to name a few—he has gone beyond it and sought out songs by Bob Dylan, John Lennon and Paul McCartney, Jim Webb, Gordon Lightfoot, Mick Jagger and Keith Richard, and even Chuck Berry. You get the sense of the larger idiom in all this, an awareness of just how closely related are the genres and styles of music represented by these various writers.

WHAT ABOUT black performers in country and western? Over the years, there have been a few. Even in the early thirties, the Mississippi Sheiks, a hot black string band that was made up of members of the very musical Chatman family, were pushed on OKeh records in both the blues and country categories. One of the original performers on the Grand Ole Opry was a black harmonica virtuoso named DeFord Bailey, who cut the first records ever made in Nashville—eight masters for Victor in 1928. Although he stayed on for years, he became increasingly bitter at the second-class treatment and payment given him on the Opry, and so he quit, and he has remained out of music—white or black—ever since. He runs a shoeshine stand in the black district of Nashville.

Lately, others have fared better. Country and western impresario Shelby Singleton has been pushing a Negro vocalist named Linda Martell; she has recorded and been on the Opry a number of times. Stoney Edwards is a much bigger name. He has had one superhit in "Odd-Job Dollar Bill Man," about a hard-working guy who makes his money any way he can (or however the rhyme goes). At this writing Edwards has had three albums issued by Capitol, and his audience is still growing; he has a real future in country and western music. This is so chiefly because he has a fine voice, a good style, and a real country feel for a song. But clearly a bit of thought and conscious image-building has gone into his selection of material. He seems to present himself as an industrious and dependable individual ("Odd-Job Dollar Bill Man") who piously honors his parents and his God ("Daddy Did His Best"), yet he also takes pains to remind his white listeners that he shares a lot with them in attitudes and country heritage ("You Can't Call Yourself Country"). It's a good image, anything but Stepin Fetchit: self-respecting, upright . . . and square. What is lacking—by intention, surely—is any suggestion of sexuality; he is strictly a steady family man in his songs ("A Kingdom I Call Home"). And this is rather rare in the country field, where many male singers play the tomcat onstage and do some rather frank sexual boasting in their material. Edwards has very wisely declined this role. A black man's position in country and western music is precarious at best; it is best not to tempt the white country audience into the sort of neurotic fear of black sexuality that has riven the South for a couple of centuries.

In this, as in much else, Stoney Edwards is simply following the lead of Charley Pride—and a good thing, too, for there is no arguing with the phenomenal success achieved by country and western's one and only black superstar. Those outside the field don't know quite what to make of Pride. Some seem content to shrug him off as an anomaly, just the sort of oddity that pops up now and again in any field to let us know there are rules operative that we might otherwise have overlooked. Others dismiss him as a kind of imitation white man, an Uncle Tom at worst and an Oreo at best.

But all you have to do is watch him in live performance to know that his success is no accident. There is something curiously and singularly personal in his appeal to the white audiences who flock in huge numbers to see and hear him. And talk to him for a little while, and you will realize that he is not an imitation anything, but the absolutely genuine Charley Frank Pride from Sledge, Mississippi. That's right. The name that sounds like a publicity agent's brainstorm is the one he was born with thirty-odd years ago in that little Delta cotton-and-corn town just south of Memphis off Highway 61.

Mention that name today in any city in the South—even one on the border, like Baltimore—and you will get the kind of immediate attention that any self-respecting name-dropper feels is his due. That was the sort of treatment I got, anyway, at the downtown Holiday Inn there when I asked if Charley Pride had registered. The girl behind the desk said no, there were no rooms reserved in his name, but added confidentially that they were sort of expecting him because there was to be a reception later on that night following his show at the huge Civic Center across the street. I knew he would be arriving shortly, for I had made a date to talk with him.

And just as I turned away from the desk, I spotted him coming in the door in the company of his manager, Jack D. Johnson, and his second-line singer, Johnny Duncan (both white). They caused quite a stir. But in the few minutes it took for Charley Pride to work his way clear of the little crowd that congregated around him at the desk, I managed to introduce myself and get invited upstairs.

On the way he was spotted through the coffeeshop window by a waitress. He smiled and gave her a wave, but before we had reached the elevator she had overtaken him and asked for his autograph. In the elevator I asked him if he grows tired of shaking hands and signing autographs. "No," he said, "I love being recognized. I don't think I'll ever get tired of that. As a matter of fact, I wish I could have more contact with people than I do. I'll tell you, what I really miss is being able to come off the stand and sit down in back and just talk to people, the way I used to when I first started out. They treat me like a star now, and that makes it hard to talk to anybody."

In the room he tossed himself down on the bed, propped a pillow behind his head, and continued in the same vein, explaining that he is a Pisces. "Very talkative. That's my nature —just the way I happen to be. I don't believe in planning your life by your sign, but I think it helps in understanding yourself and other people. I didn't even know what my sign was until about six months ago, when I read a book on astrology somebody gave me."

Anybody whose life has changed as dramatically as has Charley Pride's might well be interested in astrology or any other system that would offer him some hint as to what fate has in store for him next.

Born the son of a farmhand, he grew up with seven brothers and three sisters in the rural South and had logged plenty of hours in the cotton fields before he had even finished his education at Sledge Junior High. Nights were spent close to the radio, listening to the little radio stations around them on which he heard music of all kinds. "But the music I, personally, chose to listen to was country music," he emphasizes.

"I don't know why it was exactly. People are always saying to me, 'Why don't you sing this way or that way?' You know, as a matter of my pigmentation. Like whether you were pink or purple or whatever really should determine in some kind of absolute way the kind of music you like. That's kind of silly, isn't it? I mean it's all American music, anyway. And besides, I've always been an individualist—and that's how I try to fit into society—as an individual, and not as a pink or purple. I eliminated those skin hangups a long time ago."

But as for music in his youth, he says, he just listened and liked. Who in particular? "Oh, the whole country spectrum from the 1940s when I was growing up—Ernest Tubb, Eddy Arnold, and Hank Williams, all of them. I just loved the hits and learned them all." He had also picked up a little guitar, but insists he is no musician, and he is only embarrassed when he is described, as he has been in an article or two, as "an excellent musician."

He had no special musical ambitions, but ambition he had aplenty. "It looked to me when I was growing up that the way out of the cotton field was baseball." With blacks permitted in the major leagues for the first time during those years, he determined he would play major league baseball himself one day. And he did eventually—during a few weeks in 1961 for the then Los Angeles Angels. This was the culmination of a career that began when he left Sledge at the age of seventeen to join the old Negro American League. He played first for Detroit and then for the Memphis Red Sox. Following a stretch in the army, when he married his wife, Rozene, he got the break that landed him on the Angels. Trying too hard to please, he soon developed a sore arm and one day was taken aside and given his walking papers. They told him he just didn't have a "major league arm."

Eventually, he wound up in Helena, Montana, where he worked in a smelting factory and played semipro baseball for the Amvets. "I remember where I was living in Helena, I was working the swingshift, and I would lay down on those off-hours trying to sleep, and I couldn't because there was this country group practicing next door. Well, I figured, if you can't beat 'em, join 'em, so I went over with my old Sears Silvertone guitar and began making some music with them. That started things. We played around Helena a little, and I began singing before the ball games. One day I sang and then had a pretty good day at the plate, and they wrote me up in the papers. And all of a sudden I was a local celebrity." One thing led to another then, and people started urging him to try for the big time, and so he headed for Nashville.

An audition before Chet Atkins, the top country guitarist who bosses RCA's Nashville operation, brought Charley Pride an immediate long-term recording contract. But the question was, how could he be sold to white country and western audiences? To be honest, he wasn't so much sold as put over on them. RCA released three singles by their new artist over the course of several months—yet there was not a word of publicity on him and not a single picture. All three records hit well up on the country and western charts, purely because of Pride's fine voice and his ability to sell a song. And so by the time they got around to letting people know what he looked like he was well established as a new star in the field.

Still, when he began making personal appearances there were some awkward moments. People were always asking him embarrassing things like, "How come you don't sound like you look?" And then there was the woman who came to hear him sing his first big single, "Just Between You and Me," and took one look at him when he came on stage and groaned loudly, "No, no, it can't be!" Then he started singing her favorite song, and she began shrieking ecstatically, "It's true! It's true!" Yes, every time he opened his mouth and started singing those hits of his—songs like "The Snakes Crawl at Night," "Does My Ring Hurt Your Finger?," and "Before I Met You"—he picked up more fans and became a little less an oddity and a lot more a star.

Right now, with sixteen albums and about as many hit singles to his credit, he's in the superstar class, right up there with Johnny Cash and Glen Campbell. Interestingly enough, however, Charley Pride is purer country, both in style and appeal, than either of those two giants in the field. He sings a sweet song—much of his material is unblushingly sentimental—in a rich baritone that throbs with feeling.

He's aware of where he is in the country and western field today and what it took to get him there—and he seems to have no regrets, for fundamentally Charley Pride is a very competitive individual. "Yeah, see, we live in a world of comparison and competitiveness. And since I started out from behind right from the git-go—I don't have any harsh feelings about this, I'm just trying to be realistic—what this means is that when an opportunity comes my way I have to work three or four or five times as hard as the next guy in order to take advantage of it. This is what I've done all my life—been in competition with people, trying to learn the knack of things.

"Why, I remember once I told my Dad I could beat him picking cotton, and I did, going down the rows—but when we weighed up, he had more poundage. So he went back and showed me all I'd missed, showed me the *right* way to do it. Eventually I did it right and beat him, though."

He smiled then, summing up: "Come right down to it, I guess that's my story. I'm just an old cotton picker doing the best he can."

And that best is impressively good. It more than satisfied his sell-out audience that night at Baltimore's Civic Center. Admittedly he had some help. George Jones and Tammy Wynette, who usually headline their own show, performed like the pros they are before intermission, yet failed to cause much excitement. The audience was obviously impatient for the headliner, Charley Pride.

When, after a couple of warm-up acts, he at last appeared, the crowd (virtually all-white) went absolutely wild. The electricity generated among them fairly crackled in the air as he sang many of his old favorites and new hits—among them Kris Kristofferson's "Me and Bobby Magee" and his great recent hit, "Kiss an Angel Good Morning." But make no mistake. Charley Pride wasn't fooling anybody in the Civic Center that night—and he wasn't trying to. They knew he was a black man, and just to make sure they did, he sang Leadbelly's "Cotton Fields" and the song he says is his personal favorite, "I'm Just Me" ("It answers a lot of questions for me," he says), with its refrain:

I'm just born to be exactly what you see
Hey and every day, I'm just me.

And just being Charley Pride seemed to be quite enough for everybody there that night.

CHAPTER ELEVEN

How to begin? With that old and oft-quoted formula, "Blues plus country equals rock"? But we have already seen that country and western music is so thoroughly saturated with blues feeling that this is a little like saying that blues plus blues equals rock. Which may not, after all, be far wide of the mark but seems a little like double-talk.

And if I am to indulge in that sort of phrasemongering, what about this one, short and to the point, lifted from Michael Lydon: "Rock 'n' roll was . . . blues with a beat"? Better, for it helps remind us that back before they had even thought to call it rock-and-roll, they were calling the same music rhythm-and-blues. It was the operative phrase for *any* sort of black music that, because of some trick of tempo or style, was not instantly classifiable as blues. It was only when white kids started playing the music in the early fifties that they began calling it something else.

In a way, it all happened the way it did because there grew up after the war a solid young white audience for black music across the country. We could probably go through a record-by-record analysis as some have done (the most exhaustive and impressive of them is Charlie Gillett's *The Sound of the City*) that would show conclusively that there was a kind of a growing rebel minority out there. They were tuning into these black stations at the wrong end of the radio dial and really flipping for Ivory Joe Hunter, Hank Ballard, Lavern Baker, and maybe Muddy Waters, too. And all the while snickering contemptuously at their older brothers and sisters who sat in the next room mooning away at those sweet romantic sounds on "Your Hit Parade." This is not some retrospective fantasy of the way it *might* have been; that was the way it *did* happen with thousands of young people of high school age from Tallahassee, Florida, to Oakland, California. Why this preference for black music? It seemed funkier, earthier to them; it spoke to them of violent emotions and more direct attitudes to life and seemed free of the evasions of the romantic popular music of the period. The difference then was the vast distance that separated the raunchy hedonism of Hank Ballard's "Work with Me, Annie" from the puerile euphemism of Doris Day's "My Foolish Heart."

In its own way, of course, this sort of preference for the black "hit parade," which so often had less to do with the quality of the music than with its "outlaw" appeal, may have been simply another brand of romanticism. There was a separate, though oddly similar, development in relation to jazz and the growth of the hipster cult of "cool" and emotional detachment; it, too, had more to do with milieu than music. The two are so closely parallel in time and attitude that there is almost a high culture-low culture aspect to the phenomenon, as though the white rhythm-and-blues audience (which was the one that welcomed rock-and-roll, after all) were populist hipsters.

But when we look at those musicians and singers who were directly responsible for the rock-and-roll phenomenon, we find them much more certain of where their music came from and what it was all about. Elvis Presley, to start at the top, was from Tupelo, Mississippi, and had been turned on to the blues long before he started to record. He told one English interviewer that he "dug the real low-down Mississippi singers, mostly Big Bill Broonzy and Big Boy Crudup, although they would scold me at home for listening to them." And when he was working as a truck driver in Memphis and wanted to record, he gravitated almost naturally to Sam Phillips' Sun Records, a white-run independent label that had been active up until then recording black bluesmen from the Memphis and Delta areas. Phillips tried Presley on a country and western tune, and neither of them was happy with the results. It wasn't until Elvis started clowning around in the studio doing Arthur Crudup's "That's All Right, " the kind of music he had grown up on in Mississippi, that Phillips really got interested. He had Presley record it just as he had done it during the coffee break—and they had their first big hit. That, in fact, set the pattern, for Elvis Presley first became known in the business as a white singer of black material. His big hits for Sun and most of the best things he did for Victor were black and blues-based. "Milkcow Blues Boogie," his third release on Sun, was an old Sleepy John Estes tune. "Mystery Train," which followed it, came from blues singer Little Junior Parker. "My Baby Left Me," for Victor, was another Arthur Crudup tune from one of the Mississippi bluesman's Bluebird sessions from early in the forties. He did a couple of Little Richard tunes, too, "Tutti-Frutti" and "Lawdy, Miss Clawdy," and one by Ray Charles, "I Got a Woman." But what about the energetic "Hound Dog"? Although a couple of whites wrote that one, the redoubtable Jerry Lieber and Alvin Stoller, they had handed it over first to Willie Mae "Big Mama" Thornton. Forget about the movie star and the crooning balladeer, it was the Elvis who sang black that his real fans would remember best.

Carl Perkins? He told Michael Lydon that when he was growing up in Tiptonville, Tennessee, he used to listen to the radio a lot. "White music, I liked Bill Monroe, his fast stuff; for colored, I liked John Lee Hooker, Muddy Waters, their electric stuff. Even back then I liked to do Hooker songs Bill Monroe style, blues with a country beat." Jerry Lee Lewis, they say, was influenced by Little Richard during his early Memphis period. And Buddy Holly's favorite guitarist was Lonnie Johnson.

When rock-and-roll came along it subsumed rhythm-and-blues completely. Suddenly performers such as Bo Diddley, Chuck Berry, and Little Richard Penniman found themselves playing to white audiences, and to mixed audiences, and sharing the bill with white performers. They were instant rock-and-roll stars, and in a year's time—say, by the beginning of 1957—

nobody even remembered what rhythm-and-blues was any more.

What about their roots in the blues? They were deep and strong. Ellas McDaniel, who was known universally and apparently only by his nickname, "Bo Diddley," came up to Chicago to make it big and did just that. After playing the blues clubs for a while in the early fifties he hooked up with Muddy Waters and played guitar in his group for a while. When he made his move, it was with Muddy's blessing; he signed a contract with Chess and began recording on the company's affiliate, Checker.

With Chuck Berry the story was similar. He was from East St. Louis, Illinois, where he had a heavy local reputation. One weekend he decided to see how far it would get him in Chicago. He made the rounds of the blues clubs until he found Muddy. When he marched in with his guitar, he was invited to sit in. Muddy liked what he heard and told him to "go see Leonard" (Chess) on Monday. When he showed up at the Chess office, he had with him a tape of a tune he had written—a little number called "Maybellene." Leonard listened. Leonard liked. Leonard signed him up on the spot. And recording in Chicago, as he did, Chuck Berry would often end a day's studio work by jamming in the blues clubs. He loved that scene and was fond of referring to himself—stretching just a little—as a bluesman.

What becomes plain here, as we sift through the beginnings of rock, may not need saying at all—and that is that rock is a direct, straight-line development from the blues. Just listen to any record by Muddy, B.B., or Wolf, and then vote for the rock record of your choice. You'll find they're all running on the same ticket. It is not just that any authentic piece of rock music is almost certain to be based on blues chords (today that is probably true of *most* American music), but also that the instrumentation of the band that plays on that record will be a development of the old Chicago blues band lineup. And that guitar solo in the middle?—the one that really makes it for you? —chances are it's pure blues, strictly Buddy Guy out of Elmore James. The whole idea of rock guitar came out of Chicago, where the blues went electric. Jazz guitar, which, by the time the rock style was being shaped had been developed to almost surgical sharpness, simply had no influence whatever in the development of the rock guitar style. Plenty of accomplished rock guitarists were aware of jazz guitar, but that just wasn't where it was at as far as they were concerned.

Prove the point with any album by Jimi Hendrix, as accomplished a soloist, as certain a virtuoso, as any rock has produced. The Seattle-born guitarist died in 1970 at the age of twenty-eight. What made his death seem especially sad at the time was his great potential—he had only just begun. Nobody seemed better prepared—musically, at least—for a long career than did Hendrix. He had put in a solid apprenticeship and learned his craft well, touring with Little Richard, among others. According to legend, he had turned a feedback problem with a faulty amplifier into one of the most sophisticated techniques used by modern electric guitarists. And that, in a way, was typical of his remarkable ability to make the best of whatever he had at hand. What Jimi Hendrix had at hand when he started was the blues. He began with that. Whatever background in music he had was solid blues. He cited Albert King as the guitarist to whom he had listened longest and from whom he had learned the most. If Hendrix had had the same sort of solid background in jazz to build on, he might have been a much different sort of player, but he would not likely have been a better one. For it was his special genius as a soloist to push blues guitar to its limits, to show just how much could be done melodically and harmonically and still remain within the fairly narrow confines of the old blues structure.

The only other rock instrumentalist around today who even comes close is English guitarist Eric Clapton, fluent, inventive, flashy, and with a strain of that nonstop sitar in his style. What are his blues credentials? Clapton told *Rolling Stone* editor Jann Wenner that Little Walter Jacobs had been one of his big influences, that he had made a conscious effort to translate what Little Walter was doing on harmonica to the guitar. And others?

> At first I played exactly like Chuck Berry for six or seven months. You couldn't have told the difference when I was with the Yardbirds. Then I got into older bluesmen. Because he was so readily available I dug Big Bill Broonzy; then I heard a lot of cats I had never heard of before: Robert Johnson and Skip James and Blind Boy Fuller. I just finally got completely overwhelmed and listened to it and went

> right down in it and came back up in it. I was about seventeen or eighteen. When I came back up in it, turned on to B. B. King and it's been that way ever since. I still don't think there is a better blues guitarist in the world than B. B. King.

It wasn't long, incidentally, until such generous praise in interviews by rock disciples such as Eric Clapton began to pay off for B. B. King, Albert King, and a couple of other bluesmen. They were suddenly hot on the rock circuit. Their bookings jumped, and their record sales increased.

So it goes. There is no real point, however, in overemphasizing these tributes in print by some young rock superstar or other to certain fairly obscure black bluesmen. For let's face it, it's hip for some young fugitive from the middle-class to say, "All that I am or hope to be I owe to Howlin' Wolf." It lends a certain legitimacy to his efforts and suggests an authenticity that—who knows?—his music may lack. We could multiply such quotations endlessly, but unless there is a real blues quality to the music made by these young performers (as I honestly think there is with Eric Clapton and certainly was with Jimi Hendrix), what they say proves nothing. Honoring that, there are still a few left to talk about.

It should come as no surprise that the first of them is Janis Joplin. Yes, the late rock shouter carved a niche for herself as a sort of latter-day Bessie Smith. She never claimed the title; it was awarded her by such critics as Nat Hentoff and Ralph Gleason, who heard in her a continuation and extension of the old classic blues tradition. And sure, why not? There was a quality of utter abandon to her delivery that no white woman before or since has ever matched. It's true, too, that Bessie Smith was the model she chose. She told David Dalton, "When I first started singing I was copping Bessie Smith records. I used to sing exactly like Bessie Smith, and when I started singing with Big Brother that was the only thing I knew how to do. . . ." Well it would be wrong to pretend that she ended her short career singing "exactly like Bessie Smith." No, she was her own woman, had gone her own way, and chosen her own style by then. It was as pure, authentic, and funky as anybody's, without regard to color. Any record by Janis should be an argument-clinching affirmative to that old pain-in-the-ass question: Can white folks sing the blues? The answer is, "Sure they can, if they got 'em." And Janis Joplin sure had them. She died of them.

I am not, however, so superstar-struck as to pretend that she was absolutely unique in this. She was the best of the blues-influenced young white singers, but there are others—Ida Coxes and Alberta Hunters—to her Bessie. Tracy Nelson of Mother Earth has it all: phrasing, intonation, and feeling, and it all seems as natural—or *authentic,* if you prefer the solid-gold adjective—as can be. Bonnie Raitt is perhaps a bit more studied in her delivery, more consciously a *singer* of songs in a particular style than either of the other two, but she is such a fine singer with such good taste that she never seems to disappoint. Her choice of material is impeccable, and she is a remarkably good guitarist.

Others? Bonnie Bramlett, of Delaney and Bonnie, and Rita Coolidge—down-home girls both. And that brings up a whole category in rock that cannot be neglected even in a survey as cursory as this one, for it is steeped in the old blues tradition and saturated with the feeling. Call it down-home style, for its practitioners are young Southern whites who have listened to black music and country and western all their lives and may have sung "sanctified" in church, as well. You can hear it all there in the music of Delaney and Bonnie, Johnny Winter, and Tony Joe White—three quite different performers, admittedly, but as honest and country as they come.

And then there's Canned Heat. It is a group perhaps most important for what it was and wanted to be than for what it became. It was a white *blues* group—very committed in that—and while the band was whole it did some fine things: "Bullfrog Blues" from their first album, and "Pony Blues," "One Kind Favor," and "Refried Boogie," all from their best album, *Livin' the Blues.* The album they did with John Lee Hooker, however, *Hooker 'n' Heat,* was pure gold. It is more his album than theirs. He sings on every cut and re-establishes himself as a real force in the blues. He was a Detroit bluesman—big frog in a little pond—born in Clarksdale, Mississippi. It seems that about all that I have said about Johnny Lee, as he called himself, up to this point is that he wasn't much of a guitar player. Well, he isn't. But he surely can sing. There is that marvelous, hushed urgency in his voice that is pure Delta, and if he hasn't much guitar technique, he certainly knows how to use the little he possesses to good advantage. Canned Heat deserves a great deal of credit for presenting him as it has on this two-record album. The mood is relaxed, and they give him space enough to stretch out; and what he does on the set more than justifies the time and trouble. The credit should probably go to Alan Wilson, who played guitar and harp with the group and was acknowledged as its "musical director." He and Henry Vestine, the lead guitarist, were both out of the Boston folk blues scene, both had pursued bluesmen in the Deep South (Vestine was along when Skip James was tracked down in Tunica, Mississippi), and the two had been playing blues from high school on. Wilson died of one of those barbiturates-and-booze accidents the same month in 1970 that Janis Joplin and Jimi Hendrix died. *Hooker 'n' Heat* was the last Canned Heat album on which he appeared. And although the group has striven mightily since, they still miss him. Maybe when Henry Vestine and Big Bear Hite and the rest get it together again they'll be able to pick up where Wilson left them.

But when you talk about blues and rock you find that Muddy Waters' name is the one that comes up most. That's right, old Muddy, the alias under which McKinley Morganfield has played ever since he left Clarksdale in 1943 and came North to try his luck in Chicago. Never mind, for the moment, what he did for Chicago blues (which was to take the style that was then still in metamorphosis and shape it into the glorious, whooping electric thing it is now). What has he done for rock?

Plenty. No single bluesman has had more direct nor more personal influence on the development of rock music in America and in England than has Muddy Waters. He dates his "discovery" by the young white audience in America from the moment the Rolling Stones appeared on the scene. They had, after all, taken the name for the group from one of Muddy's tunes, and when their first LP appeared, it had one of his songs, "Just Make Love to Me." And when the Beatles came to America for the first time they told everyone they wanted to see Muddy Waters and Bo Diddley.

"Muddy Waters?" said one reporter. "Where's that?"

Paul McCartney laughed at him and said, "Don't you know who your own famous people are here?"

Muddy, as we shall see, is terribly sensitive about this. He cannot understand how and why it should be that he has become a rock-and-roll star because of the endorsement of young *English* performers.

But even if Mick Jagger, Paul McCartney, Keith Richards, and George Harrison had never heard of him, Muddy would still be a star to the young rock audience today, thanks to the earnest efforts of Paul Butterfield and Mike Bloomfield in his behalf. The leader of the Paul Butterfield Blues Band and his erstwhile sideman have made no secret of their personal debt to Muddy Waters. In the early sixties the two were down on the South Side of Chicago nearly every night digging the blues—and Muddy most of all. Butterfield, who had been a student at the University of Chicago and lived nearby, began making the blues scene with Nick Gravenites (now a songwriter and man-about-music in San Francisco) as early as 1957. Mike Bloomfield, years younger and a nervy young guitarist in suburban rock-and-roll groups, began on his own sometime later. Mike Bloomfield learned a lot of guitar out there at the wrong end of town and got what no amount of practice or instruction could have given: a real feeling for the blues. It is there in everything he plays today. Paul Butterfield? Tough and durable, one of the few fixed stars in the blinking firmament of rock; he knows what he does best, and that is what he does most—play the blues. He learned his harmonica style from Muddy's harp man Little Walter and from Rice Miller, and his love for the blues first from Muddy.

Thus Muddy Waters has become the black stepfather to them all, the putative parent of a whole generation of young blues-loving white rockers. This was made more or less official a few years ago when he got together with his half-brother, Otis Spann (who had played piano brilliantly in Muddy's blues band but died later that same year), and with Paul Butterfield, Mike Bloomfield, and a rock rhythm section; and this generation-spanning all-star group recorded an album that is easily the most successful of any such experimental session ever done. This time it really jelled. Listen to the two records in the album—all of it quite rightly Muddy's material—and you'll agree that for once the title fits: *Fathers and Sons.*

That was in April, 1969, the high point of a bad year for Muddy Waters. He had gotten out of Chicago and was doing a lot of touring with his band. It was a tough schedule of one-nighters they played, mostly at colleges and universities, with monster jumps in between, and it left little time for them at home. One night in October they were in central Illinois heading north for Chicago when they were involved in a high-speed highway collision. Muddy's driver was killed, and he himself was so badly injured that the rumor was out for a while that he would never make it back. But somehow he did. More than a year later he began playing on crutches, sitting down at the microphone when it got to be too much for him. He kept right on playing and singing those blues until he was soon able to shed the crutches and shout and pick just about as he always had.

He is a big man, a durable man, and when one meets him and talks with him, it seems that his success over the years in this grueling business may be due in no small measure to his considerable physical strength. Those old Delta cotton-field muscles have put him back on his feet again. Not long ago they took him into New York, where he played an engagement at the Village Vanguard and set a new house record. The audience was so young that it seems that a new generation may have come along to claim him as grandfather. Whatever the relationship, however, it was one that clearly pleased Muddy. He sang as well as ever, with the same deep, authoritative tone and the constant laconic half-smile that has fascinated his listeners for years.

It was in New York that I saw him—at the Albert Hotel in the Village, that favorite downtown warren of rock musicians and their followers. His room was no better and no worse than any of the rest in the Albert, yet he seemed to pay no special attention to the dismal surroundings; he carries his dignity with him and needs no fancy furnishings to tell him who he is. He holds nothing back, but he volunteers little. He sits attentively and never hesitates on an answer, but at the same time seems oddly removed from what he is saying.

I remember asking him first about the playing he had done down in Mississippi before he came to Chicago. I had heard him on an album of material originally recorded in the field for the Library of Congress by Alan Lomax. He said that was the first recording he had ever done and was just a matter of being in the right place at the right time. What year was that? The flicker of a frown comes to his face. In 1942, he says after a moment's reflection.

McKinley Morganfield was born in Rolling Fork, Mississippi, in 1915, and he told Paul Oliver that he got his unusual nickname when he was just a baby from playing in a creek that ran just behind the two-room shack where he lived. Muddy's mother died when he was quite young, and he was taken in by his grandmother in Clarksdale. "That was where she raised me," he says, "and that was where I started in to singing the blues."

"How old were you then?"

"Oh, I been singing the blues since I was fourteen. You might say I started *playing* the blues when I was thirteen, though. But I was playing harp when I started, so I didn't sing. Had my mouth full of harp all the time. I started to fool with guitar at the age of seventeen. Scott Bowhandle, who I used to play with, was teaching me. Oh, you know, there wasn't much teaching to it. We would play those parties on a Saturday night, fish fries, where there was dancing and drinking. And Scott might show me a little something on guitar when we was playing. Those were great times. I didn't have no money in my pocket, but I had a ball.

"Influences? Yeah, I was influenced by Son House. I guess he made one or two records back then, but I knew him as a kid. He was all through the Delta back then, and I used to love to hear him play guitar. He had that bottle-neck thing, and he could make the guitar real whiny."

I ask Muddy if playing the blues was how he made his living then.

"You mean down there in the Delta? Around Clarksdale?" I nodded, and he shook his head deprecatingly and said, "Not down there. I worked hard growing cotton and corn. That's some of the hardest work you can get. That'll make a good man out of you. *Had* to work hard. See, I got married down there when I was just seventeen or eighteen. I figured I was wasting my blues talent driving a tractor. So I took my wife and went up North. She came up with me to Chicago. We didn't have no kids then. Do now, though. Got grandkids now."

That was after he had cut those records for Alan Lomax down

on Stovall Plantation. The idea of recording, as he had then, seems to have given him some sense of the greater world that lay beyond the Delta. He knew he had talent. He could play good bottle-neck guitar, and everybody liked the way he sang, and so he decided to take the gamble. He and his wife moved from Clarksdale to Chicago in 1943. It was during the war, and he had no trouble finding a job for himself—in a paper factory—but he remembered why he had come North, and he began playing those house parties right away.

"I don't know," says Muddy with that mysterious smile of his, "I made Chicago like a blues city when I started playing around there. I changed the style. I think it was 1945 when I got my first electric guitar. I was playing in the clubs then. And you can't hear an acoustic in a liquor club. There's just too much noise."

In 1946, he recorded commercially for the first time. He was recommended by Sunnyland Slim to the Chess brothers, and they recorded him on their Aristocrat label. "Rolling Stone" (sound familiar?) was on that first session. Did it move? "It went straight to the market," Muddy says with dramatic emphasis. "Why, by Friday there were 5,000 records out, and on Sunday you couldn't go anyplace without hearing it all over the South Side. And it just kept right on from there."

Success in the Chicago blues world meant working regularly enough so that you didn't have to have a day job. It meant having hit records (probably selling under 100,000) so the people came to see you. Muddy Waters was a success by these standards. And yet he seldom traveled out of Chicago, because he didn't have to. Chicago was where the blues scene was. That was where the people came to see him.

I asked about Paul Butterfield and Mike Bloomfield. Did he remember them coming by to see him?"

"Sure," he says, "sure I do remember them. Why, Paul blowed on my stand many times. He plays good. Both those boys are good white musicians. Did you hear that record I made with them?" I said I had. "Was good, wasn't it? I tell you, they can *play,* those boys can. But of course they can't *sing* the blues the way we can. We are the best blues singers in the world. We—I mean the black man. Most all the white kids play good, but they can't sing the blues like we can."

I ask Muddy why that was.

"Well, that's because we *had* the blues down there. I worked as low as fifty cents a day, seventy-five cents a day, a dollar a day, from sunup right on through. And that will *give* you the blues. If that don't give you the blues, *nothin'* will."

What about the English groups? Were they playing the blues?

"Sure, same thing. They playin' them, but we singin' 'em. I will tell you one thing about those Rolling Stones and Beatles over there. They woke up our white kids over here. They got them listening to the blues. They love the blues in England. Loves to listen to it. I been there four times, and the first was in 1958."

"Muddy," I say to him then, "everybody says you're tops in blues, just the king of them all. Why? What do you suppose you've got the others don't?" I deliver the question with a wink and a grin. I suppose I had some idea of jiving him.

But you don't jive Muddy—not about that, anyway. He shakes his head solemnly and says, "I musta been born with it, I guess. Everybody says I'm tops in blues, so it must be so. Sometimes it scares me. I really don't know why it is—just a way I have with the words in a song and having a good strong voice. Oh, when I was younger I really had a voice. I could go up and down and do anything with it.

"But I don't think I'm slowing down none. Not even that auto wreck did that to me. No, I don't have no intention of giving up. I just want to stay healthy. I just want to blow until I get to be a real old man."

"Why is that?"

"Why?" The smile. "I love what I'm doing, that's why."

CHAPTER TWELVE

"JAZZ ME, BLUES"—AND VICE VERSA

THERE WAS a period in the twenties when the blues and jazz were just about synonymous. Jazz bands, white and black, recorded blues that weren't blues. Harlem honeys who had never been south of Newark suddenly found fame as blues singers when all they knew about it was that they sang the words and notes just as they appeared on the page.

This was the time that they would later label the "classic blues" period, although nobody thought of it quite that way at the time. All they knew was that everybody was suddenly crazy about the music. If you put "blues" or "blue" in the title of almost anything you could be reasonably certain of selling it to the public. The backgrounds for such early recordings were of varying quality. They were usually provided by a full jazz band, though sometimes—as on many of the early Bessie Smith records—the singer made do with just piano accompaniment. Guitar recorded badly under the early primitive conditions and was not often heard until so-called "electric recording" came in toward the end of the twenties. In any case, it was all jazz as far as the public was concerned—for after all, this was the Jazz Age, wasn't it? And if somebody black opened his mouth and sang, then it had to be the blues that came out. Or so they supposed.

With a few exceptions—most of them jazz instrumentalists who also sang—the voices heard during this classic blues period were female. They were selling sex.

If you don't like my ocean, don't fish in my sea
(twice)
Stay out of my valley and let my mountain be.

I ain't had no loving since God knows when (twice)
That's the reason I'm through with these no good trifling men.

And the public—black and white—was buying. For the first time the myth of Negro sexuality was openly and hotly celebrated—hence the women sang; it was more provocative and less threatening to the white segment of the audience that way.

The first who were recorded could hardly be considered blues singers at all, although occasionally they did sing material in the old blues form against warm jazz backgrounds. Mamie Smith and Lucille Hegamin came out of vaudeville and returned to it, more or less, when the craze died down. Edith Wilson came out of show business, did some revues—*Hot Chocolates, Blackbirds,* and *Rhapsody in Black,* that sort of thing—and went on to become Aunt Jemima in the commercials for Quaker Oats. Ethel Waters was certainly an impressive singer, though what she did had not much relation to blues or jazz; she was an actress, as she proved subsequently in *Mamba's Daughters* and *Member of the Wedding,* and it was as an actress she used her voice.

The record companies were not looking beyond New York for talent. They had to go down South to get real blues singers, and eventually that is just what they did. One of the first they brought back was one of the best: a round, homely, hoyden of a woman named Gertrude "Ma" Rainey. In her own way, her background was just as much show business as Mamie Smith's or Edith Wilson's. But she had put in her time in tent shows on the Southern circuits—the Silas Green Show, the Rabbit Foot Minstrels, and even two years with the Tolliver Circus.

She was born Gertrude Pridgett in Columbus, Georgia, in 1886. As early as 1900 she was appearing in local shows, and it wasn't long before she was out on the road learning the trade that was to be hers for thirty-five years. In a few years she married a singing comedian named William Rainey who carried the nickname "Pa," and that was how, at the age of twenty, she became Ma Rainey. They were billed as "Rainey and Rainey, Assassinators of the Blues," and that puts her pretty firmly in the showbiz context in which she worked for years under the tents.

In a way, it is remarkable that she managed to break away at all, but she did briefly when she began recording for Paramount in 1923. In a modest way she became a kind of national attraction then, playing theaters in Chicago and a few other cities in the North for the first and only time. For the most part, her appeal was to those Southern black audiences to whom she had been singing her blues for years before she was invited up North to record. And the South was in her voice. It was rough, expressive, and dramatic without ever being really a "good" voice by conventional standards. She had not much range, and even within her limits her pitch was not always good, yet she did good things with it. Even when she was unsure of her material—as she seemed to be whenever she strayed from pure blues—her experience as a performer would see her through. When she wound up talking her material, as she did from time to time, she never lost the intensity that made her a real blues singer.

She recorded a lot of traditional Delta blues material—"Levee Camp Moan," "Bo-Weevil Blues," and "Stack o' Lee Blues" among others—and she does it well in a kind of masculine style that was really natural to her. Jazz critics seem to prefer the three sides she cut with Louis Armstrong backing her up, in 1925, her "See, See Rider" usually cited as the best of all her recordings. My own preference, however, is for her last recordings in 1928, with Tampa Red and Georgia Tom Dorsey. Her "Sleep Talking Blues" and "Runaway Blues"—the same tune with different words—are as good as anything she ever recorded. Her voice is rich and full; she really sounds like the "Mother of the Blues." Those sessions in the fall of 1928 were her last. She continued to play throughout the South for five more years, however; then she retired to run the two theaters she had bought in Rome, Georgia. She died in 1939 at the age of fifty-three.

Ida Cox is harder to fix. Her style is someplace between that of vaudevillians such as Mamie Smith and hard blues shouters like Ma Rainey. She was certainly a performer in her own right; she toured the top black theaters in the country as the top attraction in her own revue—chorus girls, comedians, and second-line singers. But her voice, as it survives on records, establishes her as a much stronger and more authentic-sounding singer than you might suppose from this background. She wrote most of her own material, chose her backup groups carefully, and is easier to listen to today than most of the classic singers. She had a longer professional life than most, too, working intermittently right through the thirties and recording as late as 1961, six years before her death.

There were innumerable others—Victoria Spivey, Alberta Hunter, Martha Copeland, Clara Smith, Sara Martin, to name just a few worth attention. But the queen of them all, the Empress of the Blues, as she chose to call herself, was Bessie Smith, of course. She is one of the few of the legendary blues figures whose performances can stand up absolutely to careful listening today. If anything, she sounds even better on the recordings she made—all 160 of them have been reissued on Columbia—than one has any right to expect. There is drama and a subtlety of expression that come out in repeated listenings to them. And that in itself may seem surprising, for on first exposure what is sure to strike the listener is the raw power of the woman's voice. It practically assaults the ear, matching in strength the crudity of the lyrics she sang. She put more of herself on records than had most singers of any period up to the present. It is not just that she cut more than most, but that throughout her ten-year career as a recording artist she seemed to take more care in her performances before the microphone and the recording horn than most—she would do take after take on a session until she came up with one that satisfied her. Ma Rainey, Clara Smith, and many of the rest were very careless about what they laid down on wax; it is commonplace to hear of them that in person they were far more exciting than the recordings they have left behind indicate. Nobody has said that of Bessie Smith—not because she was an indifferent performer onstage (by all accounts she was sensational!), but because she was just as good on records. It was as though she believed that any sort of immortality she achieved would have to be through mechanical means.

She was a big woman—tall, abundant, statuesque as she struck her dramatic poses before audiences—every inch the empress she claimed to be. At the peak of her career, in 1927 and 1928, she toured with her own show and pulled close to a thousand a week for the entire package. Yet she began humbly enough down in the tent shows of the Deep South just as Ma Rainey did. In fact, she and the great Ma (who was twelve years her senior) worked together at one time in Tolliver's Circus. But she had split from it and was working theaters and bars when she was heard one night in Alabama by a scout named Frank Walker. He liked what he heard, remembered, and when he was put in charge of Columbia's Race recording operations, he searched her out and signed her up. That was in 1923. On her first session for Columbia she cut "Down-Hearted Blues," with just Clarence Williams' piano accompaniment. The song had already been recorded by Alberta Hunter, who had written it with blues accompanist Lovie Austin, so that it was just a "cover" recording, a safe choice of pretested material. But she did so well on it that, by the time it was released four months later, Walker had recorded her eighteen more times. His faith in her was more than justified: "Down-Hearted Blues," a great song with a great line—"I've got the world in the jug, got the stopper in my hand"—sold about 800,000 copies.

She was an immediate star. With her records coming out monthly, Bessie started touring through the Midwest and South, drawing huge crowds at theaters in the major cities and playing the whistlestops in between from a railroad car. She was in demand by whites as well. She did special shows for whites only in the South and played to mixed audiences in the North. As early as 1924, interest in her was so keen that the white-owned radio station WGM in Memphis (in 1924 *all* radio was white-owned) did a rare and expensive remote broadcast from a black theater, the Beale Avenue Palace, presenting Bessie Smith to the mid-South radio audience.

She recorded with top jazz musicians of the day. Fletcher Henderson and later the great James P. Johnson took over successfully as her accompanists. Joe Smith, Don Redman, Coleman Hawkins, and Buster Bailey all played behind her at one session or another. In 1925, Louis Armstrong did a session with her that really should have gone better than it did. On "St. Louis Blues," for instance, on which Bessie should have sung well, they switched Fred Longshaw, a pianist, to harmonium; he wheezes along behind her, nearly covering up her own strong voice and baffling Louis Armstrong completely. In general, she was better than the material she sang. It was only in the beginning and middle of her career that she did many true blues; toward the end she sang popular songs and lot of suggestive and downright raunchy material. The songs that she herself wrote were no closer to real blues than others she did, but a couple of them were good. Her "Blue Blue" was good and done in a spirited rendition in 1931; her "Spider Man Blues," which is a blues truly enough, is darkly paranoid in its expression, an altogether odd song.

The Depression came, and things got very tough for Bessie Smith. Columbia went bankrupt, and she did not record for the label after 1931. She was brought back by jazz critic and A & R man John Hammond in 1933, however, for a session that was cut for OKeh, which was by then Columbia's Race label. Her voice was rough—she even seems to be growling unnaturally on most of "Gimme a Pigfoot"—and there is not a blues among the four tunes recorded at the session. This seems fairly typical of what she was doing during her last years, though, for she was trying to "modernize"—keep up with the new trends in popular music. She was back to doing one-nighters in the South at the end. That came for her one night in 1937 in an auto accident outside Clarksdale, Mississippi. She was horribly mangled, an arm almost severed from her body. That was how a white doctor from Memphis found her, lying in the road. He saw her into the hospital in Clarksdale, but it would be difficult, he later said, to determine whether she died there or in the ambulance. There is no basis in fact, it seems, for the popular story that she was refused admission to a hospital because of her color.

A lot of singers were left behind in the era that followed the classic blues period. Times were hard. The Depression cut sharply into the music business at every level. Musicians and singers were playing for tips at cabarets around the country, and recording all but came to a standstill at the bottom of the slump. Because the black audience was hit hardest of all, black performers suffered most.

But tastes were changing, too. Jazz was becoming more and more distinct, a music apart from that rough-and-ready combination of blues and ragtime whence it had sprung. What was taking shape in the beginning of the thirties was a phenomenon called swing. By the end of that decade it had saved the music business. Thanks to bands like Benny Goodman's, Artie Shaw's, and those of the Dorsey Brothers, by 1939 kids around the country were dancing, swinging, and buying records as never before. But nearly all those big bands that made Swing Era history were white bands. And those few black bands that did make it then did so by managing to sound more or less "white"—Jimmie Lunceford's Orchestra is a good example of this sort of "mulatto jazz."

This trendy de-emphasis of the "blackness" of jazz was especially pronounced among the black singers. The blues was something old-fashioned or low-down. It was something they used to sing back in the twenties or maybe still did in the remote reaches of the Deep South. But the going style became gentlemanly and ladylike—they were "vocalists" who sang "ballads," but never blues singers. Ivie Anderson and Joya Sherrill of the Duke Ellington Orchestra, Maxene Sullivan with the John Kirby Sextet, Dan Grissom of the Jimmie Lunceford band—there was no black quality to their singing at all.

And there was also very little to Billie Holiday's. There has recently been a great flurry to claim her as a kind of black heroine. And while these efforts are no doubt well intended, they must have been made by people who aren't really familiar with her singing career at all. She first was heard on the Teddy Wilson Brunswick sessions of the mid-thirties. This was the politest jazz imaginable. It was almost dicty in its sweet, modulated, tasteful quality—and that was how she sang the ballads and "torch songs" they gave her, too. All that saved her as a singer was that weird tone of hers—"She sounds like her feet hurt," Ethel Waters once said of her—and her phrasing. She could phrase more subtly and with greater musical imagination than any other singer of her time or since. She was one of the first to come close to what jazz instrumentalists of her era were doing on their horns, and for this she truly deserves the "jazz singer" title that was hung on her. Billie Holiday was also called a "blues singer" in her day by some who should have known better. Although she had a couple of blues in her repertoire, she was never a blues singer. Her whole approach to music was as unlike that of a blues singer as could be. She was simply interested in other things.

There was one big band singer during this era who could, with some degree of accuracy, be called a blues singer—and that was Jimmy Rushing of the Count Basie Orchestra. The short, plump man whom they used to call "Mr. Five-by-Five," had been with the organization even before it was Basie's. In the early thirties, when Bill Basie was just the piano player with those Kansas City terrors, the Blue Devils, Rushing was discovered in an Oklahoma City café owned by his father. He joined the band, and when it began recording, went to New York, and gained national prominence, he was right up there in front of it singing his heart out. It would be a mistake to push him too hard as a bluesman; he was really a band singer—and a good one. He could do songs of all sorts with style, ease, and a certain extra grace—even down to the most banal "hit parade" material. But he could and did sing blues, too, belting out those good sounds above one of the most powerful brass sections in the business; it took a man to do the job, and he was equal to it, as he proved again and again on such big band blues as "Goin' to Chicago," "Sent for You Yesterday," and "Lazy Lady Blues."

As we go on, the relationship of jazz to blues becomes more and more tenuous. The Bebop Era made the music intellectually respectable but cut it loose from the mass audience. Moving from Swing to Bop introduced a kind of cult quality into the sociology of jazz that ultimately would prove nearly fatal to the music. Who were the singers of this period? Sarah Vaughan, certainly, Lambert-Hendricks-and-Ross possibly—but who else? The point is that it was not vocal music at all, and the music suffered when it lost the humanizing quality of the human voice. The blues? Forget it. Nobody in jazz even tried to sing them then. About the only singer who could really belt the blues and worked with jazz backgrounds was Dinah Washington. She was a fine singer, underrated by critics during the forties and fifties and largely forgotten today. She came up through gospel music, sang lead with the Original Sallie Martin Singers, and brought all that fervor and conviction with her into secular music. Her best recording was done with jazzmen, some of them as musically sophisticated as the great trumpeter

Clifford Brown. In these recordings she came about as close as anyone to hammering out a synthesis between the new intellectual music and the old blues.

THINGS HIT BOTTOM in the late fifties. The music became so introspective and inhuman that it was hardly to be listened to outside of the concert context. There remained an audience of sorts for it into the sixties, but soon that vanished, too, when the college kids found their own music—rock-and-roll. They no longer had to be quiet and attentive during Dave Brubeck's forty-five-minute piano solos (complete with quotations from Stravinsky and Bartók); they could just go out and dig the Paul Butterfield Blues Band or maybe Big Brother and the Holding Company with good old Superjanis and just *groove* on it.

Rock is the best thing that ever happened to jazz. It has removed it from the smug climate of intellectual snobbery that had almost overwhelmed it. It has put "black" back into the music (jazzmen like Cannonball Adderly and his brother Nat were working on that years before), given it balls once again, and re-established the link with the blues. The jazz-rock phenomenon—Blood, Sweat & Tears, Chase, and the much quieter Mark-Almond Quintet, as good examples—has worked a very healthy change in mainstream jazz. It is a change that is still taking shape, and so it would be difficult and probably undesirable to attempt to define it too precisely. But jazz is today funkier and more melodic—in short, bluesier than it was even five years ago.

Critics, jazz audiences, and jazzmen alike are less exclusive and less inclined toward snobbishness than before. They are less willing to exclude this bluesman or that young rocker from the jazz company because suddenly people are rather healthily uncertain about what jazz is or ever was. For the last few years, for example, B. B. King has placed highly in both the *Down Beat*'s critics' and readers' polls. That's right, B. B. King, the Beale Street Blues Boy—and not just in the male singer category, but as a guitarist as well.

And that is as it should be, for B.B. is a first-rate guitarist. Does he play blues or jazz? Well, what the readers of *Down Beat* and the critics are saying is that it really doesn't matter so very much *what* you call it, as long as it is improvised and as long as it *feels* right, as long as it is right as *music,* then we will accept it for what it is and worry about labels later. That seems satisfactory to B. B. King, too. He's not going to change to suit anybody, but he's glad for the new acceptance being given his music today. Here is what he told James Powell in a *Down Beat* interview:

> There was a time, when I first started out, when my way of playing was like the old musicians used to play. . . . And you sometimes get a little bit ashamed to play that to certain people. At some time they would look down on it, you understand, but you want to do the thing that you feel they're used to seeing or want to hear, and this is why a lot of the guys will do that. But you come to a certain age—I don't mean you have to be as old as I am (44)—after a while you get to believe that you are *you.* As regards the airs you might put on, it doesn't change the fact that you're still you: So some of us come back to earth.

You don't have to see B. B. King in action and listen to him more than once—and I have seen and heard him many more times than that—to know that he doesn't put on airs. His feet are solidly on the ground. I remember one performance in particular that did more than any other to communicate the particular quality of this remarkable man to me.

It was at Lorton Reformatory, near Washington, D.C. Lorton, located out near Interstate 95 in northern Virginia, is the "state prison" for the District of Columbia. This was the second of a long series of prison concerts that B. B. King had played and continues to play all across the country. As you read this, he has probably played the state prison or big-city jail nearest you. He works the concerts in on off-dates and layovers, brings his band out at his own expense, and plays for the prisoners under whatever conditions are permitted. They weren't ideal the day I saw him. Because there was no auditorium deemed safe, B.B. and his band had set up in midafternoon on a hot July day on the pitcher's mound of the prison baseball diamond. The Lorton inmates filled the bleachers along the first- and third-base lines as B.B. sweated to please them. Nobody sweats like he did that day.

But that doesn't mean they were a tough audience. No, they were hungry for whatever he had to give that day—and he had plenty. The music he and his band played seemed to have an almost therapeutic effect; the boys in the bleachers seemed visibly healthier when things really got swinging. Maybe that was what B.B. meant when he ad-libbed, "If you're sick, the blues will make you well!"

This, along with everything else he said, sang, or played from that point on, met with an enthusiastic response. He and his band played a long set beginning, as he always does, with the Memphis Slim tune that is his theme song, "Every Day I Have the Blues." He went on to sing all his old favorites—"Sweet Little Angel," "Sweet Sixteen," "Three O'Clock Blues," and others—as well as a few of the new tunes he is doing, like Leon Russell's "Hummingbird." And in between he kidded with the inmates like the good showman he is. He presented each member of his eight-piece, jazz-oriented band to the audience, and even introduced his guitar, Lucille.

It's a story he tells at every performance: "Oh," he will say, "you want to know how Lucille got her name? Well, that was one night in the little town of Twist, Arkansas, which is located just seventy-nine miles west of Memphis . . ." It seems there were two fellows who fell into a hell of a fight over a girl at this dance hall about the size of a sardine can where B.B. was playing one night. "One of the two fellows kicked over a kerosene heater in the middle of the floor, and the place went up in flames. Both those boys died in the fire, and all I got out with was my guitar. I asked who that girl was who had caused all that trouble—and they said she was called Lucille. And I thought, 'She must be some girl,' so I named my guitar after her."

B. B. King's history as a performer is crowded with towns like Twist and memories of gigs played in roadhouses and dance halls like that one. No bluesman today is better established than he is, yet none has worked so hard to get where he is. Years and years of one-nighters have taken their toll. In 1956 he set a personal record that few other performers would care to equal, playing 342 one-night stands in a single year. Living on the road broke up a marriage. One auto accident—"You play all night and drive all day"—left him broke; another nearly severed his right arm.

And he is still traveling today—though now in better style

than ever before, it is true. I talked with him after the Lorton concert in his suite at the rather swank Hotel Madison in downtown D. C. His valet-driver was readying his wardrobe for his next concert. B. B. King was in an expansive mood, feeling easy, and I remarked that it must be difficult to relax in odd hours like this.

"Yes," he said, "but it's how you learn to cope with the road—you learn to be yourself wherever you are. My home is usually a hotel room. My manager is up in New York, and my mother and father are on a farm that I own with them outside Memphis. But me? Well, I don't have a home, not really—I've got 300 working days this year, and recording dates on top of that. Where would I live?"

But though B.B. continues to work at just about the same grueling pace as before, the character of his audiences has changed considerably in the last few years. He has been discovered by young audiences around the country. And now, in addition to club dates, he plays colleges and universities, concerts, and festivals. How do the audiences differ? "Well, the attention is better at the concerts, of course," he says. "You take your average club-goer. He's got other things on his mind. He's got a bottle at the table and a lady along. And you may never get his full attention, but he's enjoying himself. He may yell over to his neighbor, 'Hey, Sam, listen at him.' That's his kind of appreciation. I was brought up with people like that."

He smiles. "Playing audiences is like a man planting a crop. If he's done his work right at harvesting time, he's going to get a good crop. They're going to keep coming back again and again."

I remark on the analogy to farming. "Oh, sure," he says, "I'm a country boy. Can't you tell?" Yes, he was born in Itta Bena, Mississippi, and did all the farm-boy jobs for his parents—and for a favorite aunt, too. "She was one of those hip young aunts who would let me play her phonograph. Yeah, I would do her chores and listen to Blind Lemon the rest of the afternoon. Little Riley B. King never goofed with her. He was her good boy."

Whether inspired by Blind Lemon or by the accomplishments of his cousin Bukka White, he went north to Memphis, got a disc jockey job on a black radio station—and that was when Riley B. became B.B. (short for Blues Boy). He loves the blues, and that's why it came as a shock to him when, in the mid-sixties, the taste of young blacks turned against the music that he himself had been brought up on.

It was at the Royal Theater in Baltimore. He was on the bill with Sam Cooke, as he recalls, and B.B.'s band was playing the whole show. What happened? The black kids there booed the blues—not B.B., but the blues. It shook him up. "Yes," he admits, "it really hurt in a way. I think maybe they're ashamed of the blues. They think it's some kind of old-fashioned Uncle Tom music. Well, it's not. It's the best music there is. And I got mad and told them so. Well, later I apologized for blowing up, but I still think what I told them was right."

Why do white kids feel so differently about the music? "Well," he answers, "they got used to hearing it from their own white stars, and it sounded good to them then, so they figured it must be all right. You see, they weren't thinking in terms of the past and all those associations with the music the way the black kids were. But no, I think it's changing anyway with the black kids. They're just beginning to come around to it. And it'll be good for them when they do."

I ask him the usual questions about his musical development: Who taught him? Who influenced him? How did he start?

But he's heard them all before. He gives me a wave of his hand and a wink of his eye. "Look, I learned not in school, but from the music itself. There are only seven notes of music and five accidentals—B flat up to F sharp. There's only twelve choices we've all got to work with—whether it's Beethoven or B.B. And I just started playing around when I was a youngster until I found that out, and from then on it was up to me.

"When I got my first electric guitar, though, I did start listening to T-Bone Walker pretty hard. I did love that clear touch of his, and many of us tried to duplicate it. But finally I started to move into my own direction when I began recording. But I kept right on listening to people. If you want to know the people on guitar who made a difference to me, I'll tell you it's been T-Bone, Lonnie Johnson—oh? you know him?—Blind Lemon, Django Reinhardt—yes, well, that makes two of us—and Charlie Christian. They've all been important to me one way or another."

Does he play jazz or blues? Is there a difference?

He smiles and shrugs very expressively. "Well, I'll tell you, what I play doesn't worry me, how I play does. The better jazzmen and I play about the same, but the average tries to put too much into it. I just get up there and do my best. I'm not trying to play it the same every time. I take the basic chord progressions and play it as I feel then. It's rarely I play a long, long solo in a song—twenty-four bars is the usual form. In two choruses I can be inventive. I enjoy it, man. I don't know if people know it, the way I screw up my face sometimes, but I do."

CHAPTER THIRTEEN

IT WAS one of those temperate January Sundays that only seem to happen in New Orleans. Starched white curtains hanging in the windows that faced on sunny St. Ann Street billowed slightly, lofted by the pleasant breezes that swept the French Quarter. There are no lights on in the living room where I sit, and the woman who is talking is almost hidden from me, her sharp features nearly obscured in the shadows. Her eyes are not, however; they flash at me now as she speaks, emphasizing an uncompromising, angular, even harsh quality that is certainly there in her personality. She's nobody's Aunt Jemima.

"Well, it stands to reason, young man," she says. "When people get together and start making music, they all gets to feeling happy. Any kind of music make you feel good—blues or church music. It's the sincereness of it—that's what make you feel good. It does seem to me, though, that you're bound to feel different when you sing for Jesus than when you sing the blues, because *then*"—she jabs a finger in my direction for emphasis—"then you are inspired by the Holy Spirit."

I nodded and asked if bluesmen weren't inspired, too.

She looked away from me and chose her words carefully:

"Well, being as good a musician as my husband was, that comes from inside, too. There's no doubt it takes a sort of inspiration, though I'm not sure from where."

Her name is Annie Pavageau, and she is the widow of a jazz bassist of some reputation named Alcide Pavageau who bore the nickname "Slow Drag" to the day of his death in 1968. He became best known during the forties and fifties when he played with the Bunk Johnson and George Lewis bands that toured widely in this country and Europe. He had played for years in New Orleans before that, though. Born there in 1888, he taught himself to play guitar and could be heard in dives and street corners around town from 1905 on. It wasn't until later, sometime in the thirties, that he took up bass. By that time he had met and married Annie, and the two of them had teamed up and were playing and singing around town together.

I asked about that time, and she admitted that yes, she used to play and sing the blues some. "I did one time play in a club with my husband. That was at the Autocrat Club on St. Bernard. Actually, my husband and I used to work a lot together. I learned guitar from him. I was a young woman when I was playing and singing the blues. I wasn't a church member at that time, not even a churchgoer."

Don't bluesmen go to church? "Sure they do," she snapped. It was clearly a sore point with her. "A lot of them began there. And my husband, he went when I did. I could tell you others who were church members, too. You know Punch Miller, the trumpet player? He belonged to Reverend Dunne's church. They belong to different churches around town. You know. I mean, they might be going around playing different ragtime songs and blues and all, but they call that just making a living. That's how it is."

But what about herself? Does she still play the blues? She shook her head emphatically. "No," she said, "I just like church music, religious music. I don't like blues and I don't play it any more at all. I quit. I didn't believe I could play all that ragtime music and still serve God in truth and spirit. I give all my time to the church today."

It is time well spent. She plays piano and organ ("Never took no music. All my wisdom comes from the guitar.") and serves as choir director for the Morning Star Baptist Church on Burgundy Street in New Orleans' French Quarter. I had been there earlier that day and stayed through the morning-long church service that seemed to take more than some could give in the way of endurance. They came and went. One white girl in jeans and barefoot darted in from the street and left almost immediately—looking for something but not finding it there. But I stayed on through "Amazing Grace," "Precious Lord," and all the rest—stayed on through the short sermon of the visiting Reverend Eddie Brown, who caused some stir when he said, "If you're going to be righteous, then you got to *be* righteous, If you're going to be a hellhound, then you be the biggest hellhound ever was. God don't like none of that halfway. There's right *righteous,* and there's wrong—and you got to be one or the other."

Through it all, Annie Pavageau presided at the piano; an imposing presence, she seemed as much in command of things there as the Reverend Brown. It was hard, watching her, to imagine her in that good-time life that legend said she had led before she got religion. I was curious about that. So later I asked as tactfully as I knew how if her life had changed completely when she joined the church.

She was emphatic. "It did," she declared. "It did. Of course, I was raised in the church. I sang in the choir ever since I was a girl in Columbus, Mississippi, where I'm from. I had such a strong voice they used to use me for high tenor when I was just a girl. Then I came here to New Orleans, and like any child I started going to various dances and all, and they got me to playing piano for them, and that's how I met my husband."

She half-turned in the sofa she was sitting in and looked at the large poster-sized photograph of Slow Drag that hung above her. "That's him there," she said. "Here, let me get some light on that so you can see him." She turned on a table lamp next to her, then stretched the length of the couch to switch on a floor lamp. I came over for a closer look and commented that he looked very young in the picture. "He did," she agreed, "and that's how he looked right up to the day he died, and he was eighty then."

I asked about her husband's relation to the church. Was he accepted by the congregation?

"Sure," she said, "the congregation would accept a blues

singer or a player as a member of the congregation—*if* he give it up."

And had he given it up? She was clearly annoyed by the question and felt some ambivalence about the whole matter. She seemed to feel a conflict between her loyalty to her husband, on the one hand, and, on the other, her conviction that good-time music and church music simply don't mix. And so instead of giving me a straight answer, she started preaching at me: "You know you can't serve two people. Jesus said that. You can't serve God and mammon, too. Everything that is not right is wrong. Everything that does not pertain to God is sinful. We believe the way Christ did."

She had become personal and very direct in what she was saying. She was demanding a personal response from *me,* but all I did was continue writing down what she was saying. And that annoyed her even more. Finally, she broke off in exasperation and asked, "Are you a believer in Jesus Christ?" I said I was. "Well, you better be! And you better believe in just what the Bible says. You could write all day in that book of yours, but unless you believe in Jesus it won't do you no good." She nodded emphatically and crossed her arms, and that was about all she would say to me that day.

ANNIE PAVAGEAU had made quite plain an attitude among blacks of which many whites are completely ignorant. It is commonly assumed that because blues and gospel sound so much alike many of the same people sing both. They don't. The official attitude of the black church—and I mean under that umbrella to gather the Baptists, the Methodists, and the Pentecostal sects—is that the blues is the Devil's music. It is not just the music alone that they are against. After all, not all blues are profane; not every one treats illicit love; some are simple songs of complaint, fundamental comments on the human condition. But no matter, the blues is roundly and universally condemned by the black church because of the way of life it represents—the milieu of hard drinking, loose sex, and quick violence in the city bars and country juke joints where the music is played. And the black church, as a conservative, stabilizing force in the community, has been fighting hard against this way of life right from the start. The blues is condemned because it is such a vivid reminder to so many in black congregations of the places they had been, the drinks they had drunk, and the lovers they had known, and all that they had left behind when they "crossed over."

Because whites tend to overlook or disregard such feelings, there have been some unhappy moments at concerts and folk festivals. At UCLA in 1965, for instance, blues singer Son House was to appear on the same bill with that unique spiritual group, the Sea Island Singers. When the choir saw that it was to participate in something called a "blues workshop," they got up in a huff and said they would head back to Georgia before they would ever appear on a *blues* program. It was only by renaming it a "black music workshop" that the sponsors persuaded them to stay. Even so, there were problems. During the program, John Fahey, a fine young guitarist who was then a graduate student in the University's Folklore Department, suggested that Son House and the Sea Island Singers do a number together. Fahey should have known better. Son was willing, but the choir said no, they weren't about to share the stage with a man who was a known singer of sinful songs. Son didn't take kindly to that. He called them a pack of hypocrites and told them that when the sun went down they were out dancing to the boogie beat just like everybody else. It developed into a regular shouting match before Fahey managed to calm them all down—and, of course, they never did get together and sing.

This particular incident may have been complicated further by the fact that Son House had himself been a Baptist preacher before he became a blues singer. He left the church to play sinful music and may thus have seemed sort of a pariah to the Sea Island Singers. But many blues singers got their start in church choirs—Muddy Waters among them, and Muddy will tell you straight-faced that what he plays is "sinful music." Although some of the younger bluesmen adopt a more professional attitude about the music they play and don't seem to think much about the church one way or another, many of the older men have accepted this pariah role in which they have been cast. Following the blues trail has in this way taken them beyond their pale. If they are damned men, they say, then let them at least enjoy their damnation. This has led many of them to the sort of excessive, reckless, self-destructive behavior epitomized by Robert Johnson, who sang so eloquently of that life he lived in the blues "Hellhound on My Trail."

Certainly some few bluesmen—among them the late Skip James and Sleepy John Estes—and many of the old songsters have managed to satisfy their own consciences and have sung both blues and sacred music. Nevertheless, the relationship between the two styles (and content aside, they really are only two styles of the same music) has been both complicated and ambiguous. On the one hand, you must note Big Bill Broonzy telling Studs Terkel in an interview that "The blues is a steal from the spirituals," thus acknowledging the debt of his music to the hymns of the nineteenth-century black church. And on the other hand, you must recognize the debt of the black church to the blues in the person of Thomas A. Dorsey, the man who is generally recognized as the father of modern gospel music.

He started out his career as "Georgia Tom," for he was born in Atlanta in 1889. Brought up in the church, Dorsey did not hesitate to join the local Baptist congregation when he emigrated to Gary, Indiana. He soon found, however, that he could make a good living for himself as a blues and jazz pianist around Gary and the South Side of Chicago if he put aside, at least temporarily, the prohibitions of the church against good-timing. And so that was how he happened to become one of the top piano bluesmen of his day. He was asked by Ma Rainey, then a top performer, to organize a band for her and serve as her accompanist. He put together a first-rate group with at least one soloist—trombonist Al Wynn—who went on to make a reputation for himself as a jazzman. Dorsey toured and recorded with the ebullient "Mother of the Blues" for a number of years, and the last band he led for her had in it a guitarist named Hudson Whittaker who doubled on kazoo and called himself Tampa Red. When Georgia Tom split up with Ma Rainey in 1928, he intended to give up the blues and go back to the church and religious song writing. Tampa Red, however, talked him into teaming up with him, and for a couple of years the two played and sang together and collaborated on a number of original blues, including the raunchy "Tight Like That."

Then in 1929, Thomas A. Dorsey gave up the blues life completely. ("If you're righteous, then you got to *be* righteous.") Plenty of sacred music had been written and recorded before

Dorsey turned his talents in that direction, but what he brought with him were his keen feelings for the blues and his preference for its personal, direct, and unabashedly emotional appeal. He translated all this to the sacred music he began to write and came up with a style so fundamentally different that he even gave it a new name, calling what he wrote gospel songs. During the thirties, when he did most of his work, he wrote scores of these hard-swinging gospel blues-based songs, including "I Surely Know There's Been a Change in Me," "I'm Gonna Live the Life I Sing About in My Song," and "The Day Is Past and Gone." Along with his partner, Sallie Martin, a raw-voiced shouting lady, he began touring black churches around the country, presenting his own material in revival concerts. This was the beginning of the gospel circuit, which so many great performers have traveled successfully since.

As early as 1932, the new style was so well established that Dorsey convened the first Gospel Singers' Convention and was able to attract singers and choir directors from all over the country. And it was also in 1932, under the saddest of circumstances, that he wrote his greatest song. While he was away on tour, his wife and child died in an accident, and he was brought down to a state of despair from which he rose to write his great "Precious Lord."

Precious Lord take my hand,
Lead me on, let me stand,
I am tired, I am weak, I am worn,
Through the storm, through the night,
Lead me on to the light,
Take my hand precious Lord, lead me on.

This one, a favorite of both blacks and Southern whites, is the song Martin Luther King, Jr., had just requested for the evening's service when he was shot down on the balcony of his Memphis motel room.

All gospel singers have at least the feeling of the blues in their songs. Some come by it quite naturally. The late Mahalia Jackson, the only one of them known widely to white audiences, was born in New Orleans in 1911 and grew up there listening to the records of her favorite, Bessie Smith, and absorbing the sounds of jazz and blues in the streets all around her. But she herself sang sanctified right from the start. By the time she moved North, to Chicago, in the thirties, she had a reputation as a sacred singer who could really swing. In contrast to her later appearances on the *Ed Sullivan Show* et al., in which she sang syrupy songs (much of it ersatz material manufactured to order by whites) in moony, doleful, but awfully dignified style, the early Mahalia was a terrifically spirited performer who just might pick up her robes and dance for joy when the feeling was right inside her. You can catch some of the old Mahalia on her recordings from the fifties, but by the time she had become a national celebrity outside the little gospel world, the style had changed completely. Only the voice was the same—and that remained with her until she died in 1972.

Bessie Griffin was also born in New Orleans and grew up hearing the same sounds as Mahalia. You can hear echoes of them in the fine, earthy things she does with her great contralto voice. The Reverend Alex Bradford also cheerfully admits to blues influence on his own singing and composing. He will tell you he used to spend whole days following blues singers around in his native Bessemer, Alabama, and remind you that the lady who taught him to play piano was herself a jazz pianist. Sister Rosetta Tharpe of the Holiness Church is famous—notorious in some circles—as the gospel singer who did more than just introduce blues elements into her sacred music. She kept right on playing them. Sister Rosetta is not only a singer but is a good, primitive electric guitar player, somewhat in the style of Aaron "T-Bone" Walker. The combination brought her a recording contract with Decca as early as 1938. On her records she may have been singing words as pious as you please, but when she let go on that guitar what came out was low-down, dirty blues. Decca began featuring her with the Lucky Millinder big band, and it wasn't long before she had recorded a few blues with them as well, to the great consternation of her gospel fans. Once her secular audience was established, she even began playing night clubs. Through all this, however, her basic material was gospel, with a few secular songs mixed in, so that she felt she had never really left her religion behind but had simply taken it along with her into some pretty curious places. She looked upon herself as a sort of musical missionary, and using this line, managed to talk her way back into the good graces of her church when her fling in the night clubs and on the *Billboard* Race charts was ended. Today, she is back singing her gospel songs to gospel audiences.

Although Sister Rosetta Tharpe was the first to bring sacred songs into the night clubs, she was not the last. One of gospel's finest groups, the Ward Singers, under the direction of Gertrude Ward, worked hard and was respected by all who heard it in churches and auditoriums around the country. It included not only Gertrude's pretty and precocious daughter, Clara Ward, but a girl named Marion Williams, with a powerful and affecting voice, who has since become about the finest soloist in gospel today. At that time, however, Clara was the star of the show. She had great style on the up-tempo stuff, was prettier and younger than Mahalia Jackson, and so she was considered by some to be a logical replacement when Mahalia made her way into the white world. Clara soon began acting like the new queen, swanking imperiously. She dressed up the rest of the Ward Singers like ladies-in-waiting and coiffed them in beehive wigs. This got to be a little much for Marion Williams and the rest of the Ward Singers, and together they all walked out on Clara Ward and her mother in 1958. The Ward Singers never really made a comeback in the gospel field, for Clara went into night clubs with a gospel act in 1961. Today, although Clara Ward and the Ward Singers (as the attraction is now known) continue to play auditoriums in big gospel shows, they do most of their shouting in Las Vegas and Disneyland—and have adjusted their program accordingly.

There is neither time nor space for me to attempt a survey of the huge, rich field of gospel music—and there is really no need, either, for there is already a good survey available, Tony Heilbut's *The Gospel Sound.* It is complete, offering a view of the whole field, written without pretensions but with a lot of love. You may have guessed that it is the source of much of the information that I have presented here—though the opinions have certainly been my own. A sort of minor theme that runs through the Heilbut book is the secularization of performers in gospel—blatantly, as in the case of Sister Rosetta Tharpe and Clara Ward, or somewhat more subtly, as it was with Mahalia Jackson. Then, too, there has been a steady drain of singers from the churches that started way back in the forties when

Dinah Washington left the Original Sallie Martin Singers to become the queen of rhythm-and-blues.

The music has been secularized, too, though in this case the alteration has been so complete, and the secularization so absolute, that a new label has now been applied to this new style, and it is called—soul. Heilbut remarks in passing: "The first things that will strike any newcomer to gospel are its stylistic similarities to soul music and the obvious, if not overwhelming, sexual presence of its performers." Given that sexual presence, which nobody would or could deny, perhaps the development of soul from gospel was inevitable. The important personalities in soul music, those who created the style, have nearly all been graduates of gospel. The late Sam Cooke, who comes as close as anyone to being the man who started it all, dropped out of the Soul Stirrers Quartet to become the top attraction among black male singers in popular music. Lou Rawls began with the Pilgrim Travelers; Wilson Pickett came up with the Violinaires; even Dionne Warwick, who seems to have lost the earthy gospel sound completely, got her start in the churches of Newark.

Soul music's biggest star is, of course, Aretha Franklin, and of them all, she is probably the most firmly grounded in gospel, too. She grew up on the gospel circuit. Her father was the Reverend C. L. Franklin, who for years toured with the Ward Singers and other groups, sermonizing at the song sessions. And Aretha? She traveled right along, making those long car trips and staying up to listen to her idol, Clara Ward, giving her all. With all this it is not surprising that Aretha herself began singing when she was only fourteen—or that in the beginning she sounded a lot like Clara Ward. What did surprise people, though, was that after a good beginning in gospel, she quit the field after only four years and signed with Columbia as a pop singer. She had little success, however, until she switched labels in 1966 and went with Atlantic. Then the hits—"Respect," "I Never Loved a Man the Way I Love You," "Chain of Fools," "Since You've Been Gone," and all the others—began to roll out with really astonishing frequency and precision.

Her gospel background was well known by many, though certainly not all, of her fans. It was partly to satisfy those who did know and to inform those who did not that Atlantic recently followed through on a project that had been in the planning for years. They recorded her in an all-gospel set, live, at a church location. For Aretha's part, she may have felt it was time to repay a debt of long standing to the music that gave her her start. But whatever the motives involved, the two-record album, *Amazing Grace,* which she recorded with the help of the Reverend James Cleveland and the Southern California Community Choir, succeeds beautifully. Atlantic did just right, of course, recording it in a church; all gospel albums should be recorded live before a congregation. It is this that helps make it authentic stuff. Aretha shows she has certainly not forgotten what she learned as a child all those nights on the circuit. But she also reveals what we would never have dreamed from her pop performances—that hers is not nearly as strong a voice as that of some others in gospel. Rhythmically, she cannot be faulted—she rides as few singers can, soul or sacred. Her phrasing is bold and venturesome. All that she lacks is the power and intensity of a Marion Williams—and that she will probably never have.

Her efforts seem to go over very well with the congregation. (Some credit for this must go to the choir, which performs beautifully through the whole set.) They realize who Aretha is and that this is something of an occasion for her, and they seem quite willing to forgive her her trespasses into the pop music field. In fact, they are most enthusiastic when Aretha's father, the Reverend C. L. Franklin, stands up and recalls a time when James Cleveland came to direct the choir and Cleveland and Aretha spent hours in the living room just singing sacred songs. He concludes, "If you want to know the truth, she ain't never left the church!"

BUT NOT EVERY comeback goes as well as Aretha's. The Staple Singers came out of Chicago in the fifties to become for a time just about the top attraction in gospel. Back then, the group was made up of Roebuck "Pop" Staples, the leader, and three of his children, Mavis, Cleotha, and Purvis (who has since been replaced by a third daughter, Yvonne), and they were billed as "the first family of gospel." Pop Staples did some writing, and one of his songs, "Uncloudy Day," comes about as close as anything written recently to being a gospel classic. But as performers, what they had to offer chiefly was Mavis. She has a contralto voice of immense range, one that can sweep down close to baritone, then push well up into high soprano. What she lacks in raw power she makes up in emotional intensity. Mavis was the great favorite of gospel audiences. In the early sixties, when the Staple Singers began playing the folk circuit, white audiences seemed to respond to the intimate "living-room" feeling they projected.

From gospel to "folk gospel," it wasn't far to soul, and that was where they headed next, hooking up with the new black label, Stax, in Memphis. Mavis was soon being pushed into a solo role by the company as a second Aretha Franklin. Yet partly to keep their old fans, and partly, too, because it means a lot to them personally, the Staples have tried hard to hold on to their identification as a gospel group. Toward this end, they went to Philadelphia—Marion Williams' territory—and played an all gospel program on Thanksgiving Day, 1969. What happened there, as described by Tony Heilbut in *The Gospel Sound,* was pretty brutal.

> They went back to the same routine that had sustained them for years; the Staples are probably the only gospel group who still feature the songs they sang in 1956. Mavis shook hands on "Help Me Jesus" and groaned with suffering on "Tell Heaven I'm Coming Home One Day." Philadelphia remained very still. The girls walked off stage shyly and obviously hurt. But Roebuck wouldn't give up. "Listen, church, you have to look out for yourself," he said strumming the guitar. "Don't nobody want to go to heaven more than I do, children, but we got to live down here too." The message was clear, but no "Amens" resounded. Finally Roebuck brought Mavis back to sing "Precious Lord." I've seldom seen her work harder. She was all over the audience, crying, roaring, running. Four ladies screamed, the least such effort deserved, but the rest of the church remained very still. The applause was barely polite as Cleotha led the entranced Mavis out.

Pop Staples insists that at least in intention what they are doing today is not all that different from what they were doing during the fifties in gospel. "We're telling the truth," he says, "and that's gospel."

And is gospel protest? "Sure it is—and that's what we're doing, too. Right now, today, we're trying to sing what Martin

Luther King was preaching on. I'll tell you true, I never changed from gospel. We're still preaching, and we're getting more listeners from the kids and grownups."

And there is certainly something to what he says, too, for the Staple Singers have had their greatest success with "message" songs, of which their best example is their big hit, "Respect Yourself."

If you disrepect everybody that you run into,
How in the world do you think anybody 'sposed to respect you?
If you don't give a heck about the man with the Bible in his hand,
Just get out the way and let the gentleman do his thing.
You the kind of gentleman want everything your way.
Take the sheet off your face, boy, it's a brand new day.
Refrain: *Respect yourself, respect yourself, etc.*

This is secular preaching of a sort, and it no doubt has some effect on that vast, secular, record-buying congregation out there in soul-music land. And they make it a point to include some gospel material in all their shows. It works with the audiences. I have seen a theater full of young fans react with the sort of spontaneity and personal enthusiasm you expect only from real gospel congregations.

And the Staples love being loved. Pop Staples remarks in passing on how good the audience at that soul show had made them feel. "We really had them singing along last night, didn't we?" he asks with a sudden ingenuous smile. "I can't express how well that makes me feel. You'll just never know until you've been through the ups and downs we have."

I asked if he were referring to the Staples' changeover from gospel to soul. He nods. "Well, yes. It was really kinda hard. People were so sure we couldn't do it, while in our own minds there never was much doubt. I knew we wanted to give a message in contemporary music—to really tell about what was happening right *now* in our songs. You see, when you're in gospel it's really hard to get through to the public. The radio stations didn't play it then, though it's getting better today.

Being a religious man, I didn't feel it was in no way sinful to give a message out to the public."

And what is that message? He had put it very plainly in his pitch to the audience the night before. After introducing his daughters, he went on in that low-key way of his to tell them that they had come to entertain them with some gospel and some blues that were all about love, freedom, and peace. "The main theme is unity," he admonished, beginning a kind of preaching rhythm. "Don't rip one another off. You with Pop. I want you to go to school now. Because things are changing. Because you might be president." Then, without further notice, the Staples swung into the old hymn "May the Circle Be Unbroken" (the "unity" theme)—and the house went wild with applause.

If this seems a little corny—the sort of quietistic, pietistic hogwash that kept people in their "place" for far too long—there is at least this to be said for Pop Staples' message: He really believes it. And he has a right to, for he has seen it work in his own lifetime. Ask him about how the Staple Singers got started, and he will tell you that it was when he was working in the Chicago Stockyards. "Oh, they were *hard* times, let me tell you. We were down so low we couldn't go from one week to another without borrowing. There just never was enough money back then. So one time somebody asked us would we come and sing at their church for 50 percent of the collection—see, we were known as a singing family, but it was just singing around the living room was all. Anyway, we did go and sing for them then, and we made seventeen dollars—and didn't that come in handy!

"But anyway, that was how we got started. We were just a straight-out gospel group then, but we made international tours and everything. Which is a long way to come for a Drew, Mississippi, boy."

I asked if that was where he was from. "Yes," he said, "that's right. I was born in some little town in the hills, but I grew up in the Delta—in Drew. They're all from the Delta—Big Bill, Son House, all of them. That's what inspired me, listening to all that blues down there. I started playing guitar just by ear, just what I heard around me.

"That's right, I used to listen to a lot of blues. Maybe that was why it always seemed to me there wasn't no real reason we couldn't play both blues and sacred. But there's been a change in this feeling, I think, even down South. It's not quite like it used to be."

Roebuck Staples may be right. Maybe the old attitudes are changing. The uncompromising rejection of blues and good-time music that Annie Pavageau articulated almost angrily that Sunday in New Orleans may even now seem anachronistic to younger members of the Morning Star Baptist Church. And perhaps it is just as well, too, for the Staples are at least realistic about the secular origins of their sacred music. Gospel was brought forth from the blues by Georgia Tom Dorsey, and those other songwriters and singers who helped shape the swinging sacred style back in the twenties and thirties. And so it is neither surprising nor shocking that gospel, in turn, should have spawned soul. It just reminds us once again of the continuity, the wholeness, of the music.

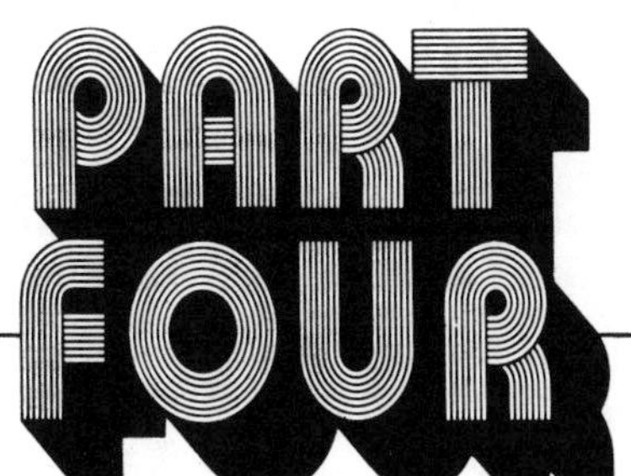
PART
FOUR

CHAPTER FOURTEEN

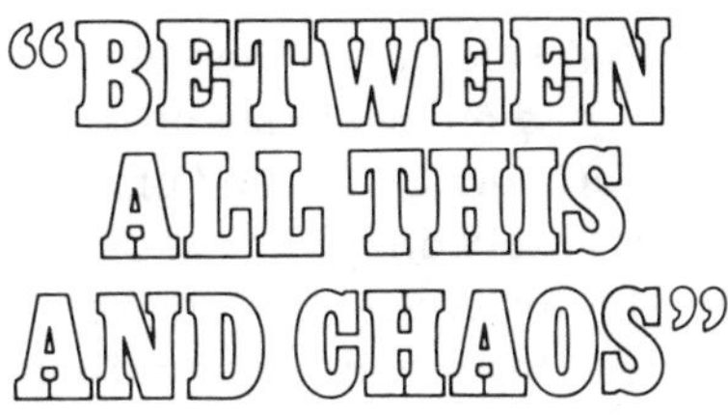

ONE FACT not widely appreciated by the general public today is that the biggest single market for live entertainment is the college circuit. More acts of all kinds are put before students at American colleges and universities than in night clubs, theaters, public auditoriums, at festivals, or at state and county fairs, or anywhere else. The kids own it all.

Of course, it was not always so. Not so many years ago, about the only contact students had with the big world of professional entertainment was when the prom committee went out timorously, check in hand, to book the big band for the big dance. But gradually television killed off the "adult" entertainment world: except for Las Vegas, Miami, and a few rooms in New York, the idea of the night club with its house band, touring headliners, and supporting acts is a thing of the past. With the single exception of Radio City Music Hall the movie houses show only movies and no stage shows. After a certain age—or perhaps it is after marriage and the first child—people seem content to get all their entertainment free right there in the living room.

During the latter fifties and throughout the sixties, as all this was taking shape, the character of a distinct youth culture was also in formation. In business they began to talk about the "youth market." What this meant was that they had suddenly discovered that kids had money to spend—a lot of it by the end of the fifties, and a lot more by the end of the sixties—and they would spend it most freely on items that gave them a sense of separate identity, of uniqueness, of being distinct from the straight adult world. This meant essentially clothes and entertainment. It was through these two that the youth culture expressed itself and began to make itself known to adult America (which, in a few years' time, it all but subdued). Although ultimately the festivals—such as Monterey Pop, and, of course, Woodstock—would be thought of as the true youth culture events, it was really the weekend concerts that were held at nearly every college in America that paved the way for them, that in a sense made them possible. For college was the place of youth; it fostered the sense of otherness that so obsessed American young people during the last couple of years of the sixties.

It has become an enormous market, no doubt about it. It is so big, in fact, that the entertainment weekly *Billboard* now issues an annual directory of "Campus Attractions." It goes out to sponsoring organizations of all kinds in colleges, and serves as a kind of catalogue to allow them to browse around in ads and listings to find out just what is available in the way of live entertainment. What is available turns out to be everything from comedians to dance troupes, hypnotists, mentalists, magicians, and lecturers. From the Ace Trucking Company to Allen Tate, it's all showbiz as far as *Billboard* is concerned, and *Billboard* is probably right.

Of course, music is what they want most at colleges and universities. And since, with student buying power, they have the wherewithal to book any acts they want, it may be interesting to see what these happen to be. In one of the brief articles in *Billboard*'s ninth annual "Campus Attractions" directory there is this: "Jay Jacobs of the William Morris Agency says that students usually decide on the live entertainment they want on campus by the artists who are on top of the popularity polls. 'For instance, we've got an overwhelming demand for Don McLean since his *American Pie* album was released.' " The title of that little article is "Booking Agent Activity Dominated by the Big Beat." Unimaginative, but it tells the story.

If this were the whole story, it would be more than disappointing; it would be tragic. But, fortunately, there is something more to tell. For many American colleges and universities offer a kind of extracurricular major in the blues. If you could do an instant survey of the boys and girls who are really into the music today you would find that something like 90 percent of them learned to like it while in college. Why should that be? Simply because they get their first exposure to the music there on records and in live concert.

The biggest and best-established of all the college blues events is the one held each year at Ann Arbor, Michigan. It is held on the University of Michigan campus, and the several sponsoring organizations are all affiliated with the University. The weekend-long affair has been held annually since 1968, and one year or another nearly every big name in the blues has appeared there—Big Mama Thornton, Roosevelt Sykes, Junior Wells, Little Brother Montgomery, Victoria Spivey, all of them. A few, such as Son House and Fred McDowell, appeared at all the festivals. Each year they have lost money. They expect to. But nobody was quite prepared for the wipeout they got in 1970, when by some unlucky coincidence the Goose Lake Festival—rock and pop—was held in nearby Jackson, Michigan, the same weekend and attracted 200,000. They were prepared to lose $5,000 that year, but the sponsors took a bath to the tune of $20,000—and that's a conservative estimate.

Nevertheless, the Ann Arbor Festival continues. Although they were forced to cut the length of the program and the number of artists drastically in the following years, they have put on representative events. The quantity may not always have been what it was during that glorious 1970 session, but the quality has remained very high indeed. And because the Ann Arbor Festival hung in there and has endured as an annual event, other colleges and universities around the country have begun to sponsor similar events of their own, making it possible for bluesmen to plan their way along a kind of short Festival circuit of their own, which may pay less, but is at least a bit steadier than the pop festivals. (Whoever heard of Woodstock II or the second annual Altamont?)

The Midwest Blues Festival, which has been held for a couple of years running at the University of Notre Dame, South Bend, Indiana, is one of those spawned by the Ann Arbor Festival. Like the rest of them, it is essentially a student enterprise. If it is held there, it is because there is enough student interest in the blues to fill a hall for one, two, or three nights running. Student promoters and their sponsoring organization depend on this interest to put such events over. How can they gauge this interest? What sort of planning goes into such a blues festival? These were things I wanted to know, and so, in advance of the event, I got in touch with the students who were putting it on and got an invitation out to South Bend for my trouble.

Owing to flight difficulties, I got there a little late on Friday, the first night of the three-day festival. Inside the auditorium things were cooking. The first night's session included a set by Mississippi Fred McDowell, another by Chicago blues harpman Carey Bell and his band, and a finale by no less than Howlin' Wolf and his Chicago band. As I listened, I kept edging my way through the half-filled circular auditorium, asking for Perry Aberli and Bill Brinkman, the two who had organized and promoted the event.

I located them at last, not long after the last set had begun, over near the side of the stage where Howlin' Wolf himself sat, legs dangling down off the apron of the stage, waiting to go on. Meanwhile his band tore through its paces, led by Wolf's guitar man Hubert Sumlin, a brilliant and fluent soloist. You could feel the electricity building up as the crowd waited impatiently for the mighty Wolf. Make no mistake—he *is* mighty. Standing a good six-five or six-six, he must weigh close to 260 without giving away much (if anything) in flab. And because he is what he is, it is a bit of a shock when he makes his entrance at last to see him crawl across the stage to the microphone on his hands and knees.

When he gets down like that he seems to be reminding the audience that he's the growling, howling wolf, that he goes about quite naturally on all fours like a beast. If that's the idea, he seems to get it across, for the young crowd loves it. He is greeted by wild cheers as soon as he comes in sight, and they keep right on cheering as he begins roaring through his repertoire—"Wang Dang Doodle," "Shake It for Me," "Little Red Rooster," and so on. He wound up sitting down at the microphone—the old ticker ain't what it used to be, boy—but seemed to lose nothing in power from that position.

But finally the set ended, and with it, the first night of the Midwest Blues Festival. At last Perry Aberli—I had stuck close to him through the Howlin' Wolf set—could tell me a little about the Festival and the way it had been organized—just a few basic questions, I assured him, as the crowd was filing out. He told me this was the second year of blues here at Notre Dame, but that it was the first time they had tried anything "on this level"—a real Festival. "Last year it was more like a two-night concert."

How did they go about lining up the talent? "Oh, well, it was mostly Dick Waterman." He said it with a shrug as if I ought to have known all about that.

But I didn't, so I asked him. It turned out that Dick Waterman managed a number—though not all—of the blues artists that were appearing on the program. Sure, he offered a package, but if they didn't want the whole package, he helped them line up the artists that he *didn't* manage, such as Muddy Waters, Little Brother Montgomery, and Howlin' Wolf. "He helped set up everything," Aberli explained. "It was all done through letters."

Then he's not here now? "Oh, sure, he's here. Would you like to meet him?" I said I would, and he led me backstage, where Wolf's band was busy packing up, getting ready for the long drive to their next date, which happened to be in Toronto. Where was Dick Waterman? Perry Aberli found him over in one corner, engaged in conversation with Wolf's piano player, Sunnyland Slim. He brought him over at the first opportunity —a middling-tall white guy in glasses with a bushy mustache and wearing a jean suit—and introduced us. I told him that I was interested in how blues festivals were put together and just how important they were to the bluesmen who played them. Instead of volunteering answers right away, he suggested that we get together the next day and talk about all this at some length.

That was how it happened that I came by for him about the middle of the next morning and waited in the lobby of his very straight South Bend hotel until the very un-straight Mr. Waterman emerged from the elevator. We found a place down the block to talk, and during breakfast I began feeding questions to him.

I asked him, first of all, whom he managed—and he seemed

to sense I wasn't exactly asking for a client list, for he answered, "I manage those I respect as people. I have a personal feeling for all these men. The only one of them all for whom I've lost any sort of objectivity is Son House. I'm just there to help out with him however I can."

Waterman has managed many, if not most, of the surviving Delta bluesmen. His enterprise, Avalon Productions, is, as a matter of fact, named after the hometown of Mississippi John Hurt, who was with Waterman until his death in 1969. The great Skip James was also with him from about the time of his exciting appearance at the Newport Folk Festival of 1964 until the time of his death in 1969. Among those with him today are Mance Lipscomb, Robert Pete Williams, Arthur Crudup, and, of course, the great Son House. I had heard that Waterman had "discovered" Eddie "Son" House, the surviving king of the Delta bluesmen, long after Son had given up the blues and become a Pullman porter, and persuaded him to take up music again. I asked Waterman if that was true.

He nodded. "Looking at it all from a philosophical viewpoint," he said, "I think that that is what I am most proud of—if that's the word—that is, proud of having brought the music of Son House back to a whole generation of people who would otherwise never have known he was alive. To some extent, this is also true of Skip James and Robert Pete Williams and Arthur Crudup, I guess. I have helped bring their careers to the point where they can be booked to play in person and younger people can talk to them and learn what it was like to be a bluesman in the late 1920s and 1930s in the South."

Son House was not to make an appearance here at Notre Dame this time around. I understood that Waterman kept the schedule of that old blues master down to a manageable minimum of concerts. However, he did have a couple of other blues attractions—the Buddy Guy-Junior Wells Blues Band and that of Otis Rush—that were a long way from the old-time blues that people expected from Son, Mance, Robert Pete, and the rest. These younger Chicago bluesmen were on the program in force.

"Yes," he conceded, "I started in band management in 1966 when Bob Koester, owner of Delmark Records, in Chicago, told me that he had just issued a record by a guy named Junior

Wells and Junior wanted to get out on the road and travel as a touring band. I started with Junior in 1966, added Buddy Guy in 1967, added the late Magic Sam in 1968 and later Luther Allison. Junior and Buddy worked with separate bands for several years until I put them into the same band in 1970 for the Rolling Stones' tour of Europe, and they have been together ever since. I've just added the Otis Rush band after having been a personal friend of his for years."

I could understand how, with all this talent at his disposal, Waterman could book a whole blues festival. And yet there were plenty of others here whom he did not handle. Perry Aberli had said that he had helped bring them all here. How? And why?

"Well, I am good friends with virtually every bluesman, whether I work with him or not. I value my long friendships with B. B. King, Muddy Waters, Howlin' Wolf, James Cotton, and many others that I don't manage or book. Many people in the business will call me for advice about recording contracts, publishing contracts, new offers, and so on. And student promoters call and ask to be put in touch with these people, too. I do what I can. I try to give back to the business this way because it has been pretty good to me over the long haul."

Dick Waterman's name for what he is is ombudsman. You must have come across that curious word of Scandinavian origin. In general, it is a public official who listens to complaints against government agencies, a middleman who helps people cope with the system—and that just about sums up his function for the bluesmen he manages. What does he do for them? Everything. He not only lines up jobs for his clients to play, he makes sure the jobs are clustered within reasonable distances for the older bluesmen to travel. He works out airline schedules and travel arrangements for these men, many of whom had never traveled out of their home states before the blues revival of the 1960s shot them into prominence. And he makes sure that none of the old-timers, all of whom are from the South and are unaccustomed to the rigors of a Northern winter, should have to work in the North between December and March.

He works just as hard for the younger blues bandsmen. He gets jobs for them at the same blues festivals that the older men play, but he has also had some success booking his blues bands on tours headlined by rock supergroups, as he did when he sent the Wells-Guy band to Europe with the Stones. Waterman serves as a maildrop for them while they are on tour and exercises discretion in forwarding letters, making sure that those perfumed envelopes don't get his guys in trouble with their wives at home.

He goes after music and record royalties for them. He reads the fine print in contracts. He handles the myriad of hassles and irritations that may arise to keep these artists away from their music. He is the intermediary between the bluesmen and the big world that frightens and intimidates so many of them.

It was as a man whose integrity is known and respected that Dick Waterman was sought out by a number of the bluesmen of lesser reputation during that weekend at Notre Dame. A couple of them had come as replacements. Others had been booked just to fill out the program. They were not his clients. I remember watching him spend a long time with a couple of them backstage that Saturday night. I made no effort to listen in, but I could tell they were talking about something that mattered. Afterward, I'm afraid I was so obviously curious about what had been discussed that he answered my unasked question: "It's really important to give the smaller-time bluesmen their time to talk and to listen to their pitch. They'll say, 'Look, I've got a truck. Me and my sidemen can make it anyplace. You just get the date for us, and we'll be there. You can count on us.' " At this point, I remember, Waterman sighed sympathetically, as though he suddenly felt burdened by all this imposed upon him.

"The trouble is," he continued, "there's a lot less work out there than they think there is. They think they can get the jobs that Buddy and Junior don't play and live pretty well just off that alone. But Buddy and Junior, and Luther [Allison] and Otis [Rush]—and all the rest of them I manage—take most of the jobs I'm able to get for them. No, it's not an easy life, being a bluesman."

I followed Dick Waterman around most of that weekend at Notre Dame, trying to pick up whatever I could from him, trying to get a fix on the realities of the professional performing side of the bluesman's life today. Around Waterman was a good place to be, for he was always close to the center of the action at the Midwest Blues Festival. He would pop out front and listen hard when somebody interesting came onstage, and the rest of the time he would hang out behind the scenes, talking with the performers and taking part in a long poker game with the boys in the Wells-Guy band. This was his life, and in spite of a kind of professional gloomy-Gus manner, he enjoyed it, you could tell. I even managed to pump him on a few points on the economics of the blues.

Sometime Sunday he came away from a discussion with Perry Aberli that was very clearly about money, and I asked him just how important the colleges were to him and his bluesmen-clients as a market for the kind of music they had to offer. "Very," he said simply. "Very important. When I started at this business, there were a few clubs in urban areas, folk music places a lot of them, that booked bluesmen, and there were festivals—maybe just Newport. There was no place else for most of these men to play until colleges started up as the big entertainment spots they are today. Today, of course, all that has changed, because there are colleges and college festivals for them. Some of the urban clubs and those around college towns are still open, but one night on a campus date like this one will bring a performer about as much as a week in a club. Plus, with an older performer, there is the question of the strain on his health. It's much easier on him to come to a place like this, play a set or a whole concert, and then return home, than it is to hang around a place a whole week and wind up playing about four or five hours a night. It's this, I think, that has made me concentrate on college bookings. It's so much easier on the older performers. For some of them it can be rather pleasant, going around talking to the kids and all. They like it.

"My biggest job is convincing these student-union boards, and other student organizations and so on, that they can have a whole two-day blues festival with a lot of really big names and all for just about the same money they would have to pay for one night with one big rock group. Not a supergroup like Creedence—just an ordinary big rock group. A lot of rock groups get $25,000 a night now. You give me $7,500 to $8,000, and I'll give you a hell of a night of blues—with some of the best and most authentic music you ever heard. And the kids might even learn something about where rock came from at a blues concert."

And is it good for the colleges? For the students themselves?

"Sure it is," he said emphatically. "The thing I'm trying to do at colleges is to help promote and present an art form that is really dying out with the men who created and practiced it. I mean, nobody's going to know about this old-time blues thing after people like Son House and Mance [Lipscomb] and Johnny Shines die off. That's why I always encourage *any* kind of filming or videotaping that any university wants to do—if they have the facilities and the inclination. All they have to do is guarantee the film will not be used for commercial use. Film is the most accurate way of keeping a record." Which is another way of saying that what they *are* is almost as important as what they *sing.*

BECAUSE I was interested in Waterman himself, I did a bit of digging and found out as much about him as I could in preparation for a meeting we arranged later. I found out, for instance, that he got into the business almost by accident. Although he had always been interested in music (a self-confessed "Buddy Holly and Bo Diddley freak" as a kid), it was always as a listener. When he started in at Boston University he became a pretty passionate folk fan. It was easy. There was a classmate of Waterman's named Joan Baez who played and sang in a coffeehouse called the Golden Vanity, which was then located next to the University. He came in a couple of nights and listened to her, and that's about all it took. But when graduation time came, he had no intention of going into the business side of music. He wanted to be a writer.

He took a job as a reporter on a small-town Connecticut newspaper for a while, and then tried free-lancing for a long, lean period. When things got too tight, he put in a stint as a publicist-advance man for the legendary Joan Baez-Bob Dylan tour of 1965. This was about as close as he had come to real involvement in the music business except for that trip he took down South in 1964.

By then blues was his music. He had picked up a rumor that the legendary and long-lost Eddie "Son" House, by reputation one of the greatest of the Mississippi Delta blues singers, had popped up briefly in Memphis. That was enough to send him and two fellow fans, Nick Perls and Phil Spiro, there in hope of finding the bluesman. It was a bad time to go. This was the summer that Chaney, Goodman, and Schwerner were murdered in Mississippi. And this was the year Violet Liuzzo was gunned down in her car. There were people down there who didn't much like white boys coming down in cars with Northern license plates making inquiries after black bluesmen. Their search took them down to Mississippi, where, with the help of the Reverend Robert Wilkins, a blues singer turned evangelist, they went from town to town and cotton field to cotton field, asking after the whereabouts of Son House. The answer, when it came, surprised them. He was living in Rochester, New York.

They found him, all right, a retired Pullman porter who had not played or sung regularly in four years. He was flattered that they had come all this way to see him, though, and so he gladly sat down and gave them a concert. As he did, the years seemed to slip away, and by the end of the afternoon he was playing well and singing in a full, strong voice. The three who had found Son House told him he ought to go back to music. Well, if I do, Son said to them, can you get some work for me? Neither of his two companions could give that sort of time to the enterprise, and so the job of finding jobs for Son House fell to Dick Waterman—and that was how he got into the music business.

This led eventually to the founding of his Avalon Productions. "At that time," he told me later, "the blues business was all messed up. Festivals were able to 'shop around' for their one token bluesman. They could get one old-time Delta artist for $250, or somebody else for $200, or somebody else for as little as $150. Or at least they'd say so, trying to whittle down the asking price. I stepped in and tried to get them all to come with me. I told them they would be working less but making more money. And this is how it has worked out for them."

It was at one of Dick Waterman's blues package shows that we arranged to meet again. The event would be held in an auditorium in Burlington, Vermont. Workshop sessions were to be held the afternoon of the concert at the University of Vermont which is located there right in the heart of town.

I began to get an idea of what the show would be like at the afternoon workshop sessions, which were held at the student union at the University. Dick Waterman was there, acting as master of ceremonies in the little mini-concert he had planned to start the session. This was to give the students an idea of what they would hear that night. He wanted the students to appreciate the sort of blues eminence he had assembled before them. After Robert Pete Williams had played and sung for them, and retired to a good round of applause, Dick Waterman got up and remarked, "I just noticed while Robert was playing that there is over one hundred years of blues-playing experience on this stage right now." And there must have been, all right, for up there with Robert Pete were Arthur Crudup, who is sixty-seven, and Son House—and blues historians only guess at his age!

Later, I asked Waterman how old he thought Son House really is, and he shook his head and said, "It's hard to tell. He doesn't know himself. He talks about living in St. Louis and working in an East St. Louis steel mill when he was in his twenties, and that was probably during World War I, so that would put him in his late seventies today. I'd guess he is about seventy-nine."

As it happens, however, Son did not take up blues or even learn guitar until comparatively late. For one interviewer he fixed the date at 1928, which, by Dick Waterman's reckoning would put Son House in his early thirties. He had stayed clear of the blues until then, for he was a Baptist preacher, and like all the rest he regarded secular music as sinful. But when he gave in, he gave in all the way, left the church, and with his partner, Willie Brown, began playing and singing all around the Clarksdale, Mississippi, area.

He got very good very fast. With barely more than a fundamental knowledge of guitar he began composing songs of his own. His blues had an easy fluent, lyrical quality to them, and an eloquence that probably came from those years in the pulpit. Some, too, were spiced with irony and humor, like his "Preachin' Blues."

Yes, I'm gonna get me religion, I'm gonna join the
Baptish Church
Yes, I'm gonna get me religion I said, I'm gonna join
the Baptist Church
You know, I want to be a Baptist preacher so I won't
have to work.

You know, one deacon jumped up and he began to grin
You know, one deacon jumped up and he began to grin
You know he said one thing, elder, I think I'll go back to barrelhousin' again.

And so on for many satirical stanzas more. In a way, this song is pure bravado, Son's nosethumb at those years he gave to the Lord. But, as we shall see, he feels a little uneasy about all that today; he seems to wish he had not shut the door quite so tight on that part of his life. Significantly, he has now eliminated "Preachin' Blues" from his performing repertoire, but makes it a point to do a hymn—"one for the Man upstairs"—whenever he appears before an audience, usually something like "John, the Revelator" or "This Little Light of Mine."

After he left the church, his reputation as a bluesman brought him in contact with the man who was then the reigning king of the Delta singers, Charley Patton. They played a little together with Son's sideman, Willie Brown, and Patton was so impressed that he recommended Son to Paramount Records. They went North, to Grafton, Wisconsin, in the summer of 1930. Son and Willie sat down and recorded nine sides, of which only four were ever released. For this he got forty dollars plus expenses, and he was delighted; this was about as much as he made in a year working in the cotton patch.

He didn't record again for twelve years—and when he finally did, it was only by accident. He happened to be nearby when, sometime in 1942, Alan Lomax, then folk curator of the Library of Congress, came through and set up his recording equipment at the crossroads which was Robinsonville, Mississippi. Word was sent to Son, and he came by with his guitar. He played and sang for him for nearly all of an afternoon thinking this was another chance to make an easy forty dollars. But then, when he finished, he was given only a bottle of Coca-Cola as payment for his day's work.

The following year he went North, to Rochester, New York. Why Rochester? Because a friend had preceded him there and said he could get him a job. Son held several, in fact, until he took one as a Pullman porter with the New York Central and stayed on until retirement. He gave up playing guitar and singing in 1948 because people up there in Rochester didn't seem to want to hear the old blues anymore. And that was how things stood in 1964 when he was found by Dick Waterman and his two friends at the end of their long search.

Although he has been performing ever since, the years have taken their toll on Son House. In many ways he is physically robust for his age, but he is quite dependent on alcohol, and this in turn has left him somewhat senile. He is a bit foggy about what did or did not happen in his past. I talked with him for a while in his motel room in Burlington, Vermont, and though he was obliging, polite, and pleasant through it all, he really didn't have much to say. And much of what he did remember for my benefit, he remembered inaccurately.

For instance, he recalled the two men with whom he played down in Mississippi: "Willie Brown and I started playing together after I learned to play guitar. Me and him played together at least twenty years. We traveled to all them places—to Europe and up to Wisconsin. Charley Patton, too. We went to Europe together, just us three—the three of us, playing them blues. Then Willie, well, it wasn't too long after that until he died."

Well, he and Willie Brown weren't together much more than ten years, and while Son eventually got to Europe after his rediscovery, neither Brown nor Charley Patton ever did. But that's the way it's fixed in the mind of Eddie "Son" House today.

In general, he was not much interested in talking, and so I didn't push him. There was only one point on which he spoke with any degree of passion, and that was his decision to leave preaching for the blues. "Oh, yeah," he said when I asked him about "Preachin' Blues." "I preached a long time before ever I get to play the blues. But I got to wanting to play the blues. I had the Bible in one hand and the guitar in the other. I knew I had to turn one loose, because you can't pretend with God. Yes, I knew I had to give up religion. You can't fool God. And it was right on behind that I started playing those old country blues."

But it is only onstage that he comes fully to life and shows live sparks from that old fire that burns within him. I found that out later on at the show. There was a terrific turnout for the Festival. Even the cop at the front door was impressed. "I haven't seen this many people," he told me, "since the last time they had wrestling here." Tickets they had been unable to sell out at the University went quickly at the box office, so that quite unexpectedly there was a sellout crowd waiting for the performers when the show began.

They were a good-natured, appreciative audience, too enthusiastic but not rowdy. They were attentive to Robert Pete Williams' distinctive blend of folk poetry and blues, appreciative of Arthur Crudup, and downright enthusiastic for Bonnie Raitt. Although she is white (records for Warner Bros.) and has a future in pop, she clearly belonged there that night. If not a blues singer, plain and simple, she sure is bluesy, for in addition to songs by Stephen Stills and Paul Siebel, her repertoire includes a lot of authentic blues material, the best of it by a neglected lady named Sippie Wallace. And can Bonnie Raitt play the guitar!

All in all, she was probably the best possible act to precede Son House. She had the crowd up and receptive, expecting something special from the man Waterman calls "Mr. Legend." What happened was special, all right, but not quite what anybody there had bargained for.

After Waterman's introduction—"the standard by which blues singers are measured"—Son swung into his first number, "Louise McGhee," with tremendous passion and enthusiasm. He bellowed forth the words and whopped away at his steel-bodied National guitar so that it whined and sang in his hands.

"You know," Dick Waterman remarked to me then, as we were watching and listening from the wings, "when he starts to sing all the aggravation and misery he gives me is worth it. I've been everywhere with him, and at every performance I'm still tremendously moved by this man as an artist."

Son did a couple of more straight blues and after the last waited for the applause to die down before he began his final number, the hymn "This Little Light of Mine." It went just fine. When he does it he lays down his guitar and does it *a capella,* but this time he got the audience clapping time with him. They continued all through the song and, bursting into a long round of applause, they kept it going after he had finished and was starting for the wings.

And then in response Son House cut a caper, doing a shuffling buck-and-wing step, and looked as if he might return for an encore. But Waterman thought that might be a bit too much for him and motioned him off. Son became momentarily addled, torn between going off and returning to the microphone. He stumbled slightly and looked as if he might fall, but two brightly dressed and bearded young black men suddenly appeared from the other side of the stage and swept him away. Nobody knew who they were or what they were up to.

They were the local militants. In the discussion that followed immediately (with Son sitting placidly outside on a bench), the two angrily accused Dick Waterman of "pushing an old man to the point of exhaustion." One, taller and leaner than his companion, was the spokesman. He asked menacingly if Waterman had a paper that said he was not legally responsible if Son House fell dead onstage.

The atmosphere in that little room was very tense indeed. But when Waterman began to speak I could tell he wasn't rattled in the least. Ordinarily he has a slight stammer that shows up from time to time in conversation, but it wasn't there as he explained that there was no paper at all between him and Son, that he did business with him, as with all other bluesmen, on the basis of a handshake. As for how strong and healthy Son was, every year he is examined by a doctor, and it is on the basis of that examination that they decide whether or not he should make the tour that year. Although he only plays a few dates every spring, Waterman added, the money he makes from these appearances eases things considerably for Son and his wife in their old age.

"Yeah," said the tall black, "and I'll bet you get a hell of a big cut out of that money of theirs."

Waterman shook his head and gave a firm no. "Because it's Son," he said, "and he and I have been together for so many years, I don't take anything. Not a thing. He's the only one I handle this way, but it's true, I take no cut."

They were impressed and began backing down a little. "Well, I'm not prophesizing against you personally. All I know is there was one mighty sick and tired old man up on that stage."

"I'm not denying there's a strain on him. There certainly is. The Mississippi Delta blues style is physically tiring. I mean I'm not being patronizing in explaining this, but it's more exhausting than other styles."

"You don't have to tell us that, man," the spokesman snapped. "We was born there." He hesitated then, wavering perceptibly, then added, "Well, we'll go out and talk to him some more about this—get his side of it."

Dick nodded. That was quite all right with him. "He'll probably make light of it, but it's serious enough. Unfortunately, he's not the best judge of his own condition." He ended by giving the two young men his card and telling them to call or write him if they wanted to discuss this further. They went outside and huddled with Son for some minutes and then left.

Afterward, Dick Waterman and I had resumed our place in the wings. Junior Wells and Buddy Guy, complete with two saxes and rhythm, were laying down some funky, heavy sounds, and the crowd out front was really taking it in. They loved it, as well they should. Waterman even seemed to be enjoying himself, relaxing a little after that encounter in the dressing room. I complimented him on his coolness down there and said he seemed quite unflappable. "I *am* flappable," he replied, "but not in my own element. When I go, everything goes." He gestured out to the stage and the audience, taking everything in. "I'm all that stands between all this and chaos."

CHAPTER FIFTEEN

SOMEBODY in Memphis gave me some advice when I said I was going to Brownsville, Tennessee, to look for Sleepy John Estes: "Find a local cop and ask him. These small-town policemen know where everybody lives." It seemed like a good idea, so when I pulled up and parked opposite the Haywood County courthouse, with its gallant-boys-in-gray statue in the front yard, I took a walk around the surrounding square and looked for a uniform of some kind.

Something struck me about Brownsville. There seemed to be a lot more black people than white out on the street, and I wondered if this reflected an imbalance in the town and in the rest of the county. Maybe not, for when I realized I was hungry and ducked into a kind of combination hamburger-joint-pool-parlor, I found all the good old boys in town, chomping hamburgers and wolfing down bowls of chili in between games of pool as the jukebox blared forth rockabilly and country and western. I did a quick check and saw that the only black man in the place was the ball-racker who worked the pool hall.

Outside again, I met a Brownsville policeman just down the street and asked him about Sleepy John. He was young and serious and determined to be helpful. There was no hint in his manner that I, a white man, should have no legitimate business with a black man there. "Well, sir, I'll tell you," he said. "I used to know where he lived, but to tell the truth, he just moved. That's a fact. Now, I know the general area where he lives now, but I don't know the house. Maybe your best bet would be to try the post office." So I took off in the direction he indicated, and as I started across the street, I happened to look down the block and got a surprise.

A car had parked diagonally at the curb and among the four people who got out was a tall blind black man. There was really no mistaking those sharp features and that abstracted manner: It had to be Sleepy John Estes. It was. I came up and introduced myself. He took the interruption in his stride, but a short, plump man named Hammie Nixon interposed himself and told me that John was just on his way to see "Lawyer Reid, up at the bank," and that I could interview him at his place after he finished. He would be happy to lead the way and show me just where John lived. That sounded good. I showed him where I was parked, and Hammie said he would get his own car, and I could follow.

But before we really got started, Hammie came back on foot to my car and told me, acting a little embarrassed, that Lawyer Reid wanted to see me, and would that be okay? He took me to the bank, up in the elevator to a second-floor office that was posh by any standard. The secretary nodded us in, and in a moment I was inside the paneled inner office, shaking hands with Lyle Reid, attorney-at-law, taking the seat opposite Sleepy John, and explaining to him just why I wanted to talk with John Estes, what I hoped to find out from him, and so on.

Lawyer Reid was okay. He just wanted to look me over. If I was going to interview Sleepy John, he just wanted to be sure that I would not be taking advantage of him, as had evidently happened in the past. What seemed to convince him was that I would not be using a tape recorder.

"No sir," I assured him. "Just a notebook. I take pretty accurate notes, and I've been around enough to know that a lot of damage has already been done with tape recorders."

He nodded. "It has," he agreed. "John has suffered some himself, and we don't want that to happen again. We're just now beginning to get his affairs in order. He's come in today to talk to me about a letter from a Mr. Carter in New York about the settlement on some royalties that are due him, and, well, we don't want him to be taken advantage of ever again. That's why I'm helping out."

He gave me his okay then and suggested that I drive out behind Hammie, as I had arranged to do, assuring me that John would be out shortly with his wife and son. I never quite got who the "we" were that Reid was talking about, but I really got the idea that he was speaking for the community, that there was genuine concern in Brownsville that Sleepy John Estes, blind as he was and at the mercy of the outside world, be protected from those who had hurt him in the past.

John Adam Estes was born in 1903 in nearby Ripley, Tennessee, the son of a guitar-playing sharecropper. When he was six, he lost the sight of one eye when he was injured in a baseball game. Not long after that, the family moved to Brownsville and John, who had been given a guitar by his father, first began playing and singing around the biggest town in Haywood County. He attracted the attention of local musicians such as Willie Newbern, who gave the boy some coaching on guitar, and mandolin-playing Yank Rachell, who began gigging around with him at country suppers and parties. Eventually, Hammie Nixon, a twelve-year-old guitar player and jug blower, joined him, and they got as far as Memphis. When Hammie was nineteen he and another Brownsville bluesman went North, to Chicago, and got a chance to record. He sent word to Sleepy John, who hopped a freight and came North and got to do some recording himself. These were his first sessions, recorded for Decca in 1934. He did them every now and again for the next six years running, when he switched to Victor's Bluebird label, recording his last for them in 1941. During the war and after, the recording industry forgot about him. He stayed close to Brownsville, though he made it as far as Memphis—was there, in fact, in 1950, when he finally lost the sight in his other eye, which had been failing gradually. Blind, he stayed close to home, and was right there in Brownsville when he was rediscovered by a documentary-film maker, Ralph Blumenthal, in the late 1950s. What followed was a series of concert, festival, and club dates that eventually took him all the way to Europe. He began recording again, found others were also recording his songs—Taj Mahal, for one, has done his "Diving Duck Blues"—and with the help of Lawyer Reid, who looks after his finances, and Hammie Nixon, who looks after his day-to-day needs, he makes a pretty good living for himself and his family.

Sleepy John Estes is no great shakes as a guitar player. His voice, somewhat thin and very intense, gives a kind of authentic urgency to the songs he sings, though it is not an exceptional voice as, say, Howlin' Wolf's is. His special talent is as a blues composer. He has written hundreds of songs, some of them improvised right on the spot, and has recorded many of them himself. Ultimately, he is the very model of the local bluesman. Although in his most active years he spent a good deal of time in Memphis and traveled as far as Chicago to record, Brownsville remained his home base. And today, since being "rediscovered," he and Hammie travel more widely than ever—to colleges, to Washington, D.C., and even to Europe—but keep coming back to Haywood County. This sort of intense identification with place has been reflected in his music, too. He has written a number of blues about persons, places, and events in the Brownsville area, a kind of blues version of Edgar Lee Masters' *Spoon River Anthology.* The best of these local blues can be heard on his Delmark LP, "Brownsville Blues."

His style of life is about average for Brownsville's black population. Approaching the Estes house from the highway, I followed Hammie Nixon's little Rambler, followed him on a right turn that took me down a dirt road. We did a bit of winding on it—he was right, I would never have found it by myself—and came to a halt at last in front of a white single-story frame house. Sleepy John moved there not long ago from a place outside of town that was pretty run down. Hammie said this place is a lot better, and he hoped John's kids took better care of it.

Hammie did quite a bit of talking that afternoon. A plump, quick man, he worries a lot—about his partner, the condition of the world today, and nearly everything else. As we waited for Sleepy John to arrive, Hammie told me a little about himself. He was born in Lauderdale County, he said, but has lived here since he was twelve. He plays harmonica, jug, tub bass, washboard, and guitar. I asked him how he first got started on the blues. He said, "That would be when Charles Barber and David Campbell of Lauderdale came through my father's yard playing. I caught that sound and I loved it. I told my father, and he said, 'Son, if you work good, I'll buy you a guitar.' He did, and that's how I got going."

John drove up in his own car, his son at the wheel, his wife—a silent, sullen woman who has been in and out of the state asylum a couple of times—in the rear seat. Greetings all around again, and John remained outside to talk with Hammie and me.

I told him that Hammie had just said he had gotten started as a bluesman. How had John Estes begun?

"Oh, I got me a cigar box with just one string, and I started whanging on that and singing along. Got me some change, and then I got a regular guitar, so I could get that real, true sound. But I just played around here until 1929, when I commenced to travel. Hammie was with me then. We was hoboing then."

Was this about the time he began to record?

"Along about this time, yes. There was this man Mel Williams of Decca. He'd give us money to come to Chicago and record, and then we'd hop a freight and save the money."

"Yes," put in Hammie, "we made a lot of trips back there then, for RCA Victor toward the end, but John's eyes started giving him troubles."

That was when people sort of lost track of you for a while?

"Yeah, I guess," said John. "They knowed of us up there because of our records. They say they looked for us for twelve years and couldn't find us. When they did, they said they heard old Hammie was ninety-five, and I was a hundred and five. Memphis Slim told them that. I guess that was his idea of a joke. I don't look no hundred and five, do I? I was born in 1903. That makes me sixty-nine this year. What would you have thought?"

I said I would have taken him for a little younger than that. He was satisfied, and so I changed the subject: What about other bluesmen from Memphis and the Delta? Had he heard them?

"Well, yes," he conceded. "I heard some. You want to remember we played all these parties and dances, and the man would say, 'Keep it up all night.' And that's what we did. The singers and players would come and go, and we'd keep right on. Yeah, for instance, Memphis Slim and Memphis Minnie, we met them before they went to Chicago."

"Robert Johnson, too," said Hammie. "He did pretty good."

John agreed. "He was good in my book. If he'd lived up to now, he'd be awful good."

People they had known. Places they had been. This got them to talking about their tours in Europe. They had liked all that traveling, and both Hammie and John were ready to go again. "Yeah, I really like Europe," said John. "I learned a lot. In London, they got a lot of nice people. We met the Beatles while we was there. We went out to their place—that was in 1964—and spent the night there. Then they had to leave and go to another part of England. Yeah, they just went crazy about our music over there. We were there in 1964 and 1966."

"Tell him about Russia," Hammie urged.

"What about it?"

"How I got lost there. You know. I did get lost. That was behind the Iron Curtain, they call it. But we did every show over there. Never missed one."

John nodded. "Yeah. We been called back several times, but we wouldn't go. Crossing that blue water scares me a little bit."

John Estes *is* sort of sleepy. It was about this time—the suggestion of peril at the crossing of the ocean—that Hammie started preaching pretty hard on when your time comes you have to go, and so on. Sleepy John acted as if he had heard it all from him before and proceeded to prove it by nodding off as Hammie talked on. I had noticed him do something similar as Lawyer Reid talked to me earlier in the office.

But making an effort to bring him back, I asked him just where he got his songs.

"You mean the blues?" he asked.

I nodded, then remembered he couldn't see me and said yes.

"Oh, the blues," he said. "The blues will never be forgotten. The blues is a feeling. You get something happen to you, and then you can sing it off. It's a feeling that comes to you when there's anything you want to do and can't do. And when you can sing it off in a song, that gives you a thrill."

Hammie nodded in agreement. "The words and music come together," he said. "We don't never have to rehearse. We just do it."

"That's right," said John. "When we're going to make records we may not know what it is we're going to do, but we know we'll get it. We could make a record about you, and this talk we're having, and everything. Or we might write a song about Lawyer Reid. He helped us a lot, getting our money for us and all. I wish we had him before. In our younger days they got a hold of us, and we never got anything from them. Now I'm stone blind and we're both sickly. . . ."

He trailed off with that, seeming to doze off once again behind his dark glasses. Hammie took up the line where John had dropped it and said they sure could use some bookings to keep themselves going. There was a pause then, and I said I thought maybe John was tired and I'd better go. He roused to say goodbye. We shook hands all the way around, and I jumped in the car. Turning it around, I had to swerve a couple of times to avoid the yard litter, so that I almost got stuck out there in the January mud.

My point in describing the situation of Sleepy John Estes in such detail is to give you some idea of the quality of life experienced by many of the surviving bluesmen today. His condition is fairly typical. Some are better off than he is. John's blindness restricts his travel somewhat, and his health, as he enters his seventies, is otherwise none too good. But in other ways, he is far more fortunate than others. In Lyle Reid, he has someone to look after his affairs, to go after royalties and fees that are rightfully his. Since he is almost totally dependent on these for his income today, he and his family would find it hard to survive without the attorney's help.

Most bluesmen need such an intermediary—an "ombudsman," to use Dick Waterman's term—to help them get by in the world. Many of these with whom I talked in the course of the research for this book have proved to be illiterate, able to write just enough to sign their names—which is, of course, all that is needed on a contract. Without someone whom they can trust to read that contract for them they cannot be sure they will receive compensation, just or unjust.

For the awful truth is that bluesmen are being cheated, ripped off, and taken advantage of today, just as they were before—or not in quite the same way, for the ground rules have now changed just a little. Let me explain. Before, it was the guys with the big black cigars who did the fleecing. They talked fast, had a score of ploys for holding onto monies that ought to have been paid out for record sales and publishing royalties, and it was all legal, of course, for they had signed contracts to back them up. But some of the more cunning, street-smart bluesmen learned how to deal with them. The Memphis Slims and the Big Bill Broonzys would dispense with contracts, demand cash, and not be put off by promises of money coming to them in the future.

There aren't many of those guys with black cigars around any more. The money to be made cheating superannuated bluesmen is nothing to that which may be picked up from underage rock-and-roll stars. But here we are in the middle of what is at least a modest blues revival, and the men who make the music are still not getting what should be coming to them. Who is?

It is, unfortunately, going to many of the very scholars, critics, and folklorists who are themselves in part responsible for this blues revival. We are not talking about great sums—the amounts involved, in many cases, would be computed in the hundreds rather than the thousands of dollars. Yet it adds up, and there seems something especially pernicious in the fact that those whose motives seem purest, who seem to be rescuing the blues from the crass commercialism that had all but stifled it in the 1930s and 1940s, are actually keeping small sums that should legitimately be passed on to blues artists and composers. There is, I'm sure, a process of rationalization involved here; it is not the sort of direct, cynical thievery that was practiced in the past.

How does it work? The blues scholar has, let us suppose, started a small record label to make available to a small public the work of a bluesman or songster he truly admires. He may even have rescued him from the obscurity of a sharecropper's cabin in Arkansas or the lowest West Side blues dive in Chicago. He pays the artist's expenses and a small advance, as much as he can afford, probably, at the time of the recording session. Although upon issue, the album has no immediate impact, as the bluesman's reputation grows through college concerts and so on, it continues to sell steadily until it has exceeded the modest advance against royalties made at the time—perhaps now a couple of years ago—when it was recorded. Our blues scholar may hardly have noticed at all. He may be plowing all he makes back into the enterprise so that he can cut more records and advance the cause of the blues. Because of his sacrifices he may have become a hero in his own eyes; and heroes put notoriously high demands on others. Without being consulted on the matter, the bluesman makes his sacrifice, too.

This is not to say that all small blues labels are run with this same careless disregard for the artists who record for them. But you cannot assume that because a bluesman has a number of albums available that he is doing well. His entire LP discography may have brought him less than a thousand dollars.

You may recall that the fact that I had no tape recorder along made quite a favorable impression on Sleepy John Estes' attorney, Lyle Reid. The sort of small, cassette voice recorder used by many interviewers was not what he was on the lookout for —most of these cannot even record music. But it takes only a little larger machine to record voice and guitar at commercial quality, if other factors are favorable. Begin an interview with a bluesman, and he will reach for his guitar and start playing to make a point. He is more comfortable singing than talking, anyway, and so with the right equipment, an interviewer may walk away with a fine collection of blues that includes personal introductions, anecdotes, bits of gossip, and so on—just the sort of back-porch concert that blues fans value for its informality and authenticity. These tapes have a mysterious way of appearing, edited, as albums on the European market. In the same way, informal blues jams at concerts, which have been recorded without permission or compensation, show up in Europe or are bootlegged here in America. Some bluesmen hold out their hands for payment whenever they see a tape recorder. They're entitled to.

And there is also the vast and troublesome area of copyright. Admittedly, a good deal of the material in some blues has come from traditional folk material that goes back well into the nineteenth century. Certain images, certain lines and rhymes, and a few whole songs have come down from those days when the laws of copyright would have been quite unknown to the black folk musicians whose work is so important to the origins of the blues. At least one latter-day blues musician has founded his reputation as a composer of traditional material that he has taken the trouble to copyright in his own name, or material that he has borrowed from long-dead blues writers such as Charley Patton, having altered it slightly in order to make it "his." Another blues player has some deserved reputation as a composer, yet he has for some years been practicing an almost childish dodge: He has been republishing his old songs, applying for new copyrights each time, while changing titles only slightly ("Someone" in one title becomes "Some One" in another).

The new breed of blues scholars and folklorists have also been guilty of questionable practices with copyrights. Let me give a specific example. As described earlier, the father-and-son collecting team of John A. and Alan Lomax have been credited with "discovering" Leadbelly, the blues singer Huddie Ledbetter, whom they first recorded in prison in 1933 for the Library of Congress. When he was pardoned in 1935, they took him North, did more recording, and helped him copyright his material (most of it unquestionably his, but some of it—"See, See Rider," for example—more likely of traditional origin). Many, if not most, of Leadbelly's songs, however, are credited in copyright to H. Ledbetter, A. Lomax, and J. Lomax. Why? How does "Death Letter Blues" belong to the Lomaxes as well as to Leadbelly? What lines did they contribute to his great song of tough teenage experiences in Shreveport, Louisiana, "Mister Tom Hughes Town"? These are personal blues that Huddie Ledbetter played and sang most of his life. How could he have divided authorship with white men whom he did not meet until he was well into his forties? And if they did not share authorship, what are their names doing on the copyrights?

There is an organization in New York called the American Guild of Authors and Composers, which exists as an auditing agency to make sure that composer-members receive the one-half of all mechanical royalties from recordings to which their copyrights entitle them. Membership in it is voluntary, of course, and its first members were jazz and popular music writers, but lately, at the urging of "ombudsmen" like Dick Waterman and Lyle Reid, blues composers have been joining the AGAC, as well. Settlements from recording companies or, more commonly, from music publishers (who withhold the composer's share of the royalties when it has been paid), are now beginning to come through. Sleepy John Estes is a member, and the "Mr. Carter" whose letter he was to discuss that afternoon with Lawyer Reid is John Carter, the managing director of the American Guild of Authors and Composers.

I went to visit Carter one day at the Guild's modest offices on

West Fifty-seventh Street, right in midtown Manhattan. We had an affable, though somewhat rushed, conversation right there, for he is one of those harried, work-right-through-lunch guys who gives himself completely to his job. He is a black man with a New York accent.

I asked how, in general terms, he would describe the AGAC and what it does. He explained: "Well, what we do is to represent the composer in an area in which he is very interested, of course—his royalties. We have 3,000 members, and among them are some of the top names, people like Ned Washington and Sammy Fain of the old guard and more modern writers such as Hal David and Bob Dylan. We audit publishers' books on a kind of continuing basis—every four years is standard, but we can go in for a special audit on a special case, of course. We also try to help our members on any contract problems they may have—anything that has to do with the collecting of recording and publishing royalties."

Since I had heard that Sleepy John Estes was an AGAC member, I asked Carter to fill me in a little on his case.

"With John Estes our work has fallen into two categories. There was one song that he had sold outright to Southern Music in New York, and, of course, he was entitled to no royalties on it, but we found out with a little digging that his bill of sale to them did not encompass the copyright-renewal period—that is, anything after the first twenty-eight years, and since it had been recorded since then, we were able to collect for him. There were also three other compositions of his that were not owned by anyone but had been recorded by Taj Mahal. We were able to collect 100 percent on these—with no difficulty at all, I might add, for Taj had credited John and was most cooperative.

"In all, I'd say we've collected about $7,000 on four compositions for him. That gave us a lot of pleasure. I remember that on that first thousand we collected for him, he was down in Washington, D.C., at a blues festival, so I took the check down to him personally."

For a special case like Sleepy John's, which requires copyright research, as well as audits and legal advice, there is a formula of payment worked out between AGAC and its members that seems quite equitable. For its work, the organization keeps 5 percent of the first $20,000 collected for the member, but only ½ percent for any amount over $20,000 up to $100,000. Anything above that goes to the member.

Dick Waterman had urged me to ask Carter about Arthur Crudup and the settlement they were negotiating on the royalties due him. When I did, Carter shook his head and said, "Believe it or not, we still haven't gotten the contract on that. It's going to be terrifically favorable for him when at last it does come through, though, and he's been very patient through all of it. Sometime in the near future he's going to be a very happy man."

The case of Arthur "Big Boy" Crudup is at once one of the most depressing and most heartening of all those with which John Carter has dealt. Probably none of the other bluesmen has been fleeced quite as thoroughly and shamefully as has this genial, relaxed giant of a man. In spite of his considerable talent as a performer and composer, he has had to support himself and his family all his life as a sharecropper and migrant laborer. He was never able to make a living in music. And the Xerox copy of the check that Carter pushed across his desk for my inspection told the story. It was made out to Arthur Crudup by Blanche Melrose, widow of Lester Melrose, and was drawn on an Orlando, Florida, bank. It was a royalty check for $1.06, meant to satisfy his claim for what was due him on his song "Mean Old Frisco." This was typical of his payments from Wabash Music. He had written one song that had become a big Elvis Presley hit—"That's Alright, Mama"—and another—"My Baby Left Me"—that was recorded not only by Presley but also by Elton John, the Grease Band, and Creedence Clearwater Revival. His "Rock Me, Mama" was a big blues hit for B. B. King. But from all these and from the many other songs he wrote and recorded, Crudup made so little that finally in the fifties he gave up music altogether. He knew he was being taken advantage of, and since he could do nothing about it, he simply walked away from a bad situation.

Unlike other Delta bluesmen, Arthur Crudup never really made a name for himself as a performer—that is, until recently, when he was "rediscovered" and his second career began. He worked almost purely as a recording artist. It all goes back to 1940, when he had been traveling around the country singing in a gospel quartet but somehow got stranded in

Chicago. With no money in his pocket, and no job in sight, he did what black musicians have been doing in this country for the past two centuries: He took to the streets with his guitar.

What happened then? Here's how Arthur Crudup remembers it: "Lester Melrose and a man named Dr. Clayton happened to come by where I was and saw me singing on the street with my guitar. They stopped and listened, and Melrose said he wanted me to sing at a party at Tampa Red's."

Melrose was, of course, the head of RCA Victor's Race recording operations on its cheaper subsidiary Bluebird label. He had, as noted earlier, gathered quite an array of talent in Chicago, a stable of steady blues singers and musicians who backed one another up on recording dates and played dates in the meantime at the gin mills on the near South Side. Tampa Red was one of these regulars; so, also, were Memphis Slim, Big Bill Broonzy, and Robert Brown (Washboard Sam).

They were all there at that party to which Lester Melrose took Arthur Crudup. "Yeah, I'd heard some of their things, too—some of Tampa Red's and Big Bill's and some others. But at the time, see, I didn't know but one or two blues myself. I had made up a song that I started out calling "Coal Black Mare" and then took to calling it "Black Pony Blues." I was so embarrassed I could hardly play, but finally I got it out, you know, and they were all very friendly to me—Tampa Red, he was a good old guy. And Melrose, he asked me if I had ever heard my own voice. 'Not more than just when I'm singing,' I told him. So he says, 'Come on up to the studio and cut some wax, and we'll see how you sound.' And that was how I started recording.

"I'll tell you the truth, it was all pretty new to me then. Why, I only learned to play the guitar six months before I started recording. And the one I had had a broken neck that I'd repaired with haywire. But I kind of liked the sound, and to this day I play with a capo on my guitar. Who taught me to play? Nobody taught me. I learned myself. I started out with four strings, added a fifth, and then a sixth when I could handle it."

What happened after that first recording session, on which he cut his "Black Pony Blues" and another, "Death Valley Blues"? "Well, I went back to Mississippi, around Forest, where I'm from, and I started traveling back and forth to make those records for Lester Melrose in Chicago. He'd send me some money, and I'd hop a train and come up and record, and then get a little more money."

But all during this period he continued to work as a farmer. He took his family and moved to Belzoni, Mississippi, and there he worked as a sharecropper. "Had to earn a living some way. I wasn't making money off those records to amount to nothing, and all those kids of mine were little then, so I just kept on recording every time I was asked and working the farm in between times. All this time I never hardly played in front of anybody, as I can remember. Only place back then was the Indiana Theater in Chicago during the war on some big blues show. It didn't amount to much. My first real performance was in Chicago, though—at the University of Chicago just three years ago. Dick Waterman got me that date, and I been at it ever since."

It was Waterman who had put me in touch with Arthur Crudup. As his manager, he had been deeply involved with John Carter of AGAC in working out a settlement for Crudup with Wabash Music, the publishing company of the late Lester Melrose. Wabash held copyrights on all the material written and sung by the bluesman during more than a dozen years of recording for Bluebird. But matters were complicated by Melrose's death. Wabash—and all its rights and obligations—had been sold to another, much larger music publishing house, which had found Arthur Crudup's claim dumped in their laps almost immediately. After their lawyers had taken a look, they admitted their liability in the case, but things were at a temporary standstill at the time I talked with John Carter while the formula for the settlement was being worked out. In any case, Arthur Crudup stands to collect a great deal of money in the near future. As royalties still accrue (Rod Stewart recently recorded "That's Alright, Mama" and made it a hit once again), his fortunes as a composer continue to grow on paper. Before the money stops, he may well get a sum in six figures for those songs he wrote between 1940 and 1955. "Arthur's is that rare case," says Dick Waterman, "where the little guy wins." Let's hope so.

Arthur Crudup has waited for the money that is coming to him for so long, however, that he tends to be a little skeptical about it all. "It's just like an old song I heard," he says, " 'You can't miss what you can't measure.' That's the same with me, see, I won't miss what I never had. I never owned $10,000 in my life at one time. I just want a little, enough to keep me till I die."

I had driven from Washington to see him, across the Chesapeake Bay Bridge, and down the Eastern Shore to the very tip of the Delmarva Peninsula. His home is in Virginia, just inland from the beach resorts where middle-class Baltimore and Washington go to splash the summer away. Take a look around and you would never guess that, though. Here, all is rural and remote and farther south than you would ever suppose from its location on the map. I had found the house with no trouble and discovered Arthur Crudup out in the yard to greet me just as soon as I emerged from my car. He steered me over to a weather-beaten building of no great dimensions removed some distance from the house. This, he explained as we settled down to talk, is where he and his boys play the country dances for the people around here.

"Your boys?" I asked. "You mean your band?"

"No, I mean my sons. They got their own band, but they let me sing with them when they're here around home. We do some pretty good stuff together. They do the playing and I do the singing." The name of the group is the Malibus. They were traveling north that day to play a job in Long Island. A couple of them had already left, but a couple more were still here, and I'd have a chance to meet them in a little while, he told me.

Now that he has been at it these three years, playing dates that have been booked for him at colleges and universities, he has decided he likes performing before audiences pretty well. He wishes he had taken it up long ago and had tried touring as his boys are doing today. "Yeah, I do," he said with a nod. "But a person just concentrates on what he's making a living out of. That's how it was with me back then. The more you do of that, the more it seems there is to do. For me, it was just farming and traveling up to Chicago to record. Now I go all over and play and sing. Why, I went to England even, just got through. They seemed to think a whole lot of me there, and I did of them, too."

I told him I could certainly understand why he had quit, but I wondered just how it had come about.

"Well, the reason I quit playing is that gradually I realized I was making everybody rich, and here I was still poor. You know, Elvis made some number of mine. He gave me credit on his records right from the start and paid money and all, but I never saw any of it."

I nodded and said I had heard that.

"Well, I guess it was that that really did it to me. I started hearing that song of mine, 'That's Alright, Mama,' just all over in Mississippi. It was a big hit, so I wrote to Melrose, who was my manager then, and asked him if I shouldn't be getting some money out of that, and he wrote me back and said he'd look into it." Arthur Crudup repeated the last four words, shaking his head in disgust. "But I never got anything extra for that, so I knew something was funny there. Five hundred dollars was the most I ever got from him, and that was mostly recording fee. No difference between hits and nonhits for me, just get the same old $200 or $110 or $90."

I asked him if he had ever gone to Melrose's office and asked to see the books.

"No, I never even been in Melrose's office once. He'd just write me and send the fare for me to come to Chicago and say to meet him at Tampa Red's, which I'd do, and then we'd go to the studio. Afterward, when the session was all done, I'd go and be paid off at the union hall. When I started, see, you had to belong to the union before you could record. The whole thing would take about five or six days, and I'd stay with a half-sister I had there or maybe with Tampa. He used to live around Thirty-fifth and State then. I think Tampa was in the same boat with Melrose I was. I never heard of him having no hell of a lot of money. He usually worked at a club at Thirty-ninth and State and had a lot of people around him. I learned to know a lot of them up at his place—Big Bill, Lonnie Johnson, Big Maceo, St. Louis Jimmy, and Memphis Minnie. Just all of them."

Just about that time Arthur Crudup's sons, George and James, came over from the house to say goodbye to their father. Their car was loaded up and ready to go, and they were ready to head for their date in Long Island. After introducing them to me, he walked over to the car with them, held a brief conversation that ended in laughter between them. He waved them off. They jumped in the car and were on their way.

He came back smiling. "They're good boys," he said. "James, he's the drummer, he learned to play on washboard or just anything he could beat on. And George, the other boy, he plays bass, only I started him on guitar and taught him chords and stuff. Jonas, the guitar, and Charles, the other brother who plays organ, they went on ahead. They sings anybody's songs, but they got their own material."

"Kind of a rock band?" I asked, and he nodded. *Down Beat* had called him the "daddy of rock"; I wanted to know how that set with him.

"Oh, well. Pretty good. You know." He ended with a shrug that told me it didn't matter to him much one way or the other. "I like what they do with my material. Elvis did a nice job on my songs, kind of a hillbilly version."

I asked if he felt bitter toward Elvis Presley and B. B. King and the rest who had made money from his songs.

"No, it's like down there in Mississippi when I was on a little farm of my own, that's when I wasn't sharecropping. They beat me out of everything I ever owned, so we just picked up and moved to Florida and then up here. I wasn't bitter over that. I'm not bitter over this. Who am I gonna get mad with? At Melrose? He's dead, so I can't hurt him. At Presley? I don't even know him. I can't get mad with a man I don't know. There's nobody around to fight, and there's no sense in getting mad if you can't fight nobody."

We talked a little longer, but nothing he said afterward stuck with me quite like that. I thanked him for the time he had given me and headed back to Washington.

AND THAT WAS IT. That was the end of my trip. Quite literally so, for when I returned from that afternoon with Arthur Crudup I started writing this book. It had begun as a kind of tour, one that would take me—and you—down to the back country of the blues, where there were still a few of the old survivors of that time when the music was first given style and shape, and into some of the back-alley bars and boulevard concert halls where the blues is still being played today. Yet it took me to a few places I had never expected to go—back into my own past, for one, because I found that the more I wrote about this music I had been hearing since I was a kid, the more personally I became involved with it. As a result, what you have read is more subjective than I ever expected it would be when I began writing.

And I have also been taken deeper into the American past than I expected to go. For the story of the blues is so much the record of black and white in America that it has been instructive—though not necessarily pleasant—to go back over that record as I have been doing here. There is a jackleg curriculum called American Studies offered at most of our colleges and universities today. It is about equal parts literature and history, and purports to communicate something to students about the formation of the American character. That sounds skeptical, I know, but my doubts are not about substance but about sources. There is such a thing as the American character, all right, although it is still in rapid metamorphosis, being shaped daily and subtly by influences that are never mentioned in the textbooks. American music is one of them. If you want to find out what America is and would like to be, the good and the bad of it, listen to its music. Listen to the blues.

A BASIC BLUES DISCOGRAPHY

While the selections below are meant to cover the blues from its recorded beginnings to the present time, it is nevertheless a personal choice and should not be taken as in any way definitive.

Son House, Skip James, Charley Patton, et al.: *Mississippi Moaners 1927–1942* (Yazoo). An anthology of historic Delta blues recordings.

Bessie Smith: *The Complete Recordings* (2 double-disc sets, Columbia Legacy). The Empress of the Blues, digitally restored.

Charley Patton: *Founder of the Delta Blues* (Yazoo). 24 remastered 78s by the first Delta bluesman to make it onto shellac.

Lonnie Johnson: *Steppin' on the Blues* (Columbia Legacy). A collection of the great blues guitarist in various contexts.

Robert Johnson: *The Complete Recordings* (double-disc set, Columbia Legacy). A necessary building block for any blues collection.

Jelly Roll Morton: *The Jelly Roll Morton Centennial* (a five CD-set, Bluebird). Mr. Jelly Lord, a great bluesman and a great jazzman.

Sleepy John Estes: *I Ain't Gonna Be Worried No More, 1929–1941* (Yazoo). The blind bluesman at his confident best; Hammie Nixon is present on harmonica on some tracks.

Mississippi Fred McDowell: *Mississippi Delta Blues* (Arhoolie). A sensitive songster and a great slide guitarist in an intimate setting.

Bukka White: *Sky Songs* (Arhoolie). A great Delta bluesman sings and talks his way through these relaxed tracks.

John Lee Hooker: *The Ultimate Collection, 1948–1990* (double-disc set, Rhino). Samples of the recorded biography of the Mississippi bluesman who went north to Detroit.

Lightnin' Hopkins: *Double Blues* (Fantasy). A great blues singer performs some of his best original material.

Memphis Slim: *Raining the Blues* (Fantasy). A.k.a. Peter Chatman, an accomplished blues wailer and pianist is presented here on his most impressive recording.

Dinah Washington: *Mellow Mama* (Delmark). The young Dinah sings the blues with solid jazz backup—minus the string arrangements which came later.

Muddy Waters: *The Chess Box* (triple-disc set, MCA Chess). The man who invented the electric Chicago blues style takes you into his laboratory.

Howlin' Wolf: *The Chess Box* (triple-disc set, MCA Chess). Chester Burnett, the most primitive of the Chicago bluesmen, at his lupine best.

Little Walter: *The Best of Little Walter* (Volume 1 and 2, MCA Chess). Little Walter Jacobs profoundly influenced other harmonica players and established a place for the instrument in the electric blues band.

Elmore James: *Rollin' & Tumblin'* (Relic). The electric slide guitarist who showed the way before his untimely death in 1963.

B. B. King: *Live in Cook County Jail* (MCA). Always at his best with his road band, B. B. shines in his first recorded prison concert.

Buddy Guy and Junior Wells: *Alone & Acoustic* (Alligator). Always in top form when they played together as they do here, informally and honestly.

Albert Collins: *Ice Pickin'* (Alligator). "Icepick" Collins on his breakthrough album—urgent, intense, and a bit mean.

Stevie Ray Vaughan: *Couldn't Stand the Weather* (Epic). Who said white boys couldn't play the blues?

Robert Cray: *Strong Persuader* (Mercury). The youngest star of the new blues scene carries on the tradition.

INDEX

Other titles of interest

MEETING THE BLUES
Alan Govenar
248 pp., over 250 illus.
80641-X $17.95

THE ARRIVAL OF B. B. KING
Charles Sawyer
274 pp., 99 photos
80169-8 $12.95

BIG BILL BLUES
William Broonzy's Story
as told to Yannick Bruynoghe
176 pp., 4 drawings, 15 photos
80490-5 $10.95

BILLIE'S BLUES: The Billie Holiday Story 1933-1959
John Chilton
272 pp., 20 photos
80363-1 $13.95

BLUEGRASS BREAKDOWN
The Making of the Old Southern Sound
Robert Cantwell
334 pp., 16 photos
80495-6 $13.95

BLUES: AN ANTHOLOGY
Edited by W. C. Handy
228 pp., 14 illus.
80411-5 $15.95

BLUES FROM THE DELTA
William Ferris
New introduction by Billy Taylor
226 pp., 30 photos
80327-5 $11.95

THE BLUES MAKERS
Samuel Charters
New preface and new chapter on Robert Johnson
416 pp., 40 illus.
80438-7 $16.95

BLUES WHO'S WHO
Sheldon Harris
775 pp., 450 photos
80155-8 $35.00

CHICAGO BLUES
The City and the Music
Mike Rowe
226 pp., 147 photos
80145-0 $11.95

THE COUNTRY BLUES
Samuel B. Charters
288 pp., 45 illus.
80014-4 $12.95

FATHER OF THE BLUES
W. C. Handy
Edited by Arna Bontemps
317 pp., 3 illus.
80421-2 $13.95

I AM THE BLUES
The Willie Dixon Story
Willie Dixon with Don Snowden
288 pp., 44 photos
80415-8 $12.95

I PUT A SPELL ON YOU
The Autobiography of Nina Simone
with Stephen Cleary
207 pp., 28 photos
80525-1 $13.95

I SAY ME FOR A PARABLE
The Oral Autobiography of Mance Lipscomb, Texas Bluesman
as told to and compiled by Glen Alyn
Foreword by Taj Mahal
508 pp., 45 illus.
80610-X $16.95

I'D RATHER BE THE DEVIL
Skip James and the Blues
Stephen Calt
400 pp., 13 pp. of illus.
80579-0 $14.95

THE LEGACY OF THE BLUES
Art and Lives of Twelve Great Bluesmen
Samuel B. Charters
192 pp., 15 photos
80054-3 $9.95

BROTHER RAY
RAY CHARLES' OWN STORY
RAY CHARLES & DAVID RITZ
THE BLUES MAKERS
SAMUEL CHARTERS
The Willie Dixon Story
I AM THE BLUES
Willie Dixon with Don Snowden
The Roots of the Blues
SAMUEL CHARTERS

CHI BLUES - MIKE ROWE

DA CAPO

BLUES F. THE DELTA - WM FERRIS